The Artifice
of Reality

The Artifice
of Reality

POETIC STYLE IN
WORDSWORTH, FOSCOLO, KEATS,
AND LEOPARDI

KARL KROEBER

The University of Wisconsin Press
Madison and Milwaukee, 1964

Published by
THE UNIVERSITY OF WISCONSIN PRESS
Madison and Milwaukee
Mailing Address: P.O. Box 1379, Madison Wisconsin 53701
Editorial offices: 430 Sterling Court, Madison

Printed in the United States of America by
Kingsport Press, Inc., Kingsport, Tennessee

Library of Congress Catalog Number 64–17769

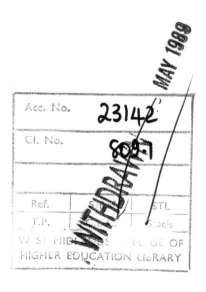

To
The Travelling Gourmands
of the Via Solenghi

T. K. K.

J. T. K.

P. D. K.

~ ACKNOWLEDGMENTS

I AM grateful to the Fulbright Commission and to the Research Committee of the Graduate School of the University of Wisconsin for generous support without which I could not have written this book. Portions of Chapter IV appeared in article form in the *Proceedings of the American Philosophical Society* (June, 1963) and Chapter Eight in the *Transactions of the Wisconsin Academy of Sciences, Arts, and Letters* (1963), and I wish to thank the editors of these journals for permission to reprint this material. It is a pleasure to acknowledge that my year in Milan was rewarding in large measure because of the cordiality of Professor Agostino Lombardo, the kindness of Professor Mario Fubini, and—most of all—the affectionate friendship which Benedetto and Mildred Salvi-Cristiani lavished on me and my family. I am indebted to Professor Glauco Cambon of Rutgers University for his keen but sympathetic criticism of the manuscript of this book and to Professor Joseph Rossi of the University of Wisconsin for his good-humored attempts to improve my Italian.

KARL KROEBER

Madison, January 21, 1964

✌ CONTENTS

☙ INTRODUCTION

I N the pages that follow I discuss and analyze some of the principal works of four early nineteenth-century poets: William
Wordsworth (1770–1850), Ugo Foscolo (1778–1827), John
Keats (1795–1821), and Giacomo Leopardi (1798–1837).[1] Two of
the poets are English, two are Italian; two belong to the first generation of nineteenth-century poets, two to the second; each of the
poets is a major figure in European literary history, and, though
the genius of each is unique, there are beneath the individuality of
their diverse works significant similarities of inspiration, technique,
and achievement which it is the purpose of this book to reveal.

I have chosen to study these four poets for several reasons. I admire
their poetry intensely; from the work of each I have gained more
enjoyment and wisdom than I can ever hope to express. And I
should particularly like to introduce to American readers the art
of Foscolo and Leopardi.[2] They are splendid poets, and if I can
interest even a few readers in their verse I shall be more than
satisfied. Finally, by studying these four poets in conjunction I hope
to show that some modern judgments of the nature and worth of
early nineteenth-century European poetry need to be modified.
Such modification may be of service not alone to our appreciation
of the past but also to our understanding of contemporary literature.
The poets studied here are among the first of the distinctively
modern era of world history, and I am interested in them not as
remote, obscure figures but as artists who first gave voice to aspirations and anxieties which have characterized the past century and
a half of the history of Western civilization.

Let me make it plain that I do not wish to force the poets into
any rigid or arbitrary relationship. For me the fascination of this
study arises from the way in which one must constantly balance
and evaluate differences and similarities of temperament, technique,
influence, and ambition in four highly original artists, two belonging
to one literary tradition, two to a very different one. Nor do I wish
to claim that the picture developed by my comparisons and contrasts
is a complete portrait of a literary epoch. I do not, therefore, use
the terms "Romantic" or "Romanticism" in the text of the chapters

which follow, though the words are unavoidable in the footnotes. I should like the reader to think of my observations as applicable to an important part of the poetry written during the first decades of the nineteenth century and not as an effort to redefine "Romanticism." Indeed, one reason for singling out this group of four poets is to provide an unusual perspective on the art of the early nineteenth century and to bring into high relief some significant qualities of that style which might be obscured by more comprehensive and conventional treatment. For this reason, too, I do not hesitate to proceed directly into the analysis of specific poems and to discuss only rarely the personal and cultural backgrounds out of which these individualized yet not unrelated art works emerged.

I cheerfully admit that my selective and inductive method has its limitations, but it does seem in one way at least peculiarly appropriate to the literature with which I am concerned. I accept the position of those modern scholars who have argued that at the end of the eighteenth century there occurred a decisive change in the theory and practice of literature, a change perhaps more momentous than any other in the history of European literature, a change from the concept of literature as formal and mimetic to a concept of literature as expressive, creative, self-assertive—"a logical inversion of the orientative patterns that had dominated the European mind from the remotest eons."[3] Since it is not my purpose to argue for the validity of this position but instead to use it as the premise upon which my work is based, it may be well to outline its salient features.

It was first adumbrated, so far as I know, by G. K. Chesterton in his book on Browning, published sixty years ago. Chesterton asserts that with Romanticism an entirely new conception of the function of poetry came into being, one that upset the most fundamental aesthetic principles of Western European literature. Chesterton contrasts Goldsmith's "When lovely woman stoops to folly" with Burns's "Ye banks and braes o' bonny Doon," observing that although the two lyrics appear side by side in Palgrave's *Golden Treasury*, few people notice that their subjects are the same. Indeed, Chesterton remarks, a man might read the two poems many times without recognizing their essential identity, because the lyrics lie on different sides of a "vast revolution in the poetical manner of looking at things. . . . And the whole difference . . . is this fundamental difference, that Goldsmith's words are spoken about a certain situation, and Burns's words are spoken in that situation." Chesterton goes on to point out, ". . . we have to arrive at the conclusion therefore, that the *vates* or poet in his absolute capacity is defied and overthrown by this new method of what may be called the *songs of experience.*"[4]

Chesterton's words, I believe, did not fall altogether unheeded, but they produced their major effects only slowly and indirectly. Since a history of twentieth-century critical evaluations of Romanticism would be out of place here, I shall leap fifty years to the work of three contemporary critics: Meyer H. Abrams, Morse Peckham, and Earl R. Wasserman. Professor Abrams' study of literary criticism, *The Mirror and the Lamp,* has decisively influenced scholarly writings about Romanticism throughout the past decade. Professor Abrams, indeed, has established a metaphoric terminology—the mirror and the lamp—which is used in all contemporary discussions of the new orientations introduced by Romanticism. Professor Abrams investigates "the displacement of the mimetic and pragmatic by the expressive view of art." According to the expressive theory,

a work of art is essentially the internal made external, resulting from a creative process operating under the impulse of feeling, and embodying the combined product of the poet's perceptions, thoughts, and feelings. The primary source and subject matter of a poem, therefore, are the attributes and actions of the poet's own mind; or if aspects of the external world, then these only as they are converted from fact to poetry by the feelings and operations of the poet's mind.

This theory, which became dominant in the early nineteenth century, transforms the way in which poems are to be evaluated. "Sincerity" and "genuineness" become the chief criteria of judgment, since according to the expressive theory a poem is no longer "to be regarded as primarily a reflection of nature, actual or improved; the mirror held up to nature becomes transparent and yields the reader insights into the mind and heart of the poet himself."[5]

Abrams is concerned above all with literary theory. Professor Morse Peckham is chiefly concerned with literary practice. His first major contribution to this topic was his article "Toward a Theory of Romanticism" (*PMLA*, LXVI, 1951, 3–23), but he has steadily developed his insights, and his original article has to be read in the light of his later "Toward a Theory of Romanticism: II. Reconsiderations," in *Studies in Romanticism* (I, 1961, 1–8), and, most recently, his volume *Beyond the Tragic Vision*. This book illustrates especially well his concern with Romanticism as supranational. Much of the strength of Peckham's criticism, like that of Abrams, resides in his ability to deal sensitively and learnedly with several literatures. Because he has this competence, and because he is imaginative enough to see relationships between diverse works in different languages, he is successful in transcending A. O. Lovejoy's argument for discriminating among "Romanticisms."[6] For example, by showing how in *Werther* "for the first time the problem of nineteenth-century man is revealed," Peckham explains the persistent international popularity of Goethe's novel. Werther's suicide, according to Peckham, symbolizes "the destruction of identity, consequent upon the failure of the vision of an ordered cosmos and of a meaningful society."[7] The solution to the problem of "Wertherian negation" was found in the nineteenth century by artists who, finding their necessary sense of identity could be "derived neither from God nor from nature," determined to

make a pure assertion of the self—to feel the sense of identity without any rational justification at all, and to perceive, to feel consciously, that the world and the divine, order and meaning and value, all emerge from this inner necessity, from the self. . . . There was . . . a logical inversion of the orientative patterns that had dominated the European mind from the remotest eons.[8]

Peckham believes in the continuing power and validity of the Romantic tradition, in which

Man therefore redeems the world; and since in the poet the imagination is predominant, the poet is the primary source of value, in traditional language, redemption. . . . Eventually this task of the artist is extended to every human being. Further, if man is to redeem the world, it is only this world which can be redeemed. . . . Nature is the source of both disturbance and equilibrium, of disorientation and orientation. To see what a gulf has here been crossed it is sufficient to call to mind that to the Enlightenment, Nature was the source of orientation only. Hence the frequent marriage of heaven and hell in the Romantic tradition.

It follows that the Romantic poet must face fully the brutality and evil of this world. He cannot be an escapist, and he must recognize the rights of others.

It is the Romantic's tradition that is really tough-minded. To him nothing is so beautiful as fact, nor does anything offer such sweet bones to gnaw on as the empirical world itself, the only world we can know, for the self can only be symbolized, not known. And hence the profoundest way to symbolize it is to recognize and assert its existence in another; and this empathic assertion is the basis of Romantic social morality.[9]

Professor Earl Wasserman's principal contribution to the definition of Romanticism is his difficult but rewarding book *The Subtler Language.* Unlike Abrams and Peckham, who both range widely and are particularly conscious of German literature, Wasserman is concentrated in his method. He analyzes intensively only a few English poems. But his analyses are for the purpose of establishing a solid critical ground for conclusions and generalizations which are close to Abrams' and Peckham's and which have broad applicability. As the title of his book indicates, Wasserman believes the new "orientative patterns" of Romanticism are manifested in the "language within language" of Romantic poetry. Once we see this subtler language, moreover, we recognize the close relation between the Romantic and the contemporary "world-picture."

The change from a mimetic to a creative conception of poetry is not merely a critical or philosophic phenomenon; the mimetic theory was no longer tenable when men ceased to share the cosmic designs that made mimesis meaningful. Now . . . the poet . . . must simultaneously employ the syntactical features of poetry to shape an order that has no assumed prototype outside the creative act, and with this internally contained order create the poem. . . . "Nature" . . . now shares with the poem a common origin in the poet's creativity.[10]

Since we today do not share "cosmic designs" any more than the Romantics did, our art must be essentially like theirs. For us as for them, "the creation of a poem is also the creation of the cosmic wholeness that gives meaning to the poem, and each poet must independently make his own world-picture, his own language within language. . . . Wordsworth's predicament is ours."[11]

Even though I have quoted extensively, I have done scant justice to three important modern critics, and of course I have omitted others of perhaps equal significance.[12] But the main outline of this contemporary position should be clear: Romantic literature is the expression of a profound change in Western man's fundamental ways of thinking, feeling, and valuing, a change, above all, toward an increased emphasis on the creative assertion of self as the basis of meaningful experience.

It is not my purpose, as I remarked before, to argue for this position. I accept it as a starting point. I want to distinguish and to characterize some of the significant qualities of the literature of the first years of the "revolution," and my contribution will be to describe more precisely and meaningfully one part—an unduly neglected part—of the total pattern which underlies the necessarily diverse and individualistic works of early nineteenth-century literature. Insofar as I am successful I shall modify the picture of the literary transformation other scholars have painted, but in the main I shall only add color and detail to their outline.

My purpose should help to explain my choice of poets. Wordsworth and Keats are among the most important English poets of the early nineteenth century, and Foscolo and Leopardi are the most important Italian poets of the same era. Motives, techniques, and aspirations common to these four are probably essential to the character of early nineteenth-century poetic style. This is particularly true since neither of the Italians influenced the Englishmen and neither of the Englishmen influenced the Italians. Furthermore, Foscolo and Leopardi, being Italians, belong to what has traditionally been regarded as the fringe of the Romantic movement, usually seen as centered in Germany and Britain. Insofar as their poetry conforms to a pattern to which Wordsworth's and Keats's conforms, we can be quite sure that we are dealing with important elements of a supranational style. And the more cosmopolitan this style is found to be, the more significant becomes the position enunciated by Abrams, Peckham, and Wasserman.

Then, too, the very unfamiliarity of Foscolo's and Leopardi's verse should help us to appreciate the almost too well-known poetry of Keats and Wordsworth, which, in its turn, may help to make more easily comprehensible the poetry of the Italians. I hope that the interplay of similarity and diversity, of familiar and unfamiliar, of central and peripheral may make it possible to break through the preconceived formulations which always block our enjoyment of the art of earlier epochs. Formulations about early nineteenth-century literature are especially dangerous, because this literature strove to escape conventional definitions and stressed originality and individualism. The more we can put aside a priori systematizations and work through particular poems toward the pattern which relates them to other, quite different poems, the more fully will we be able to enjoy both the diversity and the unity of early nineteenth-century poetry.

But it is probably futile to criticize literature without the hope of arriving at categories and generalizations. At any rate, one reason I have chosen these four poets is to make clear what seems to me an important strand in the pattern of early nineteenth-century poetry, a strand which has been, if not unrecognized, at least undervalued. It may be helpful, therefore, to summarize here the rationale of my organization. My arrangement is topical rather than chronological. I begin with the examination of works which derive rather directly from the actual social and political events produced by the French Revolution (Part One). I conclude with the examination of works which are fully "visionary" in their expression of the nature and potentiality of human existence (Part Four). I progress from the "practical" to the "visionary" first by considering some essential functions of poetry in the early years of the nineteenth century deducible from the art of the four poets (Part Two). I then investigate some important techniques by which these functions were realized (Part Three). The trend of the discussions within these sections may be summarized as follows:

PART ONE: *The Democratization of Literature: A Response to the Failure of Revolutionary Ideals.*

Many of the special qualities of early nineteenth-century poetry can be traced to the principal cultural event which precipitated the new style: the French Revolution. An impulse in most early nine-teenth-century poets is to extend to literature the ideals which gave rise to the social and political revolution which inaugurated the modern era of history. The failure of social and political aspirations frequently strengthened this impulse. The early nineteenth-century poet, whether liberal or conservative, is likely to find much to be dis-satisfied with in particular social arrangements, because he envisions an ideal civilization in which every man would be a poet, that is, a creative soul actively participating in a vital, enduring, self-conscious life. This life, though regarded by these poets as growing out of natural existence, is defined as a supranatural existence. Their effort to democratize literature and to make it expressive of a peculiarly human potentiality is, therefore, inseparable from their creation of a new cosmology. This cosmology is founded, first, on their assertion that there exists a vital principle within the apparently blind mechanism of natural forces. Then they assert that man alone—despite his physical insignificance in an infinite universe—is capable (through his imagination or capacity to create illusions) of perceiving and acting in accord with that inner vitality. Such perception and action are within the power of all men, since they are what distinguish men from other creatures. Finally, men so perceiving and so acting contribute to the intensification and the extension of universal vitality by rendering precious the seemingly insignificant and by endowing personal, private experience with suprapersonal meaning.

PART TWO: *Functions of Poetry: Translation and the Celebration of Humane Life.*

Through poetic vision, these poets believe, man attains to the possibility of the most intensely human life, a life creatively harmonized with the essential processes of a vital universe. By exercising his imaginative power man creates new life. So poetry, the expression of imaginative activity, is not a fixed thing but a translating energy. It translates the dead past into a living actuality, evanescent natural phenomena into enduring supranatural realities, and the facts of individual experience into the form of universal values. Poetry can so "translate" because it articulates an energy in the cosmos which remains latent until activated by the human imagination. In so articulating this "new" source of vitality within the systems of nature, man does not escape suffering, but he does develop his unique capacities and does establish the proper realm for their exercise. Much early nineteenth-century poetry, then, celebrates the vision of a new humanism.

PART THREE: *Time, Myth, and Total Relatedness: Essential Poetic Techniques.*

The new humanism is self-centered: its principles are revealed by particularized, individual experience. Hence the art of these poets is an intuitive one. But they believe that their art, through its intense personalization and interiorization, manifests truths of universal validity. As they strive to penetrate to the interior system of external phenomena, so they strive to pass through the idiosyncrasies of their own personalities to reach the essentially human. And to them that which is essentially human is a psychological point of view. Because a psychological point of view can be established only in relation to the total evolution of psychic processes which constitute a living mind, these poets frequently temporalize the physical. Wordsworth and Leopardi, for example, are preëminently poets of memory. But to them remembering is a creative, not a mechanical, process, a human form of resurrection. Such resurrection cannot of course restore the actuality of what is gone, but it can revitalize its significance, can establish its enduring value beyond the reach of natural destruction. This transformation of evanescent phenomena into lasting preciousness is not merely a private achievement—it also helps to articulate the artificial systems of a life superior to biological existence.

This life superior to biological existence is to these poets the true ideal misguidedly sought by political revolutionaries and social reformers. This new life does not require scorn of the world as it is, even its most commonplace elements, and this new life does not demand the rejection of the familiar and loved. The poet, inciting us to a creative revaluation of the well-known, often felt, and most sincerely believed, is a saner, freer, more humane prophet than the revolutionary or reformer, since the poet leads men toward a better life simply by seeing as all men can and should see. The poet sees the "real" in *all* its significance, as mythical in itself (not with reference, that is, to any abstract ideological or theological system), as precious simply because of its part in the total harmony of the actually existent cosmos. This harmony, however, is vital. The human being who participates in it does not sink into a passive felicity but instead engages himself completely in the hazards of a developing process. The chief characteristic of this process is its potential wholeness. Poetic vision for these poets is distinguished from political or scientific or any other kind of special vision by its search for the total possible significance of what it views. It is the ability to see the total relatedness of what he views that makes it possible for the poet to *create*, to realize the system by which mind and matter, past and present, natural and supranatural interoperate.

PART FOUR: *The Envisioned Ideal: Organic Relation of Future to Past.*

Why do some of these poets, for us notably Foscolo and Keats, so often turn to the art and mythology of earlier times as subjects of their poems? The art of the early nineteenth-century poets is visionary: it probes toward that which is not yet recognized, not yet even

in existence. Yet the visionary must be organic, too, it must be related
to previous visions. By transforming earlier recognitions of a human
life beyond biological existence into new, more complicated, re-
vitalized elements in the developing harmony of the cosmos, the poets
advance the possibilities of human experience without detaching it
from past human experience, without destroying the organic harmony of humanity's own supranatural evolution. This harmony is
particularly important since the validity of the new vision cannot be
established by appeal to any external authority. It must be self-
created, yet it must not be idiosyncratic. The "self-evident authen-
ticity" of excellent art is to these poets "beauty." But by "beauty"
they do not refer to the merely aesthetic, in the modern sense of the
term. By "beauty" they mean the compelling expression of the one
truth appropriate to modern man's potentialities, a truth which is
not and cannot be unrelated to visions of truth enshrined in the art
and mythology of earlier epochs.

Art, then, is the supreme manifestation of the evolving *power* of
civilization, which transforms the natural into something more valuable, more enduring, freer. Man, on the level of biological organization a created being, becomes a creative being through the achievement of civilization. His creativity operates not only upon natural
phenomena but also upon the already created artifices of his predecessors. Only by creatively shaping the supranatural world established
by men of the past, as well as the natural world into which he is
born, can the poet fully and actively participate in the realization of
a progressively more humane and truly autonomous life for all men.

PART

ONE

The Democratization of Literature:
A Response to the Failure
of Revolutionary Ideals

I ❧ THE COMPASSIONATE REBEL

FOSCOLO: *The Last Letters of Jacopo Ortis*

UGO Foscolo's novel *The Last Letters of Jacopo Ortis*, published in complete form in 1802,[1] is the first major work of
a young man chiefly gifted as a poet; it is principally of
interest to specialists as a biographical document and as the source
of subjects and conceptions which received full aesthetic development only in Foscolo's later poetry.[2] What I wish to call attention
to, however, are themes and aesthetic principles in *Jacopo Ortis*
surprisingly similar to themes and aesthetic principles in Wordsworth's *Prelude*, written at almost the same time. I hope to show
in Chapter II, through a study of *The Prelude*, that these similarities
are not coincidental but the product of a basic impulse in early
nineteenth-century European literature, an impulse so fundamental
as to force its way into works totally different in form, language, and
place in their authors' artistic careers. In brief, I wish to define the
likeness of works that apparently share nothing but date of composition, roughly the years 1797–1805.

The plot of Foscolo's novel is simple: Jacopo Ortis, forced to flee
Venice when the short-lived republican government he had supported is overthrown, takes refuge in his father's house in the
Euganean Hills. There he meets and falls in love with Teresa, who
has been promised by her father to Odoardo. Though Teresa recipro-
cates Jacopo's love, she is faithful to her father's command, and
Jacopo, respecting her loyalty, leaves the Euganean Hills and travels
through northern Italy. But he is unable to forget Teresa, and,
ravaged by this love and his sorrow at the divided and enslaved
condition of his fatherland, he commits suicide.

Even this bald summary suggests Foscolo's debt to Goethe's
Werther and Rousseau's *Nouvelle Héloïse*, a debt emphasized by
Foscolo's use of the epistolary form.[3] But the originality of Foscolo's

3

contribution to the tradition of the "suicide novel" is manifest from the opening sentences:

The sacrifice of our fatherland is completed: all is lost; and our life, should it be spared, will permit us only to lament our misfortunes and our infamy. My name is on the list of the proscribed, I know: but do you want me to save myself from my oppressors by entrusting myself to my betrayers? [4]
(p. 137)

These words are enough to suggest that *Jacopo Ortis*, which unlike the novels of Goethe and Rousseau was written *after* the French Revolution, will be a story not so much of sentimental suicide as of the betrayal of political ideals and the effect of that betrayal on an ardent young writer. This is also the story of *The Prelude*. And if we add to the opening quoted above the closing sentences of the first letter, we note tension between despair and love:

Since I have despaired of my fatherland and of myself, I await tranquilly prison and death. At least my body will not fall in the arms of strangers; my name will be deeply pitied by a few good men, companions in misery; and my bones will rest in the land of my fathers.
(p. 137)

This emotional conflict, central to *Jacopo Ortis*, appears in much early nineteenth-century literature. Every major poet of the time voices at least once his despair at having a glimpsed ideal snatched from his enraptured vision, and more often than not the origin of the ideal is to be found in the poet's political beliefs.

In *Jacopo Ortis*, as in *The Prelude*, the ideal is specifically political: what has been lost is political liberty. Nor does Foscolo present freedom and tyranny as abstractions; he treats them as concrete, particularized, painful and joyful experiences. He does not write from the sterilized security of political history but out of the vital confusions of personal passion. Unlike Goethe and Rousseau, Foscolo entangles real history with fiction. More than that, his sense of his personal life as a part of history permeates the novel and provides a new perspective for judging private aspirations and failure. We first see Jacopo reading Plutarch to the country folk and listening to their muddled accounts of famous local events. *Jacopo Ortis*, like *The Prelude*, strives to bring public history home to the individual heart.

Jacopo meets Teresa, "the divine girl," divine because so beautiful. Her beauty dispels his personal sorrow and revives his dreams of liberty for his country. Teresa's betrothed, Odoardo, impresses Jacopo less favorably. Odoardo is "good, punctilious, patient," but unemotional, a "calculating machine."[5] Odoardo is called to Rome on business, and Teresa's father is to accompany him part of the way. Jacopo decides to go to Padua, for he is determined "not to abuse the friendship" of Teresa's father. Such restraint shows Jacopo not to be a mere creature of his passions: he has respect for Teresa and for her father's goodness, however distorted by domestic tyranny it may be.[6] To Foscolo the true rebel is conscious of the need for genuine, if not conventional, propriety; hence much of the drama of *Jacopo Ortis* springs from Foscolo's representation of authentic passion as emotion capable of imposing limits upon itself.

Jacopo sees Teresa once more before he departs. "I was arrested by the distant trilling of a harp. O, I feel my soul smile, and running through my whole being the voluptuousness infused in me then by that sound. It was Teresa . . ." (p. 155). The essence of the description of the girl seated at her harp is expressed in Jacopo's exclamation: ". . . all, all was harmony." Teresa's beauty is a harmony of mind, spirit, and body; and the joy of Jacopo's love for her is the harmony her quiet presence imposes upon the discordant events and sensations of his life. The conflict which the novel presents is between those who would bring harmony to the world and those who deny and prevent harmony. Hence the tragic irony of the book: the tyrants, whether Teresa's father at home or the reactionary rulers of Venice, would seem to provide order and regularity to life, but loyal Venetians are in exile and Teresa's family is broken. Teresa's beauty, and Jacopo's idealistic rebelliousness reveal that deeper harmony which is destroyed by even well-meaning despots.

The next section of the novel, portraying Jacopo's life in Padua, prefigures the later more extensive and more philosophically significant journey of the hero through northern Italy. There are, however, two special incidents. Jacopo visits the boudoir of Signora M., who is, of course, a foil to Teresa's spiritual sincerity and innocent loveliness. At the end of his ironic description of how he resisted the temptations of the lady, Jacopo tells his correspondent Lorenzo: "You will perceive that this letter has been copied and recopied, because I wanted to give full expression to *'the beautiful style.'*" *Lo bello stile,* fine writing, is the *sine qua non* of contemporary society.[7] Foscolo observes that it is used to mask the crudest instincts, in this case lust. The "rational" society in which Signora M. and Odoardo flourish is a lustful society; its style is false. Emotional creatures like Jacopo and Teresa strive for relationships based on love, though their "style" is "natural." Foscolo's point is that lust is less a matter of "nature" than a product of bad society, rationalistic, tyrannous society, society that honors the artifice of *lo bello stile*. Jacopo and Teresa are drawn together by a love that makes possible the curbing of the sexual instinct. Teresa is physically beautiful, but the attraction of her beauty for Jacopo is that it manifests a harmony between sense and spirit, a harmony that would be destroyed by simple sensuality. Jacopo and Teresa are "natural" not because they are instinctual creatures but because they never behave like animals. Paduan society demands that one be either a tyrant or a slave, which is precisely the demand of lust, and Jacopo refuses: "No, neither human force nor divine power shall ever make me play the petty scoundrel's part in the theater of the world."

Jacopo meets an old countrywoman, decrepit, very poor, her family dead, who subsists on the charity of her neighbors. Sunk in apathy, she scarcely speaks, accepts charity without thanks, and clings to life with the obstinacy of instinct. This Wordsworthian figure of semi-humanity contrasted with the seductive Signora M. proves that Foscolo's ideal of "natural humanity" is not that of an instinctive, animalistic existence. Dominance of the instinct of self-preservation (the old woman) is to him a sign of incomplete humanity, as is dominance of the sensual (Signora M.). What is "natural" to man, what makes man something more than another animal, is his willingness to sacrifice his desires, even his desire for life.

Jacopo, having returned to the Euganean Hills, reads to Teresa the unhappy story of Glicera. Next, Teresa and Jacopo are visited by a woman who was formerly the love of Jacopo's friend Olivo, now deceased. The woman has forgotten her former lover and has become a Venetian bluestocking. Finally, we are given the fragmentary "Story of Lauretta," written by Jacopo himself. Glicera, Olivo, Lauretta, each suffered an unhappy love, and each in a different way illuminates the tragic situation of Jacopo and Teresa.

However, these stories and the complex perspectives they provide do not characterize Teresa and Jacopo, because Foscolo is not specially interested in psychology. The inserted stories, like the story of Teresa and Jacopo itself, are means of revealing truths about the relationship of an individual to his society, of thinking to feeling, of the human spirit to the natural world, and the like. *Jacopo Ortis* is a philosophical novel (in much the same way that *The Prelude* is a philosophical poem), and its strength lies not in its portraits of individuals but in its unabstract, emotion-charged presentation of a philosophy of life.

For example, in the long discussion Jacopo has with the Venetian bluestocking and her husband, Foscolo makes little effort at characterization or dramatic development. Rather he elaborates a philosophy of human relations. The lady who has readily forgotten her former lover is an example of society's indifference to individual constancy and suffering. Jacopo observes, "Those who have never been unfortunate are not worthy of their felicity." They are not worthy because they cannot know the value of suffering, and suffering *is* valueless unless man creates out of it supranatural value.[8]

The rich and fortunate tend to forget the personal love and compassion which alone justify suffering or give it meaning. As Teresa says to Jacopo to soothe his anger against their visitors, "If Olivo had not been unhappy, would he also have had a friend [like you] after death?" Suffering produces a compassion which transcends death. Moreover, wealth and good fortune are delusions. "I have begun the story of Lauretta," writes Jacopo, "to show the world in the mirror of that unfortunate girl's history the *inevitable* unhappiness of mortals" (p. 184). Insofar as man is a natural being he must be unhappy, for in him exists a spiritual impulse not to be satisfied by nature. Natural decay and death, supremely bitter to a creature capable of remembering past vigor and of conceiving immortality, make no distinction between rich and poor, fortunate and unfortunate. So love—not mere sensual desire—is of the utmost importance, for love is the expression of that which is supranatural in man. We are bound to suffer because we are natural beings; our compensation and highest achievement as human beings, something more than natural creatures, lies in our capacity to love. That capacity the well-to-do, the rulers of society, degrade into lust. Jacopo desires a better society, believing not in the perfectibility of man but in the beauty of compassion.

One function of Jacopo's story of Lauretta is to define compassion. The epigraph of the story is "Man will be unhappy." Human consolation is to share the feelings of others bound in a common doom, and Jacopo rejects those who with "an insolent philosophy want to rebel against human destiny, denying the inexhaustible pleasures of compassion" (p. 185). Compassion is inexhaustibly rewarding because it is inseparable from beauty and virtue.

> Oh beauty, beneficent genius of Nature! Where thou showst thy amiable smile joy leaps forth and diffused everywhere is that sensual pleasure by which the life of the universe is made eternal: one who neither sees nor feels thee is unpleasing to the world and to himself. But when virtue renders thee more shy and more dear, and misfortune taking from thee the boldness and envy of happiness, thou displayst thyself to mortals with thy locks deprived of joyful garlands . . . who could then pass before thee without offering a useless glance of compassion?
> (pp. 186–87)

Beauty, virtue, and misfortune are, of course, central to the worst sentimental eighteenth-century art.[9] But in Neoclassic art they are meant to provoke benevolence, a quality found only in people relatively satisfied and a quality perhaps never entirely free from condescension. For Foscolo beauty and virtue provoke useless compassion, for they appear in creatures doomed by their very condition to misfortune. Thus Foscolo's perspective is both more cosmic and more tragic than the Neoclassic perspective. What Dante had inscribed over the gates of hell Foscolo sees written in the eternal beauty of the heavens.

Foscolo's belief, nevertheless, derives from one of the eighteenth century's profound contributions to human thought: the conception of human brotherhood. Jacopo writes to Lauretta,

> I could have been husband, father, brother to you. The persecution of tyrants suddenly proscribed my name, and I was unable, Lauretta, to depart with a last farewell. . . . Thus poor Lauretta left forever in my heart compassion for the unfortunate. A precious heritage that I shall now share with you, men of misfortune . . . with you to whom there is no other comfort but to love virtue and to commiserate with it. You do not know me, but I, whoever you may be, am always your friend.
> (pp. 188–89)

Thus Foscolo accepts the eighteenth-century ideal of brotherhood, the belief in a common humanity which transcends the barriers of race, religion, and culture; but what had been an optimistic faith is darkened in Foscolo's mind by his broader spatial and temporal perspectives and by his experience of revolutions conducted in the name of that faith. "What can virtue do when destiny demands a victim?" The question reveals an anguished sense both of man's personal limitations and of the logic of historical necessity. Faith in progress is for Foscolo transmuted to a tragic awareness of man as victim rather than master of his fate. Brotherhood, as Foscolo understands it, rests on compassion and shared feelings, not on reason or rational benevolence. Through suffering we learn our common humanity. We learn, that is, as tragic heroes do, less with the intellect than with the heart. Foscolo believes, in fact, that a rational ideal of brotherhood must be dangerously unstable, because in his view it is all too "reasonable" for men to divide themselves from one another. To him the only stable ideal of the human community is that which can be felt along the pulse and in the heart.

Hence the climax of the first part of *Jacopo Ortis*, and the central event of the entire novel, is the kiss between Jacopo and Teresa. The complexities dramatized by the kiss are implied in the first letter which succeeds the interpolated story of Lauretta. Jacopo writes of Teresa:

I hear a voice that calls me traitor, the voice of her father! I become angry with myself, and I feel a healthy virtue rise in my heart, a repentance. . . . Then . . . at the appearance of her face my illusions return, my mind is transformed, forgets itself, and is enraptured by the contemplation of her beauty. (p. 190)

Again, Foscolo is less interested in the psychological effect of beauty and its dangers than in the philosophic significance of its dual quality. He is less concerned with the awkwardness of Jacopo's situation than with the eternal principle by which nature leads man to betray his own humanity.

And to provide for the conservation of all, [nature] rather than binding us together by reciprocal brotherliness, has constituted each man a friend of himself alone who would gladly exterminate the universe in order to live more secure of his own existence and to remain the solitary despot of creation. . . . Thus man, now openly, now secretly, is always the implacable enemy of humanity, preserving himself by any means, conspiring with the purpose of nature. . . .[10] (p. 191)

By natural instinct a man is the enemy of all other men, but a man can create the idea of an "unnatural" humanity—a relationship of love and respect between men. A man's humanity is measured by his refusal to behave naturally. The scene of the kiss is preceded by another in which Jacopo comes upon Teresa sleeping. It is a scene of sensual evocativeness in which the sensuality is intensified by the spirituality which controls and organizes it. "Her light clothing revealed the curves of her angelic body. . . . I touched like a devout believer her clothes, her fragrant hair . . . yes, and under this hand, now sacred, I felt the beating of her heart" (p. 194). But natural desire is transmuted to human love, Jacopo steals away, nature is not allowed to betray the man.

The kiss is introduced by a description of the natural setting in which it occurs, and the reflections provoked by the setting are Lucretian: "Matter returns to matter, nothing diminishes, nothing increases, nothing is lost here below." This blind materialism is the source of man's unhappiness. But when Teresa appears Lucretius is superseded by Petrarch and Sappho: "All is love, I said; the universe is only love. And who has felt this more profoundly or better depicted it than Petrarch?" (p. 198). This reference and the later one to Sappho, supreme poets of unfulfilled love, are not mere literariness. They give historical and cultural depth to Jacopo's assertion of a human love which transcends the mechanism of natural existence. Their poetry is proof that the human spirit can perpetuate itself, and testimony that Jacopo and Teresa, through their sufferings, are associating themselves with the finest and most spiritualized of human experiences. Teresa's beauty, like Lauretta's, is not mere physical attractiveness but the manifestation to the senses of a noble spiritual beauty, revealed at the very moment of the kiss by her cry, "I can never be yours." This is a nobility of denial and restraint, of the sacrifice of the strongest natural impulse to a supranatural, entirely human idealism.

There is, however, no trace of asceticism. Jacopo's kiss on Teresa's lips is no allegory; if it is a revelation of supranatural human potentialities, it is a revelation which can be manifested only in intense sensual experience. The transformation in his being, described by Jacopo, occurs only because he did kiss Teresa; what human beings can attain is to be learned only through the senses.

After that kiss I have become divine. My ideas are more sublime and smiling, my appearance gayer, my heart more compassionate. Everything appears more beautiful to my gaze, the complaints of the little birds, the whispering of the breezes among the leaves are today softer than ever; the plants grow fertile, the flowers at my feet take on color; I shall no longer flee mankind; all nature

seems to be mine. My soul is all beauty and harmony. If I could paint or sculpture that beauty I would disdain all earthly models and find them instead in my imagination. O love, the fine arts are your children; you first brought sacred poetry to the earth, the only nourishment of generous souls who can transmit from their solitude their superhuman songs to distant generations, spurring them with words and thoughts of godly inspiration to the highest ideals; you re-fire in our breasts the single genuine virtue useful to mortals, that piety which sometimes brings smiles to the lips of the unhappy condemned to sighs; and always through you revives the fruitful pleasure without which all would be chaos and death.
(p. 201)

Love, which grows from sensual experience, gives birth to art, and from art comes all that inspires man and makes beautiful a universe of perpetual self-destruction. Without love there can be no art; and art figures forth not the natural world as it is—chaos and death— but the spiritual harmony hidden (from eyes unillumined by love) within the confused discordance of ordinary appearances.

Deliciously enraptured I see before me naked nymphs, dancing, garlanded with roses, and in their company I invoke the muses and love; and beyond the banks where cascades sound and spume I see the rising bosoms, the shining hair tangled over shimmering shoulders and the laughing eyes of Naiads, amiable guardians of fountains. *Illusions!* cries the philosopher: and is not all illusion? All! Blessed the ancients who believed themselves worthy of immortal goddess's kisses, who sacrificed to beauty and to the graces, who diffused the splendor of their divinity through the imperfections of men, and who discovered BEAUTY and TRUTH by cherishing the idols of their imagination. *Illusions!* but mean- while without these I should feel life only in sorrow, or what frightens me more, only in a rigid and weary passivity; and when this heart shall feel no longer, I will tear it from my breast with my own hands, and fling it away like an unfaithful servant.[11]
(p. 202)

Love is primary. Reason is not despised, but those who rank reason above love or who believe reason alone is enough are despised. What to unaided reason are illusions, then, may be figures for truths more profound than unaided reason can attain. Reason cannot be dis- carded, however: without it illusion, which must be recognized as such, may become delusion. Jacopo knows rationally that there aren't "really" any nymphs; his illusions do not become delusions. He values illusions because they become the embodiment of his par- ticipation in experience beyond the capacity of either a merely sensual or a merely rational creature. An animal or a purely rational philos-

opher may be deluded, but neither can have illusions, for illusions
are the product of the distinctively human faculty, imagination,
which is neither sensual nor rational but is a synthesis of both. As
projections of the imagination, illusions are neither sensually nor
rationally real. Hence they vanish, and then the imaginative man
feels the deepest sorrow. But these transient illusions are valuable
because they testify to the possibility of a creative, harmonious order
in which the demands of the human spirit find, as they cannot in
the sensorily perceived natural world nor in the mechanical systemati-
zation of rational philosophy, appropriate pleasure and satisfaction.
Illusions are the fragile proof not only that man is more than an
animal but that there exist within the apparent randomness—or
worse, the apparent mechanical regularity—of the natural universe
of things, a lawful home and abiding satisfaction for the aspirations
of men's souls.

Foscolo, in other words, rejects the mechanical cosmology of the
eighteenth century but does not adopt what one might call the exis-
tentialist cosmology of the later nineteenth and twentieth centuries.
One may insist that Foscolo is a mystical or religious visionary, but
he is not a Christian writer. He finds harmony not in another world
but *within this* world. The refuge of a better life beyond the grave
to Foscolo is not a significant possibility, as is made clear by what
happens to Jacopo after the kiss.

Jacopo's ecstasy is short-lived. He has glimpsed a vision, but if he
is to be true to it he must sacrifice it.[12] He is a man with a man's
responsibility living in an imperfect world. The descriptions of nature
which express his growing sorrow and acceptance of his destiny
embody in their darkness Jacopo's sense that the price of a paradisial
vision is the recognition that man does not inhabit paradise. As a
natural creature man participates in the meaningless round of nature's fecundity and destructiveness. He must create his own paradise,
a paradise made from illusions, but to create illusions in full awareness of what they are is to recognize a human solidarity and the need
to act responsibly toward others. If Jacopo betrayed Teresa, he would
betray himself and their common humanity. Only a man can surrender what alone makes life worth living. To sacrifice what one
has oneself created is the ultimate sacrifice, since a man's own creation is all he knows that exists outside Nature's self-destroying and
self-reconstituting power. What one creates binds past to future in

the individual's vision of himself and of his fellows and their common destiny. But the sacrifice must be made. "I shall leave, I shall leave," cries Jacopo.

Italian critics agree that the second part of *Jacopo Ortis* is superior to the first.[13] There is refinement and development of ideas but no fundamental innovation in the second part. It treats of social and political affairs, but the treatment is founded upon the intensely personal evocations of part one. The structure of *Jacopo Ortis*, like that of *The Prelude*, is based on a broad movement from the personal to the social; in both works, however, the conclusion marks a return to the personal, for it is upon faith in private vision and individual experience that both poets' judgments of their world are founded. Both poets are rebels disillusioned by rebellion's aftermath but faithful to their original idealism. They became rebels because their personal vision forced them to recognize the rights of others; constancy to their ideals demands a return to the truth of their private vision of public good.[14]

The tone of part two is established when Jacopo puts Teresa before God. "I have never worshipped Him as I love Teresa. . . . I look across the universe and contemplate with astonished eyes eternity; all is chaos, all vanishes, and annuls itself. God himself becomes incomprehensible to me . . . but Teresa always stands before me" (p. 216). Yet Jacopo adheres to his decision to leave. Teresa's father is sympathetic, even apologetic, virtually admitting that Jacopo is a better man than Odoardo, but confessing that Odoardo's wealth and connections promise a tranquil and successful life for Teresa: "I beg you in Teresa's name," he says, "depart; sacrifice your passion to her felicity; and do not make of me the unhappiest father ever born." Since Jacopo knows his love is better than this shallow, anxious expediency, why does he depart? He knows Teresa will be unhappy, but she has chosen to sacrifice herself for her father. To subvert her choice would be to deny that spirit within her which makes her so precious to Jacopo: because he is more passionate than Teresa's father, Jacopo is more restrained.[15]

Jacopo travels first to Bologna and then to Florence, the sepulchre of the greatest Italian artists and thinkers. These men, says Jacopo, are now worshipped, but they were in their own times shamelessly persecuted. The one great man in modern Florence, Alfieri, is an isolated recluse because, like Galileo, Machiavelli, and Michelangelo before him, he stands for liberty, not for power. Here for the first time Foscolo begins to develop his idea of the relation of the artist to his society as the most intense and significant of *any* individual's relation to his social group. The latter portion of *Jacopo Ortis* is more openly a description of the growth of a poet's mind, and it compels us to regard the earlier section as a description of the generic sensibility out of which the artistic personality specifies itself. Yet the more concerned with aesthetics Foscolo becomes, the more he has to say about politics.

The problem of political liberty dominates the second part of *Jacopo Ortis*. Tuscany is beautiful, but its beauty is stained by Tuscan politics, and Jacopo attacks Italian particularism. The city states which fragment Italy are the social expression of selfishness, since they are sustained by politicians without ideals, especially without the ideal of national unity. Italians like Jacopo are exiles in their own land.

Italian readers have found in these pages a prophecy of a united Italy. Foscolo does condemn the dividedness of Italy; he desires the same harmonious unity for society as for the individual. But just as the individual's aspiration is based upon inspired insight into the *universal* harmony that dwells within the apparent meaninglessness of the cosmos, so social aspirations must be fitted to a *cosmic* scheme. Italy must be united, but only as one step toward the unification of all mankind. As long as Italy is politically divided Italians will be exiles in their own land; as long as humankind is politically divided all men will be exiles on the earth. Foscolo is not a nationalist in the usual sense, for to him national unity is but part of universal unity.

In Milan, where he goes after leaving Florence, Jacopo encounters Parini, an old poet-patriot. Then as now, Milan was Italy's most modern city, and here Jacopo sees Parini as one of the few exceptions in a contemporary society of tyrants and slaves. Parini's function is to challenge Jacopo's hopes for transforming this pattern. He is old but he is as vigorous an opponent of "ancient tyrannies and new license" as Jacopo. He is a great patriot and a great poet, his nobility evidenced by the wretched way in which society forces him to live. The essence of his wisdom is that rebellion produces tyranny. Parini expresses the disillusion Foscolo felt when he saw the democratic liberalism which was released by the French Revolution transformed into Napoleonic tyranny. We are equipped with more and bloodier

examples of Parini's law, so we are willing to accept it. Foscolo is not.
Parini says: "The loves of the multitude are brief and inauspicious;
they judge less by the intention than by luck; they call useful murder
virtue, and effective wickedness honesty. . . . Mortals are naturally
slaves, naturally tyrants, naturally blind" (p. 242).[16]

This view the idealistic Jacopo does not accept, though he does not
deny the *historical* truth of Parini's words and agrees that to date
humanity can only groan at the appearance of each new "liberator"
and can only look forward "to the hope of smiling over his coffin."
But there is more than history to this world: there is the unextinguish-
able passion for ideal truth.

> You few sublime souls that solitary or persecuted groan under the ancient mis-
> fortunes of our country, if the heavens prevent you from contending with force,
> why not at least reveal our evils to posterity? Raise your voice in the name of
> all, and say to the world that we are unfortunate, but neither blind nor vile,
> that we lack not courage but power. If your arms are chained, why do you
> yourselves imprison your minds, which neither tyrants nor fate, arbiters of all
> else, can ever control. Write. Persecute with the truth your persecutors . . .
> consecrate yourselves to the one phantasm that draws onward generous minds
> —glory. Condemn your contemporaries and your judgment shall enlighten
> your descendents.
> (p. 244)

So cries Jacopo. And these words enunciate the program to which
Foscolo did in fact commit himself. Unfailingly he preached his
idealistic faith in humanity, condemning his contemporaries, liberal
or conservative, who derogated his high conception of the human
spirit. And there is no doubt that his words and example inspirited
his gallant countrymen during the Risorgimento.

But Jacopo is not identical with Foscolo, though he represents an
important part of Foscolo. Jacopo's fictive existence and fate are
proof that his creator, a passionate, vital, "warrior spirit," had looked
death in the face with no unfriendly eye. For Foscolo suicide was not
simply a literary motif.[17] His choice of life was made in full awareness (of which his novel is the expression) that for man not all modes
of life are tolerable. His art, like that of most of his finest contemporaries, is characterized by its readiness to accept self-extinction as an
heroic[18] manifestation of idealism. (The "retirement" of Wordsworth is likewise meant by the poet to be affirmative and heroic,
not a retreat.)

From the moment he leaves Parini, Jacopo follows an undeviating course toward suicide, and we need not be concerned with all the psychological details of that fatal progress. But one incident is worth attention. Jacopo encounters a luckless artillery captain who recounts his poverty-stricken, wandering life with his wife and daughter. The point of the captain's story is that the "good education" of the day is a pernicious lie and that the prevalent ideal of the gentleman is fallacious. "If my father," laments the captain, "could hear from the earth where he is buried, I should denounce him with groans for not having made carpenters or tailors of his five children" (p. 252). Jacopo relieves the captain's wretchedness with gifts of clothing and money, but reflects bitterly that such temporary relief is almost worse than nothing, for in six months the family will be destitute again, still unequipped to succeed on their own, and with new regret for vanished prosperity. Yet he does not begrudge his gifts—they are the physical embodiment of "useless compassion."

Then follows an almost Sternian turn.[19] Was the captain's story a lie, Jacopo asks Lorenzo. Jacopo answers his own question by saying that it does not matter whether he believed the story or not. "I believe he was half naked and I was dressed." From this Jacopo derives a larger principle. "It is believed," he remarks with irony, "that man cannot exist without legislators and judges; and I believe it since everybody does. But I? I shall never be either legislator or judge. In this great vale where the human race is born, lives, reproduces, suffers, and finally comes to death without knowing how or why, I distinguish only the fortunate and the unfortunate" (p. 255). Jacopo is a revolutionary patriot who cannot become a Robespierre, because he sees that, bad as the old legislators and judges may be, the new legislators and judges will be no better if they are not enlightened by an ideal compassion. There can be no progress in tyranny: Napoleon can become as objectionable as Louis XVI. Jacopo declines to participate, even provisionally, in evil.

Jacopo asserts: "Each individual is the born enemy of society because society is the inevitable enemy of individuals." Each individual has the right to claim "I am a world in myself" (p. 257). What Jacopo sees further is that in claiming his individual rights denied him by society, the individual must claim the same rights for other men, and this prevents him from imposing his demands and beliefs on others. Jacopo's social beliefs are extensions of his relationship with Teresa: the strongest love is the most self-denying, and the ultimate proof of that love is the ultimate denial of self—suicide. Such suicide is neither weakness nor defeat: it is the final assertion of idealism; it implies that man can envision more worthy human relationships than those possible in present society. The validity of a man's vision is established by his willingness to prefer self-destruction to the destruction of others. Such suicide, therefore, transcends self-denial and becomes the positive assertion of a possible better self implying other better selves.[20]

The physical limits of Jacopo's journey are the boundaries of Italy, and these barren, mountainous wastes symbolize the senseless infecundity not merely of nature but of human history. In Jacopo's view man's history has been horrible because it has served the laws of nature. "It appears that men are the makers of their own misfortunes, but these misfortunes derive from universal laws, and the human race proudly and blindly obeys destiny." Man's state must be one of pitiful servitude as long as physical nature is the source and guide of his actions.

We reason about events of a few centuries; what are these in the immense space of time? Certain seasons of our mortal life appear heavy with extraordinary events, which are, however, the common and necessary effects of the whole. The universe counterbalances itself.
(p. 260)

From this general observation Jacopo passes to a rapid summary, drawn from Vico,[21] of the futility of history, concluding:

The world is a forest of beasts. . . . We pompously call virtuous all those actions which express the security of the tyrant and the fear of the slave. Governments impose justice, but could they impose it if in order to rule they had not first violated it? He who has through ambition robbed an entire province, solemnly condemns to the gallows one who stole a bit of bread out of hunger. Therefore, when power has smashed all the rights of others, to make them serve itself, it at once deludes men with the appearance of justice until another power destroys it.
(p. 261)

One must stress that Foscolo does not "hate" nature any more than does Lucretius, to whose descriptions Foscolo's are often analogous. What Foscolo opposes—and this is what puts him in opposition not only to Lucretius but also to the general trend of Enlightened thought—is the founding of morality upon natural law.[22] To Foscolo man can only define himself by asserting his independence of nature, because nature's law is that of counterbalancing forces. Man, accepting that law as his own, has made of his history a vain, blood-soaked cycle of slaughterings. Only by rejecting natural law as the basis of his morality can man attain genuine freedom and justice.

Foscolo's position is particularly interesting for two reasons. His rejection of natural law is not accompanied by any appeal to God's grace; he remains indifferent to Christian doctrine and dogma; his rejection of the eighteenth-century world-view involves no return to the medieval world-view.[23] Also, Foscolo is aware of man's minuteness within an immense universe. The nobility of the antique world's expressions of man's grandeur is limited by its relatively restricted conception of the universe. Foscolo's conception is modern; his universe is infinitely large and infinitely old. In this universe man, physically, dwindles to nothing. Yet at least as vigorously as the most humanistic of the ancients, Foscolo insists that man is not nature's slave; if he is not the measure of all things, he and he alone is the measure of himself.

This view does not commit Foscolo to a total rejection of nature. On the contrary, so soon as man is no longer subservient to nature's laws he is free to appreciate her as he could not while he was her blind, suffering slave. Free, he can choose to find in nature guidance and sources of strength, just as a child grown to independent manhood can choose to admire a parent, not following blindly as he did in his youth, but deliberately and on the basis of his own ideals.[24]

It is interesting, too, that Foscolo rejects human history as a source of moral guidance, even though he has a vivid awareness of history as a determinant in human experience. As with natural law, awareness of how historical determinism operates frees the individual from its control and permits him to understand it. Specifically, of course, consciousness of history reveals the futility of any "justice" imposed by force. The revolutionist who finds his justification in "historical necessity" enslaves himself to the meaningless law of nature, the ceaseless counterbalancing of forces, since political history is the record of human slavery to natural forces. Nor can one accept as valid the revolutionist's claim that his provisional justice, his present exercise of force, will produce a future utopia. Provisional justice is necessarily injustice. However brief its tenure, it is maintained by force; that is, by submission to the basic law of nature, which cannot lead to freedom but only to tyranny. Human freedom is rooted in the assertion of man's independence from nature in full recognition of the fact that man is a natural creature.

All this would seem to disqualify Foscolo as a rebel, and one wonders how he could have remained a liberal patriot to the end of his life. But the crisis out of which his art emerges is that, despite his philosophy, he remains passionately a rebel. Indeed, his philosophy demands that he be always rebellious. Thinking as he does, Foscolo cannot regard either the past or the present without desiring the overthrow of all that has led to and perpetuates his and others' enslavement. He must be a rebel, and one who believes in utopia now, in immediate present freedom. He differs, however, from the ordinary practical revolutionist in that his present utopia can only be established within the bounds of compassionateness. Hence for him there is no temptation to adopt the practical revolutionist's doctrine that a worthwhile end justifies evil means. To Foscolo, as to Kant, end and means should be identical: true awareness of what freedom is becomes the realization of freedom.

We can now see why Foscolo's aesthetics and politics are, at root, inseparable, and we should also be able to see that our conventional political terminology may hinder us from understanding and appreciating the value of this combination. The rebel is at least a potential artist, for to the degree that he does not accept he asserts a creative spirit. On the other hand, the artist serves as the prototype of the perfect rebel. To the artist means and end are identical in his creation, which becomes a reality simply by being expressed. The liberty demanded by Foscolo (and most other literary rebels of the early nineteenth century) is the liberty of every man to be a poet. This ideal did not come into being because the literary rebels were impractical aesthetes—Foscolo was a professional soldier—but because their idealism was innocent. They did not have behind them, as we do, the experience of 175 years of almost continuous social revolution. Hence they perhaps seem to us naïve, but their naïveté did not prevent them from perceiving—obviously it helped them to perceive—fundamental issues. Indeed, these writers are exciting today because their ideals are not corroded by too much practical experience.

One must go further. Today we can appreciate, as even our parents could not, how valuable is the penetration of these poets past the false, secondary distinctions which have multiplied through-

out our social and political life. Only a generation ago a reactionary
had to be right-wing politically, a radical, left-wing; but today we
speak of radical rightists and reactionary leftists. We can, or at least
should, understand why so many of these first artist-rebels were
driven into conservatism or a passive liberalism; but we need not
lose our sympathy for the poets because of these labels. Foscolo's
Jacopo says at the end of his life:

Lorenzo, do you know where true virtue still lives? In us few weak and unfortunate men, in us who, after having experimented with all the errors and
felt all the ills of life, know how to commiserate with them and to succor them.
Thou, O compassion, art the single true virtue! all the others are usurer's
virtues. (p. 262)

Foscolo the fighting liberal here sounds a little like Wordsworth
the retreating conservative, because each poet came to believe that
he had sustained the original and vital idealism of rebellion when
others, including successful rebels, had lost it. Liberal Foscolo and
conservative Wordsworth remain at heart idealists and republicans
because they believe that all men should be poets, but their interest
in the *individual* and his *civilization* tends to put them in opposition
to both conservative and liberal political activists, who are principally
concerned with *society*.

II ⨏ FREEDOM'S HARMONY

WORDSWORTH: *The Prelude*

I N this chapter I want to sketch a major pattern of development in *The Prelude* in order to draw attention to the way in which the relation of aesthetic principles to political aspirations expressed in *Jacopo Ortis* finds a parallel in Wordsworth's greatest work. It would be wrong, of course, to insist on too close an analogy between the Italian novel and the English poem, but the similarities that do exist are basic ones. From them derives a configuration of poetic attitudes and themes and techniques which contribute significantly to the distinctive character of early nineteenth-century European poetry. That configuration I shall describe in detail in later chapters, but first I hope to establish its foundations and origin. These are to be found in works written by men who valued their personal experiences precisely for their uniqueness. *Jacopo Ortis* and *The Prelude* are necessarily very different because both of them, the former indirectly and the latter overtly, are autobiographical works;[1] but at the center of each autobiography is one momentous public event, the French Revolution. It is not extravagant to say that much of the best early nineteenth-century poetry is the expression of an intensely personal response to an enormous cultural upheaval. Hence if we are to understand this poetry we must discover similitude in diversity, parallelism within divergencies. Any schematic description which is too simple or too general will distort the individuality which we want to make plain: similarities which are too broad will be meaningless because the poets write from personal experience. Contrarily, obvious differences may be misleading. That *The Prelude* was written by a man who later became "conservative" whereas *Jacopo Ortis* was written by a man who remained "liberal" may not be as important as it at first appears.[2] Similitude in diversity is the essential complexity of the pattern we are investigating, or at least so I believe and so I hope to prove.

21

BOOKS I AND II

The "gentle breeze" of *The Prelude's* first line is "grateful" to Wordsworth because he is "now . . . free."[3] He is not "scar'd" at his "liberty"; he feels he cannot miss his way even if his "guide" is only "a wandering cloud." The second verse paragraph again associates the wind with freedom. At the touch of the breeze he had "felt within/A corresponding mild creative breeze." But *now* that inner breeze "is become/A tempest . . . vexing its own creation." These two "powers," inner and outer breezes, having conjointly broken "a long-continued frost," bring "vernal promises" of a "holy life of music and of verse." The liberation of inner energy conse-crates the poet's outer freedom; present physical delight promises future spiritual fulfillment.

In the next verse paragraph the relations between inner and outer liberty and physical and spiritual delight are sustained by the poet's reference to himself as a "spirit" speaking "spontaneously" to the "open fields" and as a prophet taking on the raiment of holy office. The relations are further complicated and enriched by the comment:

> My own voice chear'd me, and, far more, the mind's
> Internal echo of the imperfect sound.
> (I, 64–65)

These first lines assert that the joy of liberty derives from a combination of outer and inner freedom.[4] The latter is, in part at least, produced by the former but is superior because inner freedom sanctifies outer freedom. True and complete liberty derives from a harmonious relation between physical and spiritual freedom. The story of *The Prelude* is in large measure the story of how that precious harmony was achieved.[5] The story is not simply of the evolving interplay between the poet's mind and external nature, though of course that is important. More significant is the poet's discovery of an interplay between the inward and outward energies of all animate and inanimate things, an inward energy in nature and an outward energy in his mind.[6] What begins as simple cor-respondence will become, as the lines describing the mind's response to spoken words suggest, a more elaborate harmony; but the first image of the breeze is retained throughout, so the fundamental terms in which the story is presented remain those of movement and stasis. The terms appear in different guises but are always referable to the original image of the breeze.[7] Indeed, the very structure of

The Prelude relates to this image. The poem as a whole is static in that Book XIII concludes at the point where Book I begins; yet within that "stasis" is contained the growth to maturity of a poet's mind. The essence of growth, it is worth remembering, is movement, development in time. To Wordsworth, mind is a moving force, an energy, not an object.[8] To understand a force we must attend to its manifestations, its activity, but our completed understanding must be of the force's inherent, permanent nature, that which will characterize it in all its manifestations. *The Prelude*, then, must simultaneously dramatize both the *"stable et mouvant."*[9]

The first book of *The Prelude* recounts Wordsworth's search for a subject upon which to exercise the power celebrated in the opening verse paragraphs. This seems an odd way to begin a poem, since we assume that a poet knows what he is going to write about when he starts. To Wordsworth, however, poetry is a process, a release of that energy which is the mind. A poet, therefore, cannot know exactly what he is going to write until he has written it. Poetry is not irrational, but making a poem is different, say, from making a bridge or from making a political pronouncement. Wordsworth's very manner of beginning serves to define a distinctive characteristic of that mental activity, the creation of poetry,[10] which he regards as most important,[11] namely, that it is a liberation of energy.

In searching for his "theme" Wordsworth first thinks of "some old/Romantic tale by Milton left unsung." To Wordsworth, as to most of his contemporaries, Milton was the grand republican bard of liberty, and all the heroic subjects considered by Wordsworth involve struggles for liberty: Mithridates, Sertorious, Dominique de Gourges, Gustavus, and Wallace. But none of these early champions of liberty attracts the poet's genius. Contemplating the fact that he is free to choose whatever theme he wishes but cannot find an appropriate one, he recollects the time when his liberty found expression in all his acts—his youth. So he slides into his subject, the old, Romantic tale of his own mind's freedom, enslavement, and reliberation.[12]

The first two books tell of how the "discordant elements" of Wordsworth's youth were harmonized. The harmonizing agent was the poet's visionary power which derives from love and is suprarational. Vision, as opposed to rationality, perceives "the unity of all" and is synthetic and creative,[13] whereas reason by itself is analytic and reductive.[14] Hence the weakness of reason is that it cannot explain what most interests us, the operation of the human mind.[15]

> Who that shall point, as with a wand, and say,
> "This portion of the river of my mind
> Came from yon fountain"?
> (II, 213–15)

The image of the mind as a river is scarcely original with Wordsworth, but the serious literalness with which he treats the image
is perhaps unique. Virtually all the extended metaphors and recol-
lected scenes in the first two books relate to the picture of the mind
as a river, which picture, in turn, derives from the original image
of the mind as a breeze.

> Hard task to analyse a soul, in which
>
> .   .   .   .
>
> . . . each most obvious and particular thought,
> Not in a mystical and idle sense,
> But in the words of reason deeply weigh'd,
> Hath no beginning.
> (II, 232–37)

Upon this perception depends the central argument of *The
Prelude*,[16] and the perception is true to common experience. We
do not know where our ideas come from. When we reflect on why
we do not, we recognize that any one thought is part of a moving
stream of ideas from which it cannot be separated without loss of its
special character. What is perhaps less true to common experience
is Wordsworth's conviction that the external world is like the mind,
a dynamic unity which can be enjoyed and understood only if its
parts are not separated from their matrix. To understand the special
character of any particular object one must study it not in isolation
but as an active element in its spatial and temporal context.[17]

To establish one's identity, therefore, one must harmonize the
"flow" of psyche with the "flow" of the "active universe." Such
harmony occurs naturally in earliest infancy.

> . . . blest the Babe,
> Nurs'd in his Mother's arms, the Babe who sleeps
> Upon his Mother's breast, who, when his soul
> Claims manifest kindred with an earthly soul,
> Doth gather passion from his Mother's eye!
> Such feelings pass into his torpid life
> Like an awakening breeze, and hence his mind
>
> .   .   .   .

> Is prompt and watchful, eager to combine
> In one appearance, all the elements
> And parts of the same object, else detach'd
> And loth to coalesce. . . .
>
> .   .   .   .
>
> From this beloved Presence, there exists
> A virtue which irradiates and exalts
> All objects through all intercourse of sense.
> No outcast he, bewilder'd and depress'd;
> Along his infant veins are interfus'd
> The gravitation and the filial bond
> Of nature, that connect him with the world.
> Emphatically such a Being lives,
> An inmate of this *active* universe;
> From nature largely he receives; nor so
> Is satisfied, but largely gives again,
>
> .   .   .   .
>
> . . . creator and receiver both.
>   (II, 239–73)

But this level must be transcended, the fitting of active mind to active universe must be carried out in a more complicated and significant fashion: full maturity and identity are attained if the child grows into a poet.

> . . . Such, verily, is the first
> Poetic spirit of our human life;
> By uniform controul of after years
> In most abated or suppress'd, in some,
> Through every change of growth or of decay,
> Pre-eminent till death.
>   (II, 275–80)

BOOKS III AND IV

The argument in Book III is focussed in the passage (ll. 168–94) wherein Wordsworth discusses the *necessity* for modifying the "Genius, Power,/ Creation and Divinity" of his youthful mind, the "glory" of "what passed within." This theme had appeared in the first two books but in Book III, when Wordsworth leaves the Lake Country for Cambridge, the modification is crucial. Once more the poet must harmonize discordant elements, but now on a more mature and complex level, because if he is to realize his potentialities, a "northern villager" must be transformed into a cultured man able to participate sympathetically in the highest activities of human civilization. But this change must take place without destroying the genius, power, creation, and divinity which is the poet's natural heritage. Book III and Book IV describe the halting progress, the partial success and partial failure, of this growth into a maturity which can harmonize the power of civilization with the divine power innate in the individual—a maturity which it is the purpose of *The Prelude* as a whole to celebrate.

The scene upon the poet's return to his rural home (IV, 132 ff.) reveals by its contrast with earlier similar scenes the progress in his first "humanization," his liberation from total control by nature. Now the natural setting, though not irrelevant, is subordinated to "swellings of the spirits," and serves only to comfort "A heart that had not been disconsolate." Yet, as is shown in the famous dedication passage (IV, 304–45), the value of the poet's progress lies in the fact that his new freedom deepens and enriches his heritage of natural genius, the "divinity" manifested in his youth.[18] "I made no vows, but vows/ Were then made for me." His developing humanness is still in harmony with his natural being; he can still *receive* blessings.[19]

But how far he has travelled from his thoughtless youth is revealed by the incident of the destitute soldier, which—significantly—immediately succeeds the dedication scene and contrasts with it. The poet's dedication occurs at dawn, his meeting with the soldier at the dead of night, "the fires all out." The dedication is surrounded by the practices and pleasures of communal life, "dancing, gaiety, and mirth," and "Labourers going forth into the fields," whereas the soldier appears "A desolation, a simplicity/ That seem'd akin to solitude." The focus of the dedication, of course, is the poet himself, but with the soldier—for the first time in *The Prelude*—another human being is more important than the poet, yet the soldier's individuality is not emphasized. It is his archetypal humanness which renders him memorable, and what he embodies are those features of human destiny which lie beyond tragedy: the soldier tells his story with "a strange half-absence . . . as of one/ Remembering the importance of his theme/ But feeling it no longer." The soldier's sufferings, so unremarkable, so near the basic condition of all human existence, illustrate why the poet would be "sinning greatly" did he not accept his dedication. He has been granted the opportunity and capacity to envision the relatively simple and beneficent natural harmony that attends youth, and also the more complex and painful harmony of maturity, not simply the harmony of animal vitality but also the harmony of fully developed consciousness. He has been granted the vision to perceive the inner unity which binds thinking and suffering man as an active agent (as well as a passive receptor) to the processes of the natural universe: his vision must reconcile the soldier's "ghastly mildness" betokening what man can make of man with "all the sweetness of a common dawn."

BOOK V

Book V, instead of continuing with the poet's education at Cambridge, tells of his reading, not when he was an undergraduate, but when he was an "untutored" youth. The purpose seems to be to defend children's fairy tales. The book begins with a lament for the frailty of works of art, which, Wordsworth reflects, perish easily. "Why," he wonders,

> . . . hath not the mind
> Some element to stamp her image on
> In nature somewhat nearer to her own?
> (V, 44–46)

His implied answer is that the immortality of Shakespeare, Cervantes, or Euclid depends not on preserving the physical materials containing their words but on keeping alive in the hearts and minds of men a spirit ready to receive immortal truths. As long as that spirit lives, no physical destruction can take from us our finest heritage, and that spirit is nourished by letting children read fantastic tales, even when these are written by "impostors and drivellers." Wordsworth's argument is that the human spirit requires above all else liberty. Just as he urges that children should be allowed to run about and play freely, to risk their necks physically, so he argues that they should not be shielded from emotions but should be exposed to love and hate, rage and tenderness. Analogously, their imaginations should be given complete freedom: children should be allowed to read fantastic fairy stories. Wordsworth devotes attention to fairy stories because he believes imaginative freedom is more important than physical and emotional freedom, since all other liberties derive from the liberty of the imagination. From this belief stems Wordsworth's faith that genuine freedom lies within the grasp of every man.

The last hundred lines of Book V present the outline of Wordsworth's concept of the imagination in *The Prelude*.[20] The starting point for this concept is the perception that unaided reason can find no beginning even for the most obvious and particular thought. To trace one thought toward its origin is to retrace one's life backward into childhood. The source, ultimately, of any one eddy or swirl in a river is the source of the river itself, but if one may discover the fountain from which a river originates, the fountain of the mind is more mysterious, perhaps even undiscoverable.

> . . . our childhood sits,
> Our simple childhood sits upon a throne
> That hath more power than all the elements.
> I guess not what this tells of Being past,
> Nor what it augurs of the life to come;
> But so it is. . . .
> (V, 531–36)

One must stress here the poet's confession that he does not know. He is sure that the source of man's more than natural strength lies in his "simple childhood," but from whence derives the strength of childhood he does not know.[21] He accepts the mystery; he argues for no mystical faith here; he simply establishes a limit to rationalism. Man's most essential being is mysterious—upon that circumstance will be built the Wordsworthian exaltation of humanity.[22]

Fairy tales to Wordsworth, then, are a crude but genuine expression of the mystery in which man's soul originates. However clumsily, they nourish that "poetic spirit of our human life" which must be nourished if the soul is not to wither and grow old as the body declines. It is in that "dubious hour" of childhood,

> That twilight when we first begin to see
> This dawning earth, to recognise, expect;
> And in the long probation that ensues,
> The time of trial, ere we learn to live
> In reconcilement with our stinted powers,
> (V, 537–41)

that "we feel/ We know" we have friends if the imagination is fed. Because they are not confined by the limits of rationalism, fairy tales can minister to man's noblest faculties:

> . . . that most noble attribute of man,
> Though yet untutor'd and inordinate,
> That wish for something loftier, more adorn'd,
> Than is the common aspect, daily garb
> Of human life.
> (V, 597–601)

The fully developed imagination will find *within* the "common aspect, daily garb of human life" something "loftier," but the imagination cannot so develop unless it is early encouraged to exult in the mysteries and wonders of something beyond common appearances. Just as the source of man's highest spiritual faculties must be traced back to the twilight of childhood, so the source of great art, where those highest faculties are most fully manifested, is to be found in children's stories. The mystery and wonder of the finest literature is the mature expression of the sense of mystery and wonder which is the glory of childhood.[23]

BOOK VI

The sixth book describes the poet's critical transition into early manhood, focussing on his first experience in France at a time of revolution. But early in the book there is a long passage in praise of geometry (ll. 135–87). Geometry, the poet claims, has fascinated him as it has fascinated most poets, as "an independent world,/ Created out of pure Intelligence." Such a world lies beyond the vicissitudes of time and space but is not "escapist." It is "a clear Synthesis" created out of man's mind, which transcends nature to the point of appearing as "An image not unworthy of the one/ Surpassing Life . . . out of space and time" (VI, 154–55). Rational power is essential to the poetic mind, and these lines should remind us that to Wordsworth imagination is never to be separated from reason, though he always treats imagination as superior to unaided rationality.[24]

We need this reminder, because the poet's descriptions of his joy in travelling through an exulting France during the early days of the Revolution are so rich in religious imagery that they may mislead us into thinking of Wordsworth's goal as an anti-intellectual mysticism. The culmination of this particular section is to be found in the reflections on the Convent of Chartreuse,[25] the famous monastery despoiled by the revolutionists. Here more plainly than elsewhere, perhaps, we see that Wordsworth regards the French Revolution as a spiritual event and, therefore, one which should be characterized by restraint and compassion.[26]

For Wordsworth as much as for Foscolo, the very passionate power which activates rebellion imposes a severe law upon its own impulse. The Convent was the embodiment, in crude and superstitious form, of an ideal of spiritual equality, and since such equality is the inspiriting ideal of the Revolution, the Convent should have been spared. In politics as in poetry, the dynamic, creative impulse must impose order and not degenerate into a source of anarchy. To understand this point one must grasp the central purpose of the celebrated lines commemorating Wordsworth's passage across the Alps (VI, 525–72), which fully if oracularly define imagination. Before this point in the poem, the imagination, so to speak, has not existed as a developed capacity. (The word is used only twice before this.) Whatever the sources of imagination, it cannot be possessed in childhood or youth. It is an achievement of maturity. This is so because, in the broadest terms, imagination is the human capacity which synthesizes into harmonious unity the force of impinging sensory impressions with the outgoing force of creative intelligence. Possessed of this unity, the imaginative man perceives and responds to the unity which under-lies and animates the diversity of all natural phenomena. What he perceives and responds to is not uniformity but unity—that is, a vital and meaningful system of relationships among diverse phenomena.[27] Imaginative vision does not destroy the particularity of the diverse elements of experience, but instead comprehends them as parts of a unity which could not exist except through the action of independent particularities. Hence the imaginative vision "transforms" the world at the same time that it affirms the precious existence of the world as it is.

The description of the chasm in the Alps is dominated by the attribution to natural objects of improbable and even contradictory forms of existence: "woods decaying, never to be decay'd," "station-ary blasts of water-falls," "torrents shooting from the clear blue sky," "rocks that mutter'd," and so forth. Out of these contradictions is constructed a unified impression of the chasm as a whole; and this whole, comprehending "Tumult and peace, the darkness and the light" is emblematic of the "workings of one mind, the features/ Of the same face." So the total scene endows the extraordinary sights and sounds that are parts of it not with fearful uniqueness but with the power of "types and symbols of Eternity," and the terrible chasm is humanized; that is, the most violent and fearful manifestations of external nature are perceived to be not random or only mechanically related but elements in an organic unity. The chasm, like that in *Kubla Khan* and many of the places of vision in Wordsworth's poetry, is simultaneously "savage . . . holy and enchanted," because it embodies the mysterious potency of life which is fully realized only in the harmony created when natural reality is transfigured by human imagination.

In the final portion of Book VI Wordsworth defines what he means by beauty, and, in the lines praising the Italian lake country (esp. VI, 605–10), what it means to him, what its value is. Physical beauty provides a serene accord for the senses and leads toward spiritual harmony (note ll. 661–72); yet, however much outward things may delight us, upon the exercise of our inner powers depends our success at establishing a fully satisfying existence for ourselves. So beauty at its best, like liberty, is the result of correspondent powers, is the result of mutual interchanges from within and from without. True beauty, then, is an embodiment both of the energy in substantial things and of the substantiality of spiritual phenomena, an embodiment which symbolizes the principle of harmony that orders the universe.

BOOKS VII AND VIII

Books VII and VIII tell of the poet's introduction to social life through his residence in London, and together they show us the struggle it was for Wordsworth to come to terms with his civilization. The struggle occurred, not as is sometimes said, just because the poet was a country boy who felt uncomfortable among the crowds and confusion of a great city, but because Wordsworth was a rebel. He opposed the civilization of which London was the supreme representative. When he says that what sustained him during his first months in London was his youth in the north country, he is not indulging in a homesick lament, but is reaffirming his rebellious faith that there exists a better life than that of the modern centers of civilization.

The last lines of Book VII sum up the poet's objections to urban life: the city reduces its inhabitants to "one identity," distinguishing them by differences that "have no law, no meaning, and no end."[28] This criticism is related to the poet's definition of imagination, which does not reduce the objects of its regard to "one identity" though finding them united by one life. In this life each thing has its particular place in the organized complexity of all things, to which it makes its unique contribution. The least things have law and meaning and end, in short, value—which modern city civilization denies.

It is important that Wordsworth was reared in barren country-side—barren, as we shall see, of more than vegetable life. What Wordsworth misses in the city is "among least things/ An under-sense of greatness," which is precisely the quality of a simple and unfertile landscape. In a place like the Lake Country there is never too much to distract the eye. There are only a few simple objects, such as a hill, a group of trees, a lake; hence the mind dwells upon them. In such landscapes one comes to appreciate the "majesty" that dwells in the simplest lives and natural formations. To Wordsworth it is the crowdedness and restlessness of London which typifies the spirit of modern civilization, and crowdedness and restlessness deny to the soul the possibility of envisioning that "ennobling Harmony" wherein dwells the only "enduring life."

But Wordsworth cannot, finally, deny all virtue to anything so human as a city, because for him love of nature leads to love of man. Did he remain totally negative to London he would be untrue to his deepest impulses. How he was led into active and sympathetic participation in the problems of modern civilization is revealed by the rustic fair described in Book VIII.

> . . . Immense
> Is the Recess, the circumambient World
> Magnificent, by which they are embraced.
> They move about upon the soft green field:
> How little They, they and their doings seem,
> Their herds and flocks about them, they themselves,
> And all that they can further or obstruct!
> Through utter weakness pitiably dear
> As tender Infants are: and yet how great!
> (VIII, 46–54)

For Wordsworth as for Foscolo the chief paradox of human life is man's simultaneous littleness and greatness. As the lines above suggest, Wordsworth had grown up with the paradox always physically before him, and that is why, I think, he insists that his bleak northern landscapes are "more exquisitely fair" than any of the mythical paradises of legend. What he grew up amongst was the sanctified beauty of ordinary things blessed by the presence of free men. The men who first impressed him were those closest to the ordinary workings of nature and at the same time, apparently at least, the freest.

Wordsworth's description of the shepherds and his explanation of why they so shaped his mind contrasts the reality of the poet's life in the country and the fictive descriptions of pastoral literature. The contrast is not crude, for Wordsworth does not, as some Neoclassicists do, scorn the fictive ornamentation of pastoral poetry; he speaks with sympathy and affection of this art; he appears almost to regret that plain truthfulness prevents him from joining with Shakespeare and Spenser in the delights of pastoralism. But plain truthfulness[29] combined with intense spiritual feeling is the foundation of Wordsworth's art. His nature and early environment have exiled him from Arcady.[30]

The Lake Country appears to have been without the local customs, folk-superstitions, and peasant traditions which figure so largely in the poetry and novels of Walter Scott and in almost all subsequent English literature dealing with rural life. Wordsworth mentions older people who had seen the Maypole dance in their youth, but during his own boyhood there seems to have been scarcely a trace of the local color which plays such a tremendous part, for example, in Thomas Hardy's novels more than half a century later. The absence of local tradition, superstition, and ritual in Wordsworth's early life has not been sufficiently considered. It is a key to his art. The stark, archetypal character of the people in his poetry derives from this cultural barrenness. And his ability to move from the literal presentation of a particular reality to a cosmic sense of elemental presences and emanations depends on his freedom from the restraints of any quaint localisms. In the passage we are considering, for instance, there is no peculiarity of custom to stand between the shepherds' simple, elemental humanness and the simple, elemental nature in which they live. Wordsworth offers a prayer of thanks

> That Men did at the first present themselves
> Before my untaught eyes thus purified,
> (VIII, 438-39)

for it enabled him, while seeing the reality of man in constant toil to win subsistence from an unbounteous nature, also to see man as "naturally" noble, impressive, and free from "the deformities of crowded life." Thus a shepherd might loom out of a mist, "in size a giant," or might flash suddenly from the shadow of a hill, "glorified/ By the deep radiance of the setting sun." In sum, the physical and cultural environment of the poet's youth trained him to recognize man as both great and little and to perceive the magnificence dwelling within the plainest, humblest objects. This vision is the essence of Wordsworth's imaginative power. He has the ability to see simultaneously the thing in itself and as a participant in the harmony of all things.

Given this vision, he could not fail to be led into ever deepening concern with man and all that man has made, but he admits that while his background assured him of eventual success it almost as certainly condemned him to a long period of trial and error. The falsifications of his early poetry (VIII, 511–41) sprang from too great a love for nature. To this error London offered a corrective. The great metropolis (VIII, 678–836) brought a sense of living history into the poet's heart. The crowds and monuments, present realities, carried home to him, as books never had, a *vital* sense of that unity amid diversity which, heretofore, he had experienced only in natural surroundings. In London it dawned on him that the beauty he had found in natural relationships exists also in social relationships, that beauty finds expression in time, the dimension of human history, as well as in space, the dimension of natural experience. But "this scale of love, though filling daily," was still light compared to that of nature. It was to be the revolution in France, an historical event, which would tip the balance.

BOOKS IX–XI

The rhythm of the books describing Wordsworth's experiences during and immediately after the French Revolution, is that of a succession of hopeful exaltations followed by plunges into despair,[31] and the alternations culminate in the black hopelessness with which Book XI closes. To outline as briefly as possible the pattern of these developing oscillations, and its significance, one may observe first the way Wordsworth was drawn into intense personal commitment to revolution and second the nature of the final despair to which his commitment led. One of the few individuals named in *The Prelude* is Michel Beaupuy, the French officer who probably as much as any other single person developed Wordsworth's revolutionary ardor. Beaupuy aroused Wordsworth to the necessities and opportunities of the historical moment. Wordsworth had not followed the political events in France with the excited interest of his contemporaries because he took liberty for granted.[32] He had been reared, he says, in what was almost a natural democracy (IX, 221–25), and his youthful experience of democracy was reinforced by the intellectual democracy of Cambridge (IX, 225–29). Hence to Wordsworth the events of the French Revolution and their impact on English society

> Seem'd nothing out of nature's certain course,
> A gift that rather was come late than soon.
> (IX, 252–53)

Beaupuy presented the historical moment of French social life to Wordsworth, and in a fashion that accorded with the poet's early experience. The "hunger-bitten girl" (IX, 510 ff.), for example, combines the simple particularity and universal significance which Wordsworth had found in the shepherds of Cumberland. And her suffering from hunger he knew and understood.[33] More idealized appeals for the overthrow of traditions and superstitions left him cold because he possessed no intimate experience of such tyrannies. Under Beaupuy's guidance Wordsworth became a revolutionary in somewhat the same way he became a poet, slowly, one might say, prosaically, through the accretion in his mind of specific and concrete observations coalescing almost of themselves to establish a general significance.

But this significance was upset by the very success of the Revolution, which produced specific and concrete evils. When the French at last discovered in Napoleon a leader as viciously oppressive as the leaders of England, the poet was driven to search for a philosophic justification for his revolutionary faith. Discouraged by the actual political events of the moment, he sought for hope and satisfaction in a purely rational understanding of the means and forms a man might properly use to assert his right to freedom. But as a poet, a thinker, even as a mystic, Wordsworth was happy and successful only when he could find general truth embodied in the actual, the specific, the physical. Detached intelligence, rational schemes, philosophic abstractions led him only into moral frustration.[34] For Wordsworth, all philosophical speculations on man's right to freedom and his ability to attain it separated from actualities produce finally reasons why man must be and remain a slave. In the 1850 version of *The Prelude*, Wordsworth uses words like those of Shigalov in *The Possessed*: "Starting from unlimited freedom, I arrive at unlimited despotism." (Cf. *The Prelude*, 1850, XI, 306–20.) To Wordsworth such a conviction carries the horror of blank hopelessness because it negates not alone his revolutionary aspirations but also the very foundation of his personality, his youthful experiences in the "natural democracy" of the Lake Country amidst the "awful" yet strangely beneficent powers of nature. At the end of Book XI, Wordsworth's condition is analogous to that which brought Jacopo Ortis to suicide.

BOOKS XII AND XIII

Wordsworth's recovery from despair, described, explained, and celebrated in the final books of *The Prelude*, is in one way a complicated process and in another way a simple one. It is simple in that it is a return to his youthful values (notice X, 922–30), but the return is complicated because it is a conscious return, not a mere regression. It is the wise and deliberate choosing by a free adult of a style of life which was his when a child.[35]

Community with others is now established deliberately, not unconsciously as in childhood, by something other than rationality. This is not a "rejection" of reason but a recognition of its limits. In trying to find a rational scheme of liberty, Wordsworth now understands, he and other theoretical libertarians were engaged in a self-contradictory project (XI, 74–95), since it is "those mysteries of passion" which have made "one brotherhood of all the human race." Thus Wordsworth arrives at the position which is central to Foscolo's idealism. Accepting the eighteenth-century ideal of brotherhood, Wordsworth denies that it derives from reason and affirms it to be a spiritual attainment, an imaginative ideal, to be known through experience, not abstract rationalization. An imaginative ideal, as distinct from a rational ideal, is one which excites man's whole being, his mind, his emotions, his spiritual aspirations, and which beckons man forward yet does not make him dissatisfied.[36]

The praise of "a maid" (either Mary Hutchinson or Dorothy Wordsworth) compliments above all else her ability to accept, to welcome "what was given," and Wordsworth goes on to assert (XI, 224 ff.) that at his best he had the same capacity to accept without judging and criticizing. If there is a harmony in the universe, a concordant relation between all elements, the perception of that harmony will render judging, comparing, or criticizing superfluous.

When we are in perfect harmony with our surroundings we do not find fault, we are serene, benign, and tolerant.

Wordsworth, moreover, insists that from this benign serenity arises creative power (XI, 251–57). Because the poet is receptive to harmony he can by his harmonious utterance transmit the joy of his vision to others. In the well-known spots of time passage (XI, 258 ff.) he identifies "this efficacious spirit" with

> . . . those passages of life in which
> We have had deepest feeling that the mind
> Is lord and master, and that outward sense
> Is but the obedient servant of her will.
> (XI, 270–73)

The mind, then, operates with "Liberty and Power" when it rises superior to the tyranny of mere sense impressions,[37] when, through "wise passiveness" it grasps the harmony of relationships among sensible objects.

Such suprasensory insight and activity impose upon the mind significant restrictions. The sources of the mind's power are shrouded in mystery beyond rational articulation, darker for the free adult than for the submitting child, and the mind must not play the tyrant in its turn. The mature vision of nature's inner harmony requires accompanying respect for those particular, external things and functions amongst which that harmony dwells and without which it could not exist. So for Wordsworth the vision of the universe as meaningfully concordant—as moral—accompanies a respect for that which is in itself amoral, for that which appears to be merely physical, merely external.[38]

Hence Wordsworth, unlike the French, who have fallen from their idealism into despotism and slavery, has become a truer democrat than he was in his days of revolutionary ardor. He asserts that the worth of any individual man is now higher for him than it had been before, that common things have now a more intense preciousness, and that everywhere he sees beauty and pleasure which previously had been invisible. He has strengthened his original idealism, while the men who pretend to fight for liberty have in actuality betrayed their original ideal.[39] They kill and oppress, though always in the name of some chimerical utopia, but he labors to make every man a poet and to find poetry in everything.[40]

The opening lines of the twelfth book stress the need of "Genius" for the "interchange/Of peace and excitation." From nature's gift of emotion, the poet "receives/That energy by which he seeks the truth," and by nature's equally valuable gift of "happy stillness of the mind" he is fitted to "receive it, when unsought." Wordsworth desires to establish these conditions so as to claim for every man the possibility of artistic vision. A poet is simply a man who has learned to look through "the busy dance/ Of things that pass away" to the "temperate shew/ Of objects that endure" (XII, 34–36) to see the falsity "in what we blazon" as "power and action" and the true preciousness of "unassuming things, that hold/ A silent station in this beauteous world." This is the essence both of Wordsworth's "realism" and his "democraticness."[41] He claims that he sees in the simple, ordinary, humble lives of simple, ordinary, humble people profound beauty and profound wisdom which we too may see if only we look. If we look we shall see the quiet lives of unextraordinary people to be rich with honors more worthy than those that crown the rulers of the world.

Having found joy and serenity within himself, the poet was moved to enquire "What one is/ Why may not many be?" He found that he was not unique, found that his strength and sensitivities were shared by other men—of all types and classes. Indeed, he discovered these strengths and sensitivities most prominent in unpretentious people whose native intelligence and imagination had not been deformed by abstract theories, whether of aesthetics or of politics.

At this point one understands that Wordsworth's concentration on the growth of his own mind is not merely egocentrism.[42] It is, paradoxically, his unwillingness to regard poetry as the specialized craft of an elite which makes him appear egocentric. Consideration of the visions of Stonehenge and Snowdon may help to illuminate this democratic personalism.

Wordsworth approaches the Stonehenge scene with a statement, first, of what poetic vision enables us to see externally.

> Nature through all conditions hath a power
> To consecrate, if we have eyes to see,
> The outside of her creatures, and to breathe
> Grandeur upon the very humblest face
> Of human life. . . .

> . . . meanwhile the forms
> Of Nature have a passion in themselves.
> (XII, 282–86, 289–90)

Then he suggests the more creative, active vision of inner truth which accompanies such responsiveness.

> . . . Poets, even as Prophets, each with each
> Connected in a mighty scheme of truth,
> Have each for his peculiar dower, a sense
> By which he is enabled to perceive
> Something unseen before. . . .
> (XII, 301–5)

Thus each poet possesses

> A privilege, . . .
> Proceeding from the depth of untaught things,
> Enduring and creative [to] become
> A power like one of Nature's. . . .
> (XII, 309–12)

Then follows the illustrative description of how, wandering on Salisbury plain, his imagination created the compelling vision of the past (the poet's experiences in London and France have not been wasted— he can penetrate into time now as well as into physical appearances) with both its "midnight darkness" represented by the "dismal flames" of the sacrificial altar and its bright aspiration represented by

> . . . bearded Teachers, with white wands
> Uplifted, pointing to the starry sky.
> (XII, 349–50)

The poet, concentrating on "the vulgar forms of present things/ And actual world of our familiar days" (XII, 361–62) attains to a "higher power" and actively participates in the bright vitality dwelling within the dreary, the commonplace, even the apparently incomprehensible. The success of this personal vision enables the poet to transmit to others what can never be conveyed by "practical" or rationalistic men, the wonder of familiar things and the marvel of man's creative capacity to enter into the life of all times and all things. Poetic vision is the capacity to recognize that the external and inanimate possess also an inner life, and that the internal and psychic possess also external, physical, suprapersonal functions.[43]

> . . . in life's every-day appearances
> I seem'd about this period to have sight
> Of a new world, a world, too, that was fit
> To be transmitted, and made visible
> To other eyes, as having for its base
> That whence our dignity originates,
> That which both gives it being and maintains
> A balance, an ennobling interchange
> Of action from within and from without,
> The excellence, pure spirit, and best power
> Both of the object seen, and eye that sees.
>   (XII, 369–79)

Such a conception of the poetic spirit is democratic in the sense that all men, at least potentially, must be possessed of it, because it is, simply, appropriate human participation in the system of the cosmos. And such a conception detaches poetry from the exclusive possession of special classes or castes established by social distinction or educational training. Furthermore, it makes the ever-broader diffusion of the poetic spirit an obvious benefit and goal. Yet poetic vision remains a matter of personal experience, of individual activity, so that the social significance of each man, each potential poet, is enhanced at the same time that privileges of particular castes or classes are eliminated.[44] In other words, the conjunction of Wordsworth's poetics and politics, like the similar conjunction of Foscolo's, is less an event in social and political history than an event in literary history: a decisive phase in the democratization of literature.

This democratization, as I have suggested, rests upon a cosmological conception, the essence of which is that the universe is vitally, actively harmonious. This harmony is not the simple adjustment of similar parts,[45] but the organic interplay of different kinds of energy, in Wordsworth's own phrase, "a harmony finer than that of contrast." Especially important is the "ennobling interchange" of inner and outer energies.[46]

It is the organic interplay of "action from within and from without" which is conclusively celebrated in the Snowdon vision in Book XIII. This vision reveals the universe to be harmonious, not meaningless or chaotic; morally beautiful, not inertly mechanical. The vision is attained by an unremarkable, even uninteresting, climb up the mountain. The sight that bursts upon the poet is not to be detached from the "trivial" ascent.[47] That is, the chief dramatic circumstance of the vision is the insignificance of the man who possesses it and is possessed by it. All the heavens and all the earth reveal their utmost beauty to a single, unimportant man. Everything conspires to show how trivial in the vistas of cosmic time and space is the individual human being. Yet simultaneously to the man "By sensible impressions not enthrall'd" this infinity becomes the embodiment of his particular imaginative vision and, therefore, his appropriate and delightful home. This supreme satisfaction is open to all men, since any man may see the infinite beauty that necessarily resides within "unassuming things" and any man may see the infinite, cosmic splendor which alone can appropriately represent and satisfy the visionary aspirations of his soul. This is true because the natural harmony of the universe is but the physical emblem of the indwelling power of life which finds its fullest and most intense expression in man's imagination (XIII, 84–119).

Upon this correspondence of external and imaginative energies depends what Wordsworth calls the beauty of "refined humanity," a gracious beauty from which terror has been purged.[48] This humanized beauty, revealed in an "exquisite regard for common things," in the perception of which what Wordsworth later called "the incumbent mystery of sense and soul" becomes serene delight, is the final "discipline/ And consummation of a Poet's mind." For the glory of the poet (that each man may become) rests, finally, on the affirmation of the mind's superiority to its physical environment.[49] The inner harmony of imagination is true harmony because it participates in the inner harmony of the natural world, not its merely physical manifestations but the meaningful system of relations that is "law and impulse" to those manifestations.

> . . . the mind of man becomes
> A thousand times more beautiful than the earth
> On which he dwells, above this Frame of things
>
> . . . .
>
> In beauty exalted, as it is itself
> Of substance and of fabric more divine.[50]
> (XIII, 446–52)

I have discussed *The Prelude* with few references to *Jacopo Ortis* because I have not wished to force any close parallelism between Wordsworth's poem and Foscolo's novel. But I want to summarize a few of the common elements in these writers' diverse contributions to what I have called the democratization of literature, which I believe to be an underlying process in most early nineteenth-century poetry and prose.

Foscolo and Wordsworth are equally committed in different ways to an ideal of freedom for all men, both tending to emphasize its spiritual-aesthetic implications when the political movements they had supported seem to them to have betrayed that ideal and left little hope of its achievement. But their belief in freedom is not purely literary, because it cannot be detached from the social ideal of human brotherhood on which it is based. Both poets, however, affirm the brotherhood of man not as an abstract idea rationally deduced but as a fact of spiritual experience. Private and individual experience is the cornerstone of their assertion of a universal community. Wordsworth's *Prelude* concentrates on imagination, or the *act*—Foscolo's *Jacopo Ortis*, on compassion, or the *result*—of intense personal experience. It is particularly interesting that the two so nearly agree as to the nature of valuable experience and the attitudes and actions toward which it urges us.

Both deny that reason, separated from other faculties, can adequately order human life. Both believe man functions best when the suprarational and suprasensory power (imagination) resulting from the harmonious cooperation of all faculties is dominant. To both the proof of imagination is beauty. Beauty is, externally, the naturally harmonious relationship among all things; internally, it is the active harmony of all the faculties—moral, sensual, rational, emotional— within man. Imaginative vision, then, cannot be a special gift of particular men, but must be a capacity latent in every man,[51] since it is, simply, the power to recognize one's privilege and duty to participate in the universal vitality of the cosmos.

Jacopo Ortis and *The Prelude* are personal responses to the cultural upheaval of the French Revolution. The French Revolution was conducted in the name of reason, and its chief symbolic act, possibly, was the execution of God in the person of a divine monarch.[52] What Wordsworth and Foscolo attempt, it seems to me, is the rescue of divinity by a reaffirmation of what they believe to have been the original and essential revolutionary vision.[53] They insist that whatever name the Revolution used, its inspiriting force was an idealistic assertion that all men had the right and power to be free.

In calling a king no better than other men they would not deny his divinity but affirm the divinity of all men. This, they believe, is not merely an abstract concept but a visionary truth. To know personal freedom from sterile conventions of thought, feeling, and behavior is to know that all men can and should be free, because such freedom is the experiencing with one's senses and feelings as well as with one's intellect the vital harmony of our multitudinously diverse and infinitely extensive universe. Such experience is exhilarating, liberating, but humbling and not anarchic. Pure reason, that is, rationality free from any limitation or restraint, *is* in the broadest sense prideful and anarchic, and, therefore, requires artificial and violent control, hence any scheme of human life that is purely rational must triumph at the cost of becoming tyranny.[54] To deny divinity—the total, active harmony of all—in the name of reason is to make one part of life superior to the whole and to produce in literature the sterile tyranny of Neoclassicism and in politics Napoleonic rulers and Benthamite legislators.

Wordsworth and Foscolo argue that we must transform the ancient experience of divinity into something newer, subtler, more profound. This new experience of divinity will make precious the humblest human life, will create value in the most simple object, and will render significant the most personal feelings, sensations, and thoughts.[55] In so doing it will bring us not only refreshed life but also a new kind of immortality by making us creative participants in an eternally vital cosmos. Desire for this kind of immortality is the underlying impulse of much early nineteenth-century literature.[56]

TWO

Functions of Poetry:
Translation and the Celebration
of Humane Life

III ❧ TRANSLATION AND ORIGINALITY

FOSCOLO: *The Sepulchres*

D ESIRE for creative participation in the eternal vitality of the universe, I have suggested in the first two chapters, is an important impulse in early nineteenth-century poets. A man, they believe, so participates by exercising his imagination, in other words, by making poetry and by making the world poetic. In this chapter and the next I shall try to define what "making poetry" and "making the world poetic" meant to these poets, how they discovered and created a new reality. In this chapter, organized around an extended discussion of Foscolo's great poem *The Sepulchres*, my aim is to show that for these poets "making poetry" means releasing what I shall call a *translating* energy; and in the next chapter, organized around briefer discussions of several poems by Leopardi and Keats, my aim is to show how the release of translating energy for these poets makes the world poetic by articulating a latent source of vitality within it. With these definitions established, it will be possible in subsequent chapters to evaluate the poets' specialized techniques of "translation" and "articulation."

Foscolo's *The Sepulchres* has been acclaimed since its publication in 1807 as a masterpiece of Italian poetry.[1] Carducci's judgment— *"The only lyric poem*, in the full Pindaric significance, which Italy possesses"—is not unusually laudatory. Nor has the praise been confined to the poet's countrymen. Foscolo's poem won him an international reputation which made it worth the Austrians' trouble, when they reoccupied Milan after Napoleon's fall, to treat Foscolo with circumspection at a time when their courtesy to outspoken Italian patriots was not conspicuous.[2] And it was as the author of *The Sepulchres* that Foscolo, after he had chosen exile in preference to Austrian tyranny, was warmly received in England.[3]

Unfortunately, this poem of less than three hundred lines is virtually untranslatable. Its untranslatability springs from the particular

47

vision of the poem and is not simply a function of the untranslatability of all lyric verse. Foscolo was fluent in several languages and was throughout his life an active translator. He believed with Coleridge, however, that a poem was a unique and untranslatable statement, not to be reworded even in its own language.[4] Yet *The Sepulchres* is a special kind of translation.

The poem opens with a series of questions. "Beneath the shade of cypresses and within urns comforted by tears is death's sleep perhaps less desolate?"[5] This general query is followed by a more personal one. The poet refers to the beauty of the natural universe and the joy of art and asks: "What recompense for lost days will be one stone distinguishing my bones from the infinite number death sows on land and sea?" These questions provide the familiar motivations of elegiac verse. Like most elegists Foscolo combines intense personal sorrow with cosmic pessimism: "A relentless force transforms [all things] from one movement into another; and time transfigures the last relics of man and his tombs and the features of the earth and sky." But because nothing later in the poem refutes the darkness of this original view, *The Sepulchres* does not sustain the traditional pattern of the Christian elegy. There is, for example, no structural reversal of the kind signaled by the line "Weep no more, woeful shepherds weep no more" in *Lycidas*.

That there will be no simple Christian consolation is foreshadowed by the last of the introductory questions: "But why, anticipating time, will man deny himself the illusion which halts him, though dead, at the threshold of the underworld? Does he not perhaps live even underground, when for him day's harmony is stilled, if with soft anxieties he can awaken that harmony in the memory of his friends?" Life beyond death, the poet implies, can be a reality only if man recognizes it to be an illusion. In time the operation of universal forces will destroy any particular existence, but we need not deny ourselves the illusion that the memory of our existence, in the minds of our family and friends, preserves the best part of our being from the total extinction to which our bodies are subject. So sepulchres, which might seem in their cold, stony blankness to be gloomy reminders of death, serve instead, by sorrowfully reminding survivors of the departed, to keep the dead "alive."

Life in memory is a life in this world, in the natural world, not in a supernatural realm such as the heaven of Christianity. Man's imagination, though it may transcend the natural world, cannot exist except through its participation in the processes of the natural world. As Foscolo says, a man may live in the minds of other men only "if reverently the earth which cradled and nourished him as a child, offers him a final refuge in her maternal lap, protecting his sacred relics from insulting storms and the profane feet of the multitude, and if a stone preserves his name, and a kindly tree, fragrant with flowers, consoles his ashes with their soft shade."

Tombs, then, are the embodiment and inspiration of man's more than natural life within nature. "Only he who leaves no heritage of affections takes little joy in urns." So, too, the evil of the new laws— the inspiration of the poem—which forbid the burial of the dead in marked graves within the precincts of the city. The evil of these "progressive" statutes is illustrated by the fate of Parini in Milan. The body of this great but gentle poet-patriot was dumped into a common grave outside the city walls, where at night one hears "a vagrant bitch scraping in the burial pits and howling hungrily," and where the bloody head of some decapitated thief may stain the bones of the good old man. From such disposal of human flesh, as if it were only waste matter, no good nor beauty can come, only a spiritual as well as a physical wasteland: "No flower rises over the dead unless it is honored by human praise and tears of love."

From the dawn of history sepulchres have served as the material focus for the spirit of civilization.

From the day that marriages and courts of law and altars made human beasts feel compassion for themselves and others, the living protected from corrupting airs and wild animals those pathetic remains which Nature in her eternal changefulness destines for other purposes. Tombs were the testimony of high enterprise and altars for sons, and from them came forth answers of the house-hold gods, and an oath sworn by the ashes of ancestors was sacred; this religion, mingling in diverse forms civic and familial love, preserved intact through the long succession of years.
(ll. 91–103)

Ancient cultures instead of teaching superstitious dread of death sought to beautify it. In antique cemeteries

. . . cypresses and cedars impregnating the breeze with their pure fragrance stretched their evergreen branches over urns perpetually remembered, and precious vases received votive tears. Friends stole a spark from the sun to illuminate the subterranean night, because the eyes of a dying man seek the sun; and all breathe their last sigh for the fading light. Fountains pouring lustral water nourished amaranths and violets on the turf of the grave; and whoever sat there to pour out libations of milk and to share his sorrows with the cherished dead, sensed about him a fragrance like the air of blessed Elysian fields. (ll. 114–29)

The custom is maintained in the suburban cemeteries of England, which, significantly, has produced the greatest warrior of the age, Nelson, who "hewed his coffin from the tallest mast of a conquered ship" while leading the fight against the tyranny of Napoleon. In Italy there are only pompous monuments, "inauspicious images" of spiritual death in a land where the rich are gluttons infatuated with "emasculated singers," where pedants are thought wise, and where the "nobility" are parasitic riffraff.

Sepulchres link present with past and inspire ardor for a better future: "heroic souls are fired to noble actions by the tombs of heroes." Italy's tomb of heroes is Florence. Within its walls stands Santa Croce, where the memory of Machiavelli, Galileo, and Michelangelo is honored, and without its walls flourishes the lovely Tuscan countryside: "hills exulting in their wine harvest, and . . . sloping valleys, clustered with homes and olive groves, pour forth to the sky the incense of a thousand flowers." Florence is the altar of Italian aspirations, and the proof of its holiness is that from it have sprung the great poet-patriots of Italian civilization—Dante, Petrarch, and most recently, Alfieri. "Ah, yes, from that religious peace a God speaks."

The god who speaks is the one who "nourished Greek valor and anger against the Persians at Marathon, where Athens consecrated tombs to her heroes." For Foscolo, Marathon was preëminently the battle in which free men repelled the onslaught of tyranny and in so doing founded Western civilization. With the defeat of Darius, the Greeks achieved political autonomy and security, the physical body, one might say, of that spirit which is expressed in the poetry of Homer.

The Iliad, which provided a continuous influence upon Foscolo's imagination, says much about funeral rites and the treatment of the dead.[6] Homer's poem teaches that man is more than a beast because he honors his dead, even enemy dead, making of a corpse a shrine whereon is renewed the pledge of common humanity. This Homeric ideal is reasserted in *The Sepulchres* in modern language and for modern civilization. Such translation from the classic and heroic to the contemporary Foscolo saw as the central function of the poet, who should thus affirm men's community with the past while inspiring them to new heroism. The poet, more fortunate than the ordinary man, may, if he fulfills this most important function of "translation," look forward to life after death, not only in the memory of his friends, but in the memory and actions of all noble men whose lives his works have touched.

> . . . let me be summoned to make the heroes live again by the Muses, inspirers of human thought. They are enthroned as guardians of sepulchres, and when time with his cold wings has brushed away even their ruins, the Muses gladden the deserts with their song, and harmony conquers the silence of a thousand centuries.
> (ll. 227–34)

The continuing vitality of Homer's poetry is proof to Foscolo of the immortality of art: "Today in the untilled Troad one place shines immortal." Foscolo returns to Homer by way of the mythical history of Troy, the tragedy of which extends into modern times. Troy is "immortal through the Nymph [Electra] to whom Jove was husband, and to Jove she gave a son, Dardanus, from whom sprang Troy, Assaracus, the fifty bridal beds, and the empire of the Julian race," that is, the Roman empire from which evolved modern Europe. The nymph Electra, dying, asked that Jove keep alive her fame, which he did by consecrating her tomb. Around the tomb were later buried and worshipped the great men of Troy until the fatal day of the Grecian sack. In *The Sepulchres* that catastrophic event is recreated through Cassandra's prophetic prayer at the yet undesecrated tombs.

> . . . she sang a song of love to these spirits, and guided here their grandsons and taught the youths the loving lament. And she spoke, sighing: Oh, if ever heaven permits you to return from Argos where you will serve the horses of Tydeus' and Laertes' son, in vain will you search for your fatherland. The walls built by Phoebus shall smoke beneath their ruins. But the Penates of Troy shall dwell in these tombs, because it is the gift of Gods to preserve their proud name in misfortune. And you, palms and cypresses, which Priam's daughters plant, and which will grow, alas so soon nourished by widows' tears, protect my ancestors.
> (ll. 260–75)

At last Cassandra foretells the far-off day when Homer will find in the tombs of Troy inspiration for his song, through which the glory and agony of the Trojan War (even then "ancient history") will become an inspiration to future generations of mankind.[7]

One day you shall see a blind beggar groping under your ancient shadows, and, muttering, penetrate the burial vaults, and embrace the urns, and question them. The secret recesses shall groan, and the tombs tell all, Ilium razed twice and twice re-risen magnificently above its silent roads to make finer the final trophy of the fatal sons of Peleus. The holy bard, calming those tormented souls with his song, shall make immortal the Argive princes through all lands embraced by the great father Oceanus. And you, Hector, shall be honored by tears wherever men lament and hold sacred blood poured out for a fatherland, and as long as the sun shall shine on the calamities of man.
(ll. 279–95)

At the conclusion of the poem we do not know, any more than we know in the last books of *The Iliad*, whether we weep for the endless repetition of human suffering or for the heroic spirit which transcends the worst sufferings that nature or man can inflict.

This presentation of *The Sepulchres* will have been successful if it suggests to the reader the question which has always been asked about *The Sepulchres*: what kind of poem is it? Despite Foscolo's complaint that it was not his fault if people referred to it as an elegy, there is much evidence that he was influenced by elegiac literature and that he knew well Thomas Gray's *Elegy Written in a Country Churchyard*.[8]

Foscolo knew Cesarotti,[9] who had translated Ossian and had propagandized for all the English "pre-Romantics" of the mid-eighteenth century. It happens, moreover, that Gray translates into Italian fairly well, and by the end of the eighteenth century his poetry was well known in Italy. By 1806, too, Foscolo had some competence in English. Without doubt *The Sepulchres* owes much to Gray's poem.

Before Gray, the elegy was traditionally a lament for some specific person, though, as in *Lycidas*, the ostensible subject usually served to objectify the poet's own situation. Gray is unspecific; he elegizes the "rude forefathers"; he addresses an anonymous class—yet at the end of the poem he elegizes himself. Gray's elegy is at the same time more generalized and more personal than any of its famous predecessors.

To the degree that *The Sepulchres* is elegiac it follows and develops Gray's pattern. Gray elegizes a class, Foscolo his nation. Gray is circumspect in speaking of himself; Foscolo addresses his poem to a specific friend, Pindemonte, and takes advantage of the personalness "allowed" by the poetic epistle. But the differences between *The Sepulchres*, even if we regard it as a kind of elegy, and Gray's poem are striking. Gray modulates and qualifies a single mood, whereas Foscolo depends upon a play of contrasting moods and of specific scenes, times, and persons. Gray restricts himself to a single, generalized setting and situation. The poems begin very differently. Gray opens with a descriptive statement which sets the tonal limits of the entire poem, and his success lies in maintaining the accents of calm assertion without ever becoming trite, trivial, or didactic. Gray accepts and affirms. Foscolo begins with interrogatives; his art is problematical, dramatic, dialectical—he questions, protests, exhorts.

Foscolo denied that *The Sepulchres* was an elegy and sometimes claimed it was a revitalization of the Pindaric ode. Some distinguished Italian scholars and critics have accepted the claim.[10] Yet many readers have asked, without eliciting any very specific answer, if the adjective "Pindaric" is really more than a rhetorical flourish of praise.

Foscolo probably follows Pindar in making an individual stand for the best in his civilization. Like Pindar, Foscolo identifies the function of poetry as the binding together in spiritual concord of noble souls and the extending of their influence so that the material success of a polity reinforces, rather than limits, man's freedom and power to be civilized. Like Pindar, Foscolo interweaves diverse legends and myths throughout a single lyric and relates immediate actuality to a complex body of mythological tradition. Foscolo seems to have appreciated the way in which the real man whose triumph Pindar celebrates becomes a means for making the audience feel the living reality of ancient traditions—feel the present vitality of ideals and attitudes that otherwise would be only abstractions.[11]

The person celebrated in a Pindaric ode, the ostensible subject, needs little more than brief mention. Were his personality and accomplishments emphasized too heavily the traditions which he embodies would be obscured. The poet is free to move from story to story, from brief allusion to brief allusion, because the triumph he celebrates is above all a cultural one. Pindar does not celebrate boxers as boxers or owners of successful horses as horse-owners but as representatives of their cities' or states' virtues as cultural entities. The individual celebrated stands for his *polis*, which is culturally complex, and proper praise of the individual must, therefore, praise the complexity for which he stands.

Pindar accomplishes this without difficulty because he has a special attitude toward the past. To Pindar, present relates to past genealogically; legendary heroes are actual ancestors, culturally if not biologically. Past relates to present through exemplary actions that are not abstract, like medieval *exempla,* but concrete. The anger of Achilles, for instance, seems to have been to Pindar's audience neither merely an interesting tale nor merely a piece of history but a living lesson in the nature and effects of wrath. It was not an abstract lesson because its applicability depended less on its general truth than on the "fact" that Achilles and the present-day audience belonged to the same "family."[12]

Because of this "genealogical" relationship, the myths and legendary figures of Pindar's odes are not dead but living and imbued with a warm, familial contact with the present. Pindar's treatment is not scholastic and static. Later European writers have known the Greek myths only in the form of relatively untransmutable stories, and we tend even today to think of a myth as one fixed story which has different versions. What to the Greeks was definite but dynamic has been to most later writers multiform but static. Foscolo had the advantage over many of his contemporaries of having read Vico. Vico, if no one else, would confirm the hopelessness of any attempt to imitate the poetry of a different civilization.[13] But precisely because Foscolo did not believe in imitation, he could think of translation in a broader and more philosophical fashion than had his Neoclassic predecessors.

The Sepulchres is full of classical references. But very little in the poem seems hackneyed, even though the most commonplace scenes and figures of ancient civilization are used: Marathon, the fall of Troy, Cassandra, Hector, blind Homer, etc. These classical commonplaces are suited to a treatment somewhat analogous to Pindar's: they are familiar enough to arouse a definite response but are general enough to give the poet leeway for the dynamic particularization of his special purpose. Foscolo introduces his commonplaces by means of unfamiliar and dramatic details. He forces us to see the familiar in unusual perspective.[14] The struggle between Odysseus and Ajax for Achilles' armor is recalled by the picture of the waves carrying the armor to Ajax's tomb; Homer is presented only through Cassandra's prophecy (Foscolo's invention) inspired by the pre-Homeric tombs of Troy; or, to choose an example we may pursue in detail, Marathon appears in a strangely personalized vision.

Ah, yes, from that religious peace a God speaks; and nourished Greek valor and anger against the Persians at Marathon, where Athens consecrated tombs to her heroes. The sailor coasting that sea under Euboea saw through the vast darkness sparks flashing from helmets and clashing swords, fiery smoke fuming from pyres, saw spectral warriors glaring with steely arms seeking the battle; and through the horror of night's silences the tumult of phalanxes reverberates across the plain, and the trumpets' sound, and a charge of rushing cavalry, trampling the helmets of the dying, and lamentation, and hymns, and the song of the Fates.
(ll. 197–212)

We are introduced to the battle by the voice of a god speaking from the "religious peace" of an Italian church. The formal connection between Marathon and the preceding portrait of Vittorio (Alfieri) is, of course, that the same god speaks from tombs separated by 2500 years: Alfieri and the triumphant Athenians were patriots. But Athenian patriotism is not directly represented. Instead, adapting a superstitious story from Pausanias, Foscolo presents the battle after the combat through the fearful vision of a sailor coasting at night near Marathon. The swords clashing and the cavalry clattering over the helmets of the dying are phantoms. In the tumult of battle, pyres flame and smoke, hymns of victory and lamentations for the dead are heard, while over all sounds "the song of the Fates," and this song impresses us with the sorrow of fact—it does not strike us as a learned allusion. We have been made to experience Marathon as a mixture of myth and history and individual experience. But there is no formal, literary myth and no historicity. Personal experience is primary. The passage "works" because we feel that process of a simple man's superstition investing a dreadful place with phantasms created by his awe and fear and wonder. We see Marathon through the eyes of "the sailor" and through him hear the voice of the god.

Foscolo recreates this primitive response within his natural manner, which involves elaborate syntax and formal diction. He is unlike some modern poets, who imitate stylistically the primitivism of their subjects. He does not exploit symbols that may be expected to arouse response from the primitive part of our minds. He remains literary. His aim is to lure us into an imaginative experience of what happened 2500 years ago, told within the form and tradition of modern literary language. Because his poem is, above all else, a celebration of civilization, he cannot abandon the language, the artifice, which expresses that civilization.

This "primitivism-within-literariness" is perhaps the chief obstacle to our appreciation of Foscolo and—insofar as his art is typical of his epoch—to our understanding of much early nineteenth-century verse.[15] Italian critics point to the creative, myth-making cast of Foscolo's mind, but Foscolo is never more original than when he affirms the vitality of literary tradition. Like most of his contemporaries, he contributes to the destruction of the concept of art as imitation and simultaneously pioneers in the revival of forgotten or underrated writers of the past and in a revitalization of some of Western Europe's literary traditions.[16]

It is not surprising that one finds ambiguity in Foscolo's opinion of the nature of his own poetry, as in his variable classifying of *The Sepulchres* as an original work or as a revivification of Pindar's art.[17] In fact, *The Sepulchres* is original because it "translates" Pindar. To explain this paradox, it is necessary to go beyond the poem itself and to explore Foscolo's philosophy of art. He believed that poetry is not a special gift or a particular inheritance, like blue eyes. Rather, to be a poet, a man must be fully a man, not an average man, but manly beyond the average, more humane, more totally and freely himself.[18]

Such a belief does not, as it might at first appear, eliminate inspiration. According to Foscolo, poetry could be successfully composed only at those times—alas, too rare in our imperfect societies—when all of the poet's faculties were conjoined in an active harmony. It is that harmony to which Coleridge and Wordsworth refer when they say poetry can be composed only under conditions of health and "joy." They are particularly concerned with the psychological state of the poet, and so is Foscolo, but, more than his English contemporaries perhaps, he also sees the importance of historical or cultural factors. Disharmonies, political as well as psychological, can disturb the poet's power to create.

For Foscolo great monuments of literature are rare and valuable confluences of fortunate circumstances. They present a poet at harmony with himself at a moment in history which allows that harmony to be expressed. Foscolo emphasizes that the critic's function is to recreate the historical or cultural milieu out of which a particular work of art emerged. To understand Dante, say, one must understand the civilization of which Dante was a part,[19] but Foscolo is equally emphatic that each great work of art is autonomous and individual.[20] Partly, of course, this separateness is the product of the autonomy of the "cultural moment." The civilization Dante lived in existed only at one time and in one place; the good critic distinguishes the special characteristics which make "Dante's civilization" different from the generic "medieval civilization." Because history never exactly repeats itself and because an artistic creation is to some degree the product of historical forces, a work of art must have an existence all its own.

But the autonomy of the work of art derives also from the autonomy of the man who creates it. To Foscolo men share a common humanity, and poetry is the language which expresses their spiritual community. We thrill to Dante's poetry because we are men and he speaks to us as men. But we are not Dante. Each man is an independent being, hence each man's creation will necessarily differ from all other men's creations. The great poet is the man able to give unique expression to the spiritual community of mankind, which is, like the inner harmony of diverse faculties that constitute imaginative power, a concord among diverse and independent energies. To experience the spirit of humanity is not to surrender one's own particular personality but, quite the contrary, to feel one's own personality in the full strength of its individuality in harmonious relationship with other, diverse, equally autonomous personalities.

Imitation is futility. Yet the understanding of previous works of art is of the highest importance, for in them is enshrined the voice of our common humanity. To the degree that we do not comprehend the great expressions of the human spirit we are hindered from bringing our particular personality into harmonious relationship with that spirit. The poet must translate, then, not imitate; that is, he must re-express in his own individual fashion what great poets of the past have expressed in their own, inimitable ways.[21]

Here we return to the paradox: Foscolo and his contemporaries devoted much attention to translation while insisting upon the untranslatability of any authentic work of art. We are now in a position to understand the paradox, if we stop to consider how, in the Foscolian view, one should read poetry of earlier epochs. To comprehend *The Divine Comedy*, for instance, we must not only read it with our rational intelligence but we must also experience it with our whole being. Such experience is possible only if we read imaginatively, which means we must read with awareness of the dynamic complexity of each individual word.

It was Locke, probably, who taught Foscolo that the meaning of a word is determined by the ideas of the man who speaks it. So dictionaries are fraudulent; their definitions render only the abstract signification, whereas the true vitality of words resides in their particularity, in the specific signification that they have for each speaker. Understanding *The Divine Comedy*, then, is not a matter of understanding the abstract signification of all the words in the poem but of responding fully to the complex and particularized meanings the words have been given by the mind of Dante. The function of an actual translation is to render available as many as possible of those complexities which are concealed beneath the abstract signification of the individual words.[22]

One must observe that Foscolo goes beyond Locke in finding positive value in the dynamic complexity of words. Foscolo is a poet, interested not only in how to comprehend in reading, but also in how to express in writing. To him the finest poet is the one who can render with perfect clarity the greatest complexity. Poetry is the exploitation of the potential complexity of words,[23] and each true poem will be a new world, a harmonic system in which verbal complexity forms a dynamic unity.

Each authentic poem is, to use a Coleridgean term, a linguistic "recreation"; the poet does not, in general, invent words, but he endows them with the vitality which in dictionaries or in ordinary discourse they lack. That is why poets are the best critics of poetry—they are trained in re-creation, and good reading, like good writing, is a re-creative process. But the reader's re-creation of the poet's experience does not entail loss of independence. The reader does not reproduce the poet's experience, does not become the poet; instead he experiences the poet's experience. That is why literal translation is impossible. As Foscolo puts it, translations of *The Iliad* by different poets, however alike, will be totally unlike.[24]

The value of translation, which is simply the most active form of attention to past literature, simply creative reading, is that it brings the autonomous personality of the translator into a positive relation with the autonomous personality of the original author. By so doing, the translator adds another dynamic element to the harmony in man's spiritual existence. This process is true of an original poem, which also leans in its composition upon earlier literature. Or if it does not, it will be an incomplete or bad poem, because made in ignorance of the historic-literary harmony which an artist must know and feel if he would write well. The new poem, the original poem, will be composed of elements found in earlier works but will have re-ordered them into a new unity, original and autonomous. What this boils down to, is that Foscolo's conception of the way the imagination works on literary tradition is parallel to the definition of the way the imagination works on nature as enunciated by Coleridge: "It dissolves, diffuses, dissipates, in order to recreate."[25]

Foscolo would not have written *The Sepulchres* as he did without his knowledge and understanding of Pindar. It stands, nonetheless, squarely original, un-Pindaric or supra-Pindaric, with a meaning and unity new and wholly its own. Pindar, although very Greek, very pessimistic, celebrates success. Foscolo, although positive in his attitude to life, makes his lyric from life's failures and tragedies.[26] Pindar's odes are in praise of the victor in his triumph; Foscolo's lyric is to men who suffer, who are destroyed, or who sink under some failure of their civilization: Nelson is dead, Homer is seen as a blind, aged outcast, and the heroes of Italian civilization emerge from the ruins of its present dissolution.

But Foscolo does not celebrate fact in itself. Whether the person of whom he writes be historical, like Parini, or fictional, like Hector, his significance lies always in his assertion of a spiritual truth. The "facts of life" to Foscolo are evil and sorrowful, leading swiftly to the blank extinction of death. From this view derives the realism of *The Sepulchres*. But beyond the facts of natural life are the illusions of human life; idealism transcends realism. Hence the central paradox of the poem is its affirmation that tombs are a source of life. The tomb of a worthy man is an inspiration of enduring human civilization. This paradox reminds one of *The Iliad*, and it is appropriate that the most powerful image in *The Sepulchres* is that of Homer finding inspiration for his immortal poem among the sepulchres of Troy.

Homer is but one of the dramatic persons within the poem. *The Sepulchres* does more than restate an Homeric creed; the structure of the poem, which is a private meditation, gives it a wider scope, in one sense at least, than that of the heroic epic. Foscolo's poem includes all of history, not a single event. Its dynamics are the confrontation of the individual with the whole of human history. To use current jargon, what Foscolo says about tombs, though very close to what Homer says, has a different "frame of reference." Both Homer and Foscolo assert that what makes a man worthy is a loyalty to humanity that transcends particular loyalties. To both poets, a man's worth is in his humanness, not his special abilities or his nationality or race. But Foscolo asserts this in a cosmic frame of reference which is un-Greek. Foscolo's cosmos is larger than the Greek and it is more complex. Foscolo's man has not a secure place within the vastness of universal time and space, but *he is all that matters within the vastness.* Foscolo's assertion, therefore, has in it a doubt and a degree of consciousness of doubt never suffered by Homer, whose intensity, though not his grandeur, remains correspondingly less than Foscolo's.

The epic is very different from the intense and restricted form of the lyric *Sepulchres,* which implies that man's development is by way of private and personal experience. Understanding of human nature, of an all-encompassing humanity, comes as personal experience or revelation to an individual, singly, privately, if at all. It is a vision, it is an ideal, it is an intensely personal apperception.

As men together we can observe nature and history in their cyclic perpetuations and dissolutions, reconstitutions and changes: under the dark influence of time man's memorials and the earth and sky themselves pass away and are transformed into "that which recalls them not." When man no longer merely observes but participates in the changing cosmos, then he begins to create, and he survives in what he creates: in his affectional relations with friends and family, in his art. For then he is participating in the eternal, unchanging realms of the supranatural and the suprahistorical. To operate however modestly in such realms, man must be truly affectionate, he must truly love his fellow men, he must be imaginative, and he must be steadfast to his ideals learned from his own subjective experience. This is the stuff of heroism which concerns Foscolo, a heroism at once unostentatious, intense, and interior.

It is not surprising, then, that his "heroes" are frequently women.[27] The final Homeric episode of *The Sepulchres* is born of Electra's prayer and is told in the words of Cassandra. Both women are (except for their passionate utterances, which are the more powerful for being untouched by recrimination) passive sufferers. Cassandra, to be sure, has often symbolized innocence victimized by men and gods.

But Foscolo endows her with an intense womanliness which transcends the limitations of her traditional symbolic role: without Cassandra (and Electra), we feel, there would be no Homer. Without the subjective suffering of "unimportant" individuals there would be no supranatural, humane existence for poets to celebrate.

Foscolo's emphasis on the personal origin of an envisioned supranatural, purely humane way of life explains why *The Sepulchres* is in a profound sense unique. That uniqueness, ironically, identifies the poem as typical of its time, when poets strove to create a new ideal of life for all men out of private, even lonely, experience.[28]

IV ❧ POETIC HUMANISM

LEOPARDI: *The Broom*

FOSCOLO: *To Luigia Pallavicini*
To a Friend Restored to Health

KEATS: *Ode to Psyche* / *Ode on Melancholy*
Ode to a Nightingale / *Ode on Indolence*
Ode on a Grecian Urn

ONE purpose of this chapter is to suggest how the uniqueness of *The Sepulchres* identifies Foscolo's poem as characteristic of its era, which, while reviving the medieval and Hellenic past, sought for originality and rejected the public and formal traditionalism of the preceding age. Composed nearly three decades after *The Sepulchres*, by a poet as different temperamentally from Foscolo as night from day,[1] Giacomo Leopardi's *The Broom* is most like the *The Sepulchres* in being a personal meditation upon all human history and the entire natural cosmos. And the structural principle which shapes Leopardi's poem is like that which shapes Foscolo's, the contrasting of elemental opposites: destruction against fecundity, vastness (both spatial and temporal) against minuteness, beauty against chaotic ugliness, compassion against hatred, selfishness against generosity, vain pride against humble courage.[2]

In the first section of *The Broom* the stony wasteland of the Vesuvian slopes is dramatized by the recollection of what the lava destroyed, a luxurious and easeful civilization, the memory of which is rendered intangibly specific by the fragrance of the broom. The lava beds are the vast natural sepulchre of mankind's "magnificent and progressive destiny."

Here on the arid spine of this fearful mountain, Vesuvius the destroyer, which no other tree nor flower gladdens, you scatter your solitary tufts, fragrant broom, contented with the wasteland. Thus I have seen your shoots make lovely the barren fields round that city that was once mistress of mankind, by

62

your grave and silent aspect testifying to her vanished empire. Now I encounter you again in this soil. . . faithful comrade of afflicted fortune. These
fields . . . were once the farms and homesteads . . . were once gardens and
palaces . . . were once famous cities which the haughty mountain, pouring
fiery torrents from its burning throat, obliterated together with their residents.
Now a single ruin buries all. In this you root yourself, O gentle flower, as if in
pity for the doom of others, flinging toward the sky your sweet perfume to
console the wasteland. To these slopes let him come who exalts with flattery our
mortal state, let him see how loving Nature cares for humankind. . . . Depicted on these slopes is man's *magnificent and progressive destiny*.

Against the background of this opening scene Leopardi's satiric
condemnation of his contemporaries' schemes for the rational perfection of society takes on cosmic significance. Like Foscolo, Leopardi
carries satire beyond immediate evils and transforms scorn into a
bitter affirmation of mankind's tragic condition.

Gaze here and see yourself, proud and stupid century, you who have abandoned
the path marked out for you before by reawakened thought, you who have
turned back your steps, vaunting your retreat as progress. . . . You dream of
liberty while you enslave once more that thought through which alone our
civilization grows, and through which alone the public destiny is guided on
toward better things. The truth displeased you by displaying the low condition
and the bitter fate that nature gives to us.

Leopardi's attack, be it noted, is not against reason. He objects to that
which masquerades as reason. The so-called rationalists refuse to face
the truth revealed by honest intelligence—that man's condition is
"low" and his fate "bitter." True reason sees and proclaims the
tragedy of man; it does not disguise the facts of life with utopian
abstractions.

Nor do I think a creature great of soul, but stupid, rather, who, born to die,
reared in pain, says: "I was made for pleasure," and out of festered pride
scrawls reams promising lofty destinies and new delights, of which this globe
and heaven itself know nothing, to peoples whom one wave of the plunging
sea, one breath of air diseased, one tremor of the earth destroys so that even the
memory of them will scarce survive.

To Leopardi a man's reasoning is fantasy if it is not based on the
most obvious and logical of truths: man must suffer because he is
subject to nature's mechanical laws although he possesses powers that
enable him to conceive subtler and more vital systems. Genuine
wisdom is tragic wisdom, and genuine idealism is the affirmation
that all men are brothers, not because they are alike as natural crea-

tures, but because they are alike in being something more than natural creatures.

A noble soul is he who burns to lift his mortal eyes against our common doom, and who with open speech, detracting nothing from the truth, confesses the evil lot assigned to us by fate and our depressed and frail condition; he who is strong and enduring in his suffering nor will add fraternal hate and wrath—the worst of evils—to his other miseries by blaming mankind for his sorrow, but casts the blame upon the truly guilty one, the power that is our mother by birth, in will our stepmother. Her he calls enemy, and thus believing, as is the truth, the human company was from the first united and arrayed against her, he esteems all men confederated, embraces all men with truest love, offering and expecting prompt and effective aid in the dangers and vicissitudes of the common war. . . . When thoughts like these shall be, as once they were, made manifest to people everywhere, that horror which forced mortals into social fellowship, joined against pitiless nature, shall be in part restored . . . justice and piety shall root themselves in other soil than the madnesses of pride. . . .

Leopardi's social ideals and ethical principles, like Foscolo's, are founded on a cosmological conception essentially modern in its comprehension of both spatial and temporal infinitude and in its sense of man's state as problematical.

Often on these desolated slopes, which the hardened flood has clothed in black, still seeming to move undulating on, I sit at night, and above the melancholy slope in the deepest blue I see the flaming stars, which the distant sea mirrors, and the whole world shining with wheeling scintillations through the empty vault of heaven. And when I fix my sight upon those lights, seeming but points, which are, in truth, immense, so vast that to them this earth and sea are but a point—to which, indeed, not man alone but this whole globe whereon mankind is nothing, is entirely unknown; and when I see, beyond these, still infinitely more remote, those knots of stars which to us appear like clouds, wherefrom not only man, nor earth alone, but this universe of stars, infinite in number and in mass, our golden sun but one among them all, is unknown or seems, as they seem to the earth, a mere point of doubtful light; to my thought then what do you seem, O son of man? And remembering your lowly state, of which the soil I tread bears testimony, and that you—in contrast—think yourself the ruler, the final purpose of the Whole, and that you have often pleased yourself with fabling how to this obscure grain of sand named earth the authors of the universe of things descended, for your good, often chatting pleasantly with you, and how this present age, that in knowledge and civility seems most advanced, insults the wise by reviving these derided dreams; what feeling then, unhappy mortal children, what final thought assails my heart? I do not know if laughter or if pity then prevails.

What matters most in this passage is the paradoxical diminution and exaltation of man. Leopardi's ostensible purpose is to make us recognize our insignificance in the cosmic scheme, yet the passage contains more than this single purpose. The imaginative power which conceives and represents with such splendor the unfathomableness of infinity is itself testimony of man's supranatural capacity. Leopardi's ability to express his sense of the material enormousness of the universe which so dwarfs man as a physical being testifies to the power of the human mind.[3] For Leopardi, as for Foscolo, man exalts himself in his comprehension of that which humbles him.

We have here something more than an incidental similarity between two Italian poets. We have instead the basis of the early nineteenth-century exaltation of imagination. For the poets of this era imagination is more than sensory perception and more than reason but it is not separable from either sensation or reason. It is the *process* by which sensation and reason transcend themselves to become a fusion of super-reason and super-sensation. Imagination permits us to know and to feel, within the well-known and the often-felt, what ordinarily would be beyond our knowing or feeling. Above all, imagination permits us to know and feel the paradox of man's simultaneous littleness and greatness, his simultaneous existence within and beyond nature.

The paradox is central to the "Titanism" of the epoch, the "Promethean striving" represented by Goethe and Byron: all the Faust, Prometheus, and Satan figures so characteristic of the early nineteenth century represent their creators' awareness of man as a limited creature possessed of infinite powers. The four poets with whom we are concerned, however, never employ the Satan, Faust, or Prometheus archetypes.[4] Our poets prefer to represent the infinite grandeur revealed by imagination within familiar situations, humble occurrences, and unremarkable personal experiences. Even when Keats turns to stories of Greek mythology or when Foscolo turns to the epic events of ancient history, what impresses us is not the grandiose and heroic externalities but the deep, private intensity of something close to ordinary human feelings.

Leopardi, sitting alone on the slopes of Vesuvius, watching the scintillations of the infinite universe mirrored in the sea that cradled human civilization, and contemplating modern man's misguided self-aggrandizements, symbolizes in more than a superficial way the place and purpose of the poet of his era. Leopardi regards his society as evil because it obscures those elemental truths of the human situation which are apparent to any man who contemplates, as he does, the most open manifestations of the natural universe. The plain fact is that, physically, man is too minute to be of any significance; but that recognition, instead of producing despair, should bind men together in brotherhood. That brotherhood, being based on man's hostility to nature—not, as in the minds of many eighteenth-century writers, on man's adherence to natural law—will become a positive assertion of the capability within man which makes him finally more significant, even more powerful, than all the blank infinitude of natural space and time.[5]

The view of the stars in *The Broom* is followed by a picture of an anthill destroyed by a falling apple. This leads, by the poet's mode of contrast within similitude, to the picture of incandescent lava and choking ashes overwhelming Pompeii. To nature, man and ants are alike: "if one is massacred less frequently, there is no cause but that man breeds not quite so fast." But to man there is, or ought to be, a difference. The society of ants is natural, but man's society is anti-natural—a weapon in man's struggle against his natural destiny, because unlike ants, men are aware of a conflict between their goals and nature's.[6] Perhaps the simple man sees this most clearly. Leopardi shows us a modern peasant who scratches a bare subsistence from the stony hillsides of Vesuvius and who

still raises suspicious glances toward the fatal peak, which, no more kindly now, still looms terribly, still menaces disaster for himself, his children, and his impoverished farm. And often the poor man, on the roof of his miserable hut, lying sleepless all the night in the wayward wind, many times leaps up, watches the course of the fearful boiling flood that still pours out of the un-exhausted womb over the sandy ridge and shines from sea-girt Capri across Naples Bay to Mergellina. And if he sees it nearing, or if in the depths of his household well he hears the water seethe and gurgle, he wakes his children, wakes his wife in haste, flees with whatever they can snatch, and sees from far off his cherished home, his little field—their sole guard against famine—prey to the ruinous flood which, crackling, overwhelms it, spreads inexorably and everlastingly above it all.

Then follows the description of the traveller viewing the ruins of Pompeii, exhumed by "piety or greed," which extends the lesson of the single peasant to comprehend the history of the race.

From the deserted forum amidst the ranks of upright broken columns, the traveller contemplates the distant cloven summit and smoking plume still hanging in menace above the shattered ruins. And in the awfulness of secret night, through the emptied theaters, through the mutilated temples, and through the blasted houses where the bat conceals its young, like a baleful torch flickering darkly among abandoned palaces, runs the shimmer of the ghastly lava that distantly through shadows reddens all the ruins.

The human present and the human past are linked by the perpetual menace of natural catastrophe, which flickers darkly over a single poverty-stricken peasant and the proud metropolis of the most famous of civilizations.

. . . ignorant of man and the ages he calls ancient and the succession of generation after generation, nature stays forever young, or, rather, follows a course so long she seems forever young. Meanwhile empires crash, languages and people pass away: she sees them not: and man presumes to vaunt his immortality.

To Leopardi the ultimate truth attainable by imaginative intelligence is that man, the sole possessor of imaginative intelligence, is not immortal. Leopardi does not even turn to the Foscolian solace of art. But Leopardi's pessimism, like Foscolo's suicide motif, is heroic rather than nihilistic.[7] One might argue that *The Broom*, like *The Sepulchres*, looks back to Homeric realism rather than forward to twentieth-century negativism, and one must admit that stylistically Leopardi is closer to the tragic simplicity of Greek art than to the complicated symbolism of modern art.

At the conclusion of the poem Leopardi returns to the modest beauty of the gentle flower that rises from the waste of unfecund lava.

And you, supple broom, who with fragrant shoots make beautiful these despoiled fields, you, also, will soon succumb to the cruel power of subterraneous fire returning to familiar haunts, extending its greedy edge over your gentle tufts. And you will bow your innocent head under the burden of mortality, not stubbornly, but not until that time bowing in vain and cowardly supplication before your future conqueror, and not rearing in mad pride against the stars nor against the wasteland—your birthplace and your home by fortune, not by choice; wiser and less weak than man in not believing your frail race to be given immortality by destiny or by yourself.

Man's duty lies in accepting his lot, and the outcome of this acceptance will be the brotherhood of man. Leopardi promises no utopia. We are men, therefore we should be brothers; this is the only imperative imposed by a perception that nature's hostility has always been successful: we have always been defeated both as individuals and as builders of suprapersonal civilizations. Yet a sense of defeat is not the only feeling aroused by *The Broom*. The realism the poet demands is not merely a matter of seeing things in the proportions in which they appear to everyday vision. First and last in the poem the little yellow flower is more important than the menace of Vesuvius and all the unfecund testimony of its destructive power. The poet's mind spans history and probes interstellar space, but at last returns to the gentle flower whose fragrance consoles the wasteland. The imagination, able to comprehend infinite time and space, finds its abiding home in what would seem to be most frail, transitory, and insignificant.

The effect of the poem can best be explained, perhaps, by an analogy. Consider how the first living organisms on our young planet must have appeared: frail, transitory, and insignificant, with no hope of survival against the massive mechanisms of brute matter, so much older and more enduring. But how would those first organisms have appeared to an imaginative mind, one capable of grasping the amazing potentialities of life? The analogy is not far-fetched, since what *The Broom* makes us feel is the potential power of conscious life, of life capable of recognizing the hazards which encompass it and its own frailty. So endangered it can scarcely hope to triumph, but it can and should assert its difference from other orders of existence. That assertion makes *The Broom* what it is, not merely a cry of despair, but a proclamation of human potentiality.

Leopardi's poem reveals the true revolutionariness of much early nineteenth-century poetry, which is something more than a plea for social improvement.[8] This poetry above all else expresses and encourages a new advance in reflective, self-conscious life. That is why it is a poetry which rejects traditional "reason." It replaces reason not with irrationalism but with imagination, suprarationalism, reason functioning harmoniously with the processes of sensation, emotion, and the promptings of spiritual aspiration—reason, that is, become synthetic and subtly responsive to new possibilities of experience and a new kind of dynamic existence.

This revolutionary spirit modifies literary form. Both *The Sepulchres* and *The Broom* are lyric meditations, and in both the poet reveals the particularity of his individual ideas and emotions. But in both poems the meditation concerns cosmic issues and comprehends enormous vistas of time and space. It is not surprising, then, that both poems are formally free[9]—they do not closely adhere to any classical genre. They are, in fact, developed examples of what Samuel Johnson identified as a "new scheme of poetry" and named "local poetry."

This poetry focusses on a "particular landscape to be poetically de-scribed" and adds to that subject "historical retrospection or incidental meditation." This is what Professor Langbaum calls "the poetry of experience," remarking that ". . . we can only wonder . . . whether the poetry of experience is not itself a new genre which abolishes the distinction between subjective and objective poetry and between the lyrical and dramatic or narrative genres."[10] Because the poetry of experience or local poetry aspires to new consciousness, it seeks new form, even when adhering to traditional patterns. This may be illus-trated in the odes of John Keats.

Keats, like most of his contemporaries, turned to the ode not as a source of formal structure (few if any early nineteenth-century odes follow the accepted tripartite structure of strophe, antistrophe, epode) but as a source of freedom. The ode was perhaps the one conven-tional genre which required the combination of personal and pro-phetic utterance, which allowed the poet as a private individual to express religious, social, philosophic, or aesthetic truths. The ode was thus the traditional genre best suited to the expression of a new fusion of objective and subjective experience and the dramatic definition of a new form of suprarational life. Keats's odes, like those of his contemporaries, are impressive and original not merely be-cause they express actual personal experience, but because they express a new kind of personal experience.

For example, the subject of Keats's *Ode to Psyche* appears to be a mere fancy. The poet, "wander'd in a forest thoughtlessly," sees Cupid and Psyche asleep in one another's arms; he reflects on how the ancient deities have "faded," then promises to create a fitting landscape and shrine for Psyche "in some untrodden region" of his "mind." In the other great odes the object which calls forth the poetry—the urn, the nightingale, the melancholy, and the indolence —is actually present as Cupid and Psyche could not be, for they are merely literary reminiscences. The other odes, it has been suggested, are filled with realistic tensions not to be found in the *Ode to Psyche*, which is sometimes associated with Keats's immature poems.[11]

To Psyche is, perhaps, the most simply delightful of the great odes, but it is not merely fanciful, for external reality—sense data and historical circumstances independent of the poet's dreams—plays an important role in the poem. The "forest" with its "hush'd, cool-rooted flowers" is not a fantasy forest; it is historically true that

"Olympus' hierarchy" has "faded"; and the relationship of Cupid and Psyche is not etherealized—on the contrary, its warm sexuality is emphasized.

These various kinds of realism need to be observed, first, because the total structure of the ode is founded upon a contrast between the future psychological reality of the end of the poem and the past physical reality of the beginning, and, second, because there is an important truth dramatized by Keats's apparent fancy. We *are* in "these days . . . far retir'd" from the "happy pieties" of Greco-Roman paganism. It is literally true that we can experience the delight of that religion only through an act of imagination. The ode embodies the process of imaginative transformation by which the divine power of an obsolete religious system is experienced poetically.

Biologists are aware that as its environment alters a species persists as a species by transforming itself. And any individual organism matures by developing from an immature condition. It is a law of life that one remains the same by changing. Keats's treatment of Psyche conforms to the organic law. Keats does not imitate the form of the old mythological story; he does not admire the Cupid and Psyche tale as a beautiful pattern of dead ideas and vanished feelings. He finds in it the inspirational source of immediate and personal imaginative experience.

The change wrought by Keats which preserves Psyche's divinity may be suggested by contrasting the ode to its primary source, the story of Cupid and Psyche as told by Apuleius. Probably Keats accepted the opinion of Adlington, the Elizabethan translator of *The Golden Ass* whose version he knew,[12] that Apuleius' purpose was religious.[13] But it must have been plain to Keats that for Apuleius the true divinity is Isis. He does not worship Cupid and Psyche; at best their story is for him illustrative allegory;[14] it is not the object of devotion. To Keats, on the contrary, Psyche is a "true" divinity. If we assume that Cupid and Psyche were once worshipped by religious believers, we must recognize that Apuleius has transformed sincere belief into illustrative art, and that Keats transforms Apuleius' allegory back into the passionate utterance of genuine adoration, though of a new kind. The ode is a prayer.

The nature of Keats's religiosity is indicated by the two examples of oxymoron in the opening lines.

> O Goddess! hear these tuneless numbers, wrung
> By sweet enforcement and remembrance dear.[15]

Although compressed antithesis appears again in the poem, i.e., "delicious moan," "pleasant pain," the rhetorical figure is less important per se than as a hint as to the total dynamics of the ode. A publicly unworshipped deity will be resurrected to divinity by means of private devotional experience. So the poet at once asks pardon that the goddess' "secrets should be sung/ Even into thine own soft-conchèd ear." Even if the last phrase is overly literary, it is functional, since the poet's temple to the goddess will be a mental one and his worship will be a form of self-communion.

Next Keats asks:

> Surely I dreamt to-day, or did I see
> The wingèd Psyche with awaken'd eyes?

The poet's doubt is meant to emphasize the extraordinariness of his sight when he "wander'd in a forest thoughtlessly." The revelation came unsought. And the following description is unintellectual too, in that it is directed entirely to sensory evocation. Its most famous line compresses the sensations of sound, sight, touch, and smell into a single phrase that rises to an intricate synaesthetic climax: "'Mid hush'd, cool-rooted flowers, fragrant-eyed."

Keats identifies Cupid at once, but stresses the special wonder of Psyche with a rhetorical question:

> But who wast thou, O happy, happy dove?
> His Psyche true!

One can understand why Keats's taste erred at this point. Psyche is his subject, not Cupid, although, as the poem's last lines prove, it is not his intention to make us entirely forget the divine love story. But the second and third stanzas speak only of Psyche:

> O latest born and loveliest vision far
> Of all Olympus' faded hierachy!

Why Psyche never received formal worship, though the youngest, hence presumably the most vital, and the most beautiful of "Olympus' faded hierachy" is explained by the opening of the third stanza. She was born "too late for the fond believing lyre,/ When holy were the haunted forest boughs,/ Holy the air, the water, and the fire." Yet, says the poet, I now see Psyche: "I see, and sing,

by my own eyes inspired." This passage returns us to the present
time of the poem's first lines. After the invocation Keats moves to
the immediate past, recounting his view of Cupid and Psyche earlier
in the day, and then goes back to the distant past of antiquity. In
stanza three he returns to the present, and throughout the remainder
of the poem he speaks in the future tense, predicting what he will
do under the inspiration of his vision. But the vision which inspires
that prophecy is not his first sight of Cupid and Psyche. By his
own eyes inspired, the poet sees Psyche "among the faint Olympians," not "on the bedded grass" with Cupid. The original sight
of the lovers is a prelude, a sensory intimation of the true vision,
which is a self-inspired insight into the supranatural beauty that is
Psyche.[16] This progress from sight to vision parallels Psyche's progress from mortal to immortal in Apuleius' story.

The poet's worship, then, will not be worship of the natural world,
which was the object of adoration for the "fond believing lyre" of
ancient rhapsodists. Keats will "build a fane" to her "in some untrodden region of my mind." So in the final stanza the natural
world only provides metaphors to express Keats's now prophetic
vision; the "real" nature of the first stanza has been transcended:
"the gardener Fancy . . . breeding flowers, will never breed the
same."[17] When, therefore, in the last lines another embrace between
Cupid and Psyche is foreshadowed—"a casement ope at night,/ To
let the warm Love in!"—the poet is not returning to his original
sight in the forest. What had happened externally before will in
the future take place within the poet's mind. The action of the
poem is a process of interiorization.

Thus we may summarize what occurs in the poem in a new way.
Within a natural setting the poet sees Cupid and Psyche embracing:
his senses respond to spirits or powers in nature that are not themselves natural beings. From this sight arises his inspired vision of
love and beauty as supranatural, divinely eternal. He determines
to shape his mind to be a haven for the joyful mingling of love
and beauty, so that when they have mingled in his mind he will
become, literally,

> Thy voice, thy lute, thy pipe, thy incense sweet
>   From swinged censer teeming;
> Thy shrine, thy grove, thy oracle, thy heat
>   Of pale-mouth'd prophet dreaming.[18]

What had been objective will be subjective and what had been subjective will be objective. The old distinctions between mind and external world will be fused in a new life.[19]

It may be illuminating at this point to consider briefly Foscolo's two most famous odes, for different as they are from Keats's, they express a similar aspiration within an analogous form. *To Luigia Pallavicini* is a hymn to the recovery of a beautiful woman who had been seriously injured and disfigured by a fall from a horse. The poem begins with a prayer to the Graces to prepare the same healing ointments they applied to Venus when a thorn pierced her foot, while, distracted, she lamented Adonis. Cupids weep for the lady and bring offerings to Apollo's throne, and the spirit of the dance calls for her, recollecting her free beauty in movement, reminiscent of Athena and Venus together. Then follows a narrative of the frightful ride on the maddened horse, then a description of the present languor of the lady's face and her "love-filled eyes searching the doctors' looks for a flattering hope of her original beauty." In the final three stanzas the poem turns to another myth.

One day the stags drawing Diana's golden chariot, driven mad with terror at the howling of wild beasts, plunged the goddess over the Etnian cliff. The other Olympian goddesses rejoiced with envious smiles when the immortal face, silent and pallid, appeared veiled at the banquet of heaven. But bitterly they wept the day she returned happy among the worshipping virgins at the Ephesian dances and rose even more beautiful into the sky as the sister of Phoebus.

Foscolo's ode is certainly in some ways closer to Neoclassical practice than Keats's. But, as Italian critics have stressed, Foscolo's poem is not Neoclassical.[20] His originality is illustrated by the concluding story of Diana, which is not traditional but his own invention. The culmination of his mythological references (as in *To Psyche*) is a new, private myth.

It was not an uncommon Neoclassic practice to compare eighteenth-century ladies to classical divinities, and in the earlier part of *Pallavicini* Foscolo makes such a comparison. But in the last stanzas there is no comparison; there is no mention of the lady, who becomes Diana—perhaps it would be better to say that Diana becomes the lady. The transformation occurs, as Professor Fubini has observed, first, because the mythology in the early part of the poem is not called on to adorn the reality of actual life but the reality of actual life is perceived mythologically.[21] To put it stiffly, the lady's accident represents the violent perils which circumscribe the transient manifestations of beauty in the natural world. Then, too, the final transfiguration in the Diana myth is the culmination of a process of interiorization. The poet begins with *pictures* of the Graces preparing healing oils for Venus and of the weeping cupids making offerings, and then the lady's former beauty is recalled in the image of her dancing, an image that calls forth *comparisons* to Athena and Venus. Next follows the *narrative* of the fatal ride, with few classical allusions, and finally we arrive at the psychological *dramatization* with the pallid sufferer's mute look of questioning appeal. We progress from abstraction to particularity, from public panorama to inward emotion, and the new myth arises from the poet's penetration into the personal anguish of the lady, so that the myth of Diana expresses both her hopes and the poet's faith that there is a spiritual, enduring beauty transcending mere physical appearance.

This process of interiorization is the key to Foscolo's other great ode, *To a Friend Restored to Health*, which celebrates the recovery from serious illness of a woman Foscolo loved. In this ode, a shimmering fabric of mythological allusions sustained by the poet's Greek parentage and childhood on Zante, the lady scarcely appears in her own person. She is perceived as the embodiment of divine beauty, but this is not merely the conceit of conventional flattery. Foscolo thinks his beloved to be equal to the goddesses of ancient mythology, a new goddess, because he believes the old goddesses were themselves once mortal women, destined like his beloved to the "eternal peace" of death. They were deified by the songs of ancient poets. Because he is a Greek, and because he was reared amidst the beauty of Grecian sea and land, he, too, can deify his beloved. The poem is the process of deification, the process of increasingly intensified understanding by which the imagination creates out of the reality of natural existence a more vital and enduring supranatural life.[22]

This vital, supranatural life Foscolo, like Keats, identifies with beauty. Foscolo and Keats perhaps differ most from modern poets in their explicit celebration of beauty. They use the word freely; we shy from it. They unashamedly seek for manifestations of beauty;[23] we accept these uneasily, and often as secondary attributes of physical efficiency or moral subtlety. But if Keats and Foscolo celebrate beauty they are not therefore remote from reality nor indulging a detached aestheticism. They did not believe in or practice what later was called "art for art's sake," yet we tend to read them as if they were latter-day aesthetes. We do so because we misunderstand their feeling for beauty and because we have come to believe, with Auden, that "poetry makes nothing happen."

It may not be a coincidence, however, that in history an efflorescence of lyric poetry, surely the most "useless" kind, often does precede and accompany a powerful thrust of material and intellectual culture. This is not surprising if lyric poetry is the spark which ignites creative consciousness. And why should it not be? Why should it not be the rendering explicit and transmissible of new self-awareness and consequently of new awareness of the individual's relation to his environment? And is it not from such decisive mental (and, therefore, originally personal) stimuli that the great material transformations of civilization derive? If human evolution is biological evolution advanced to a new level of self-reflection, if man is evolution become conscious of itself (in Julian Huxley's phrase), lyric poetry may have a very practical function. It may be the means of increasing man's mental awareness. This is what seems most to need doing, man having advanced biologically so far as he has, and so far ahead of other species.

At any rate, this is a function and effect of much early nineteenth-century poetry, one indication of the process being the interiorizing and personalizing, the "localizing" in Dr. Johnson's terminology, of traditional themes and motifs.[24] For example, the theme of Keats's *Ode on Melancholy*—that joy and sorrow are inseparable—is an old and familiar one. But the intensity with which the poet feels the inseparability of melancholy and joy makes us forget how trite his theme is and from what diverse sources he may have drawn in creating his poem.

It is important that Keats locates Melancholy's "sovran shrine" *within* "the very temple of Delight." What is original in Keats's poem is the energy with which he insists that melancholy, though absolutely distinct from joy, is contained within delight and is to be attained, therefore, by a process of penetration. The emphasis upon penetration is reinforced by the total structure of the ode and by the careful arrangement of key details. The word "melancholy" is not used in the first stanza; in the second it is employed without capitalization; only in the final stanza does "Melancholy" appear. Stanza one, in fact, says less about melancholy than about suicide.[25] The melancholy of the first stanza is to be inferred: the advice not to seek death implies that he who is so advised suffers from melancholy. It is noteworthy that the person so advised is the reader. *Melancholy* is the only one of the five "great" odes which is not about Keats, in which the dominant personal pronoun is "you," not "I."[26] Dominance of the second person forces us to recognize that *Melancholy* does not focus on a single experience; instead it dramatizes the principle by which all precious emotional experience takes place. It dramatizes the nature of the psychic system upon which depend the particularized experiences that are the subjects of the other odes. It is the most impersonal of the great odes because it is the most abstractly psychological.

Because *Melancholy* sets forth a psychological system, it progresses to a climax that seems at first glance to be Neoclassical. The final stanza is almost a tableau of personifications,[27] yet these last lines are far removed from the cool, static clarity of Neoclassical art. Keats's personifications express a dynamic psychology. That is why they are inseparable from vigorous renderings of the most intensely personal of sensory experiences.

The first eight lines of the poem, though concerned with an apparently personal matter, suicide, are dominated by three classical references: Lethe, Proserpine, and Psyche. But these traditional accompaniments of "sorrow's mysteries" are to be rejected, lest

> . . . shade to shade will come too drowsily,
> And drown the wakeful anguish of the soul.

Probably we should not read too much into this turning away from three primary elements in the pagan mythology of death, yet Keats's lines recall the shadowy underworld of the pagan after-life and in so doing may subtly remind us how insubstantial are the dead ways of thought of ancient civilization. At any rate, the personifications of the third stanza (which, significantly, concludes as the second opens, with an image carrying the mind skyward) plainly are not resurrected classical deities; they are embodiments of new powers, psychological powers which synthesize the shadowy traditions of antiquity with the sensory vividness of immediate experience.

Instead of drowning "the wakeful anguish of the soul" one should, the second stanza advises, "glut" one's "sorrow" on the beauty of fleeting phenomena: "a morning rose," the "wealth of globed peonies," or the "rich anger" in a mistress' "peerless eyes." The importance of Keats's word "glut," sustained by "feed deep, deep" in line twenty, must not be overlooked. The phenomena are impressively lovely because they are transient. One feeds his sorrow to satiety by dwelling intensely upon—as it were, participating fully in —this "Beauty that must die." The beauty of the phenomena does not *compensate* for "the melancholy fit." On the contrary, the transience of the beauty will "foster" the melancholy, just as "a weeping cloud . . . fosters the droop-headed flowers." And as the cloud in fostering the flowers destroys them (suggested by the phrase, "hides the green hill in an April shroud") so the beautiful phenomena in fostering "the melancholy fit" destroy it by bringing it to fulfillment.

In stanza three the lovely phenomena of stanza two and the traditional death images of stanza one coalesce into personifications —Beauty, Pleasure, Joy, Melancholy—which are given force and vitality by their association with climactic images of taste: "aching Pleasure" turns "to poison as the bee-mouth sips," and "Veil'd Melancholy" is

> . . . seen of none save him whose strenuous tongue
> Can burst Joy's grape against his palate fine.

Here, even more than in the first two stanzas, powerful images of eating and drinking, of the act of nourishment, sustain Keats's abstractness with sensory substantiality.

Taste is the most personal and probably for many of us the most specific of our sensations. We can share sights and sounds, odors and tactile sensations with others, but not tastes. Throughout *Melancholy* Keats fleshes his psychological abstractions by appealing to our sense of taste, and when in the third stanza he reaches the zenith of his abstraction, "Veil'd Melancholy" in the "temple of Delight," he provides the climactic sensory figure of the grape bursting against the palate. And this figure reminds us that eating and drinking differ significantly from seeing, touching, hearing, or smelling: tasting is a process of transformation.

Melancholy and delight, joy and sorrow, are represented by Keats not as states of mind but as processes by which the mind passes from one condition to another. Joy is the action by which the mind becomes sorrowful. Melancholy is the action by which the mind becomes joyful. But are we not, then, caught in a vicious circle, joy becoming sorrow and sorrow becoming joy? Yes, and that vicious circle is precisely the "wakeful anguish of the soul." Ultimately, of course, this cycle ends in the quiescent shade of death, but he who dares to follow not the "drowsy" way of suicide—shrinking from the "anguish" that is life—but the "strenuous" way, bursting "Joy's grape," shall win a place among the "cloudy trophies" of that melancholic "might" to which at last all men must submit. To commit suicide is to deny life, to make human life as shadowy as that of the ancient underworld. Those who choose the way of "wakeful anguish" adorn and dignify by their acceptance their inescapable destiny.[28]

Keats's conception of the emotions as acts by which the mind changes its condition is in itself interesting. It becomes even more interesting when we observe that this conception, presented abstractly in *Melancholy*, is the psychological foundation for the specific experiences celebrated in the other odes.[29] The *Nightingale* ode, for example, treats not joy and sorrow but inspired and realistic apprehension.[30] To envision is to become aware of the sensory reality of things, and sensuous awareness, in turn, is a process conducing to visionary apprehension. When the poet cries to the bird, "I will fly to thee . . . on the viewless wings of Poesy," he suggests that poetry is the human equivalent of the bird's ecstatic song but not that they are identical. Nor does the exclamation, "Thou wast not born for death, immortal Bird," leading to the observation that perhaps the "self-same song" was heard "in ancient days," mean that he regards this nightingale as beyond nature. His view is more poignant. The song heard by Ruth was identical with the one heard by him now, because ancient and modern nightingales are not, like Ruth and himself, separated by the march of hungry generations. The song of the nightingale is immortal in the sense that every nightingale sings the same song, and that repetitiveness is a function of the bird's freedom from "the weariness, the fever, and the fret" of mankind's existence.

To this natural immortality is opposed the more problematical but more meaningful immortality of Poesy in the form of the ode itself. The opposition is not simple, as is an analogous kind of opposition in Renaissance pastoral poetry, for the inspiration of Poesy is found in that sensual ecstasy with which nature surrounds the poet and of which the nightingale's song is the supreme manifestation. The ultimate achievement of the bird's singing is to carry the human mind through nature into a visionary realm, to charm "magic casements, opening on the foam/ Of perilous seas, in faery lands forlorn."[31]

"Thou wast not born for death, immortal Bird," means, then, that the bird's song does not, as some have thought, urge us toward death but toward a new life. Properly understood, understood by the poet who does not "have ears in vain," the song leads on to the visionary realm where he may be, through his creative consciousness, more than his "sole self," but that realm is one of "faery lands forlorn." The poet's visionary existence is not his natural existence. He must return to his "sole self," his conscious isolation, from which the nightingale as a purely instinctual (natural) creature is saved.[32] Not until, possibly, the final transition of death will he know whether his vision is delusive or a foresight of a more intense and enduring reality: "Do I wake or sleep?" To the poet, the man of high sensitivity, this must be the most persistently agonizing of questions, if for no other reason than that his awareness forces him to recognize that there can be no answer before death.[33]

The *Ode to a Nightingale* is complex and fascinating because it celebrates the process by which the human mind, aroused by circumstances external to itself, creates a "visionary existence" for itself beyond the natural, external stimulus, only to return once more to the natural confines.[34] The mind is not identical, however, with what it was before its rise. There has been "a step forward in articulation,"[35] the sign of which is the final emotional ambivalence. On the one hand, the poet is happier because of his momentary transcendence, and, on the other hand, he is sadder because of his increased awareness of the inherent transience of such conquest.

In the *Nightingale*, then, Keats extends the psychological principle stated in *Melancholy* (that joyful and sorrowful emotions are actions of transition from one state of being to another) to man's dealings with the natural universe. In the *Ode to a Nightingale* Keats makes us feel that truly to sense ordinary reality is to transcend it, and that such transcendence returns us with heightened awareness to our sense of ordinary reality. The very action by which we fully apprehend the sensory reality external to us, that which is not our "sole self," is a mental exertion by which we penetrate within the mere sensory appearances of things. This apprehension of the inner being of external reality, however, carries us back to our "sole self," our awareness of the sensory surface of things different from ourselves. But the fact of the transcending experience remains in memory, carrying with it both a haunting sense of loss and the bright promise of possible attainment.

In the odes *On Indolence* and *On a Grecian Urn* Keats concentrates on art, in the former on the process of creation, in the latter on the created work. The *Ode on Indolence* is complicated in its temporal ordering, and it may be helpful to trace the "narrative" which is its structure.[36] "One morn" three figures were seen by the poet. A tone of passiveness is established at once. Where or how the figures appeared we are not told; the mood of indolence dissolves sharpness of outline. The figures "pass'd, like figures on a marble urn," twice, but "they were strange" to the poet, as figures on a Greek vase might be "strange," familiar but unidentifiable, to a student of sculpture.

"How is it, Shadows! that I knew ye not?" asks the poet. Was his inability to recognize the figures the result of some "deep-disguised plot" to leave him "without a task"? At the time of this vision, the poet then tells us, he was relaxed, "Benumb'd," and he complains that the figures disturbed this "blissful cloud of summer-indolence":

> . . . why did ye not melt, and leave my sense
> Unhaunted quite of all but—nothingness?

The poet regrets the appearance of the shades because they disrupt his tranced apathy.

But a third time they appear, "Alas, wherefore?" He describes his condition *before* their appearance (hence his use of the pluperfect tense), the bliss of his indolence, and then the lazy luxuriance of the natural surroundings in which the "shades" intrude. This was "a time to bid farewell!" especially as from the poet "had fallen no tears" for the figures: he had not invoked them.

The fourth stanza returns to the third appearance of the figures and describes how they turned "Each one the face a moment whiles to me;/ Then faded." At this instant the poet recognized the three, and "because I knew the three," he says, "to follow them I burn'd."

He identifies the figures at last as Love, Ambition, and Poesy, although, in keeping with the indefinite imagery of the poem, he does not identify their sex—it is only from Keats's letters that we know the figures comprise two women and a man.

"They faded, and, forsooth! I wanted wings:/ O folly!" *Now* the poet's complaint is not that the figures appeared but that their appearance tempted him, even momentarily, to follow them out of his "honied indolence." In the concluding stanza the poet says:

> So, ye three Ghosts, adieu! Ye cannot raise
> My head cool-bedded in the flowery grass.

He does not wish to be "dieted with praise," just as at the end of the preceding stanza he prays not to know "how change the moons," not to "hear the voice of busy common-sense!" He is determined to luxuriate in his indolence; so he commands the figures to "Fade softly from my eyes," to reassume their strange, unrecognized positions in which they first appeared, "masque-like figures on the dreamy urn." The poet bids the figures an unregretful farewell because he has, in his indolence, "visions for the night" and "for the day faint visions there is store." So he concludes by repeating his command, "Vanish, ye Phantoms! . . . and never more return!" Love, Ambition, and Poesy do not succeed in drawing him from his mood of indolence.

They fail because they are "shades," "shadows," "ghosts," "phantoms." In short, they are unreal. Keats makes no claims for the "visions" of his indolence: they are "nothingness." But Love, Ambition, and Poesy are likewise illusions, are no more substantial than the day or night dreams of luxurious relaxation. It is "the voice of busy common-sense" which insists that Love, Ambition, and Poesy are "realities" for which it is worthwhile to yearn, struggle, and suffer. The poet knows better. He knows that all human achievement, even that of the art to which he is profoundly dedicated, is illusion, is "nothingness." Even when his friends praise his work and shower affection upon him he recognizes the falseness of this glory: "A pet-lamb in a sentimental farce!" In fine, the *Ode on Indolence* expresses the same kind of wisdom to which Prospero gives utterance.

> . . . like the baseless fabric of this vision,
> The cloud-capped towers, the gorgeous palaces,
> The solemn temples, the great globe itself,
> Yea, all which it inherit, shall dissolve,

And, like this insubstantial pageant faded,
Leave not a rack behind. We are such stuff
As dreams are made on, and our little life
Is rounded with a sleep.

Can there be a greater artistic maturity than this, wherein the
poet accepts the insubstantiality of his labor? Yes, as Shakespeare's
Tempest shows us—and Keats's *Ode on Indolence*, too. There is
a fundamental paradox in Keats's poem that has never been remarked,[37] even though many critics have noticed the same paradox
in a different form in *The Tempest*. Prospero's assertion of the
illusoriness of art and life is the speech of a dramatic character within
the larger "illusion" of a fabulous drama. As for Keats, we may
define his paradoxical situation by a simple question: does it take
more energy to write an *Ode on Activity* than to write an *Ode on
Indolence*? Keats's very celebration of indolence and rejection of
poetry in a fine poem is an expression of energy and a validation
of poetry.

This paradox is of the utmost importance not alone for one poem
but for all Keats's art. The paradox upon which the *Ode on Indolence*
is founded is one source of Keats's admiration for Shakespeare,
his theory of "negative capability," and his desire to attain "disin-
terestedness." These last terms may be difficult of exact definition,
but their function in the Keatsian aesthetic is clarified as soon as
we read the *Ode on Indolence* in the light of the psychological
theory dramatized by the *Ode on Melancholy* (that is, as described
earlier, the process by which sorrow becomes joy and joy becomes
sorrow). In the *Ode on Indolence* he transfers this "process" psychology of the emotions to the total act of artistic creation. To be
actively creative is to pass into passive indolence, and to be passively indolent is to become artistically creative. Were this not so
Keats would have been simply lazy, and we should have had no
Ode on Indolence.

Although the "negative capability" expressed in *Indolence* seems,
and indeed is, paradoxical, at the same time it embodies a simple
truth about art. Music cannot exist without silence, that which is,
aesthetically, a "nothingness." What is true of the created work
of art is probably true of its creator. For example, were the poet
not sometimes indolent, he could never express, in his creative phase,
the attractiveness of indolence as personal experience. When he is

not creating, then, the poet is necessarily, in Keats's phrase, "the most unpoetical of any thing in existence," just as, analogously, only he who can "burst Joy's grape" can know "Veil'd Melancholy" and "taste the sadness of her might."

The product of the creative process is dramatized in the *Ode on a Grecian Urn*.[38] The work of art is, above all else, "a thing of beauty," and a thing of beauty is neither simply a physical object, a mere artifact, nor simply a mental construct, a mere psychic entity. It is instead a dynamic intermediary, a focus for the interplay of mind and matter, of natural and supranatural realities. The work of art is fragile as a dream yet more enduring than natural objects or creatures, because it is a created mode of being. Man alone makes it and enjoys its existence, but it is not fully separable, anymore than man is, from the natural mode of existence.

The work of art is the expression of the inner system of vitality of the natural universe which is present only latently until man, by means of his imagination, recognizes it and brings it into fully realized being. That which impels man to recognize and bring forth this inner system of energy is love. Beauty, hence art, for Keats and his contemporaries is inseparable from love.

In the *Grecian Urn*, a poem about a work of art, there is a basic contrast between the ecstasy and limitations of real, natural love and the different ecstasy and limitations of love as it appears in art.[39] The chief unstated question of the poem is, are the figures on the urn, "For ever panting, and for ever young," who will never know sexual consummation and its concomitant, "a heart high-sorrowful and cloy'd," more or less fortunate than we? The central subject matter of this poem about art is not separable from the problem of human love. Thus there is a complex balance of forces in the *Ode on a Grecian Urn*, but the balance pivots on the basic contrast-in-similitude between the figures on the urn and the viewers. These latter, like the poet himself, can experience love's consummation but must in consequence suffer its aftermath, "a burning forehead, and a parching tongue." But they, like the poet, appreciate and draw satisfaction from the perception of the other form of existence represented by the urn's figures. Beauty in art and beauty in nature, beauty in time and beauty *sub specie aeternitatis*, can balance because they are alike. The beauty of enduring art is like the beauty of transient human passion because both derive from love. Sensual

activity within natural reality and spiritual activity within supranatural reality are different but not incompatible, for they are both
manifestations of love. The two manifestations unite in the truth
of art, which embodies supranatural truth in natural truth, actual-
izing the potentiality of the real.

Because the work of art dramatizes this similitude in diversity
it is a dynamic paradox, a vital structural intermediary between
different but interdependent modes of life.[40] Thus the work of art
which is Keats's subject, the whole urn, is described paradoxically,
as an "unravish'd bride" and a "Cold Pastoral." And the work of
art which is the ode itself is paradoxical, since what the urn finally
tells us, "Beauty is truth, truth beauty," does not definitely answer
the pivotal question of the poem—as innumerable diverse interpretations testify.[41]

Yet the *Ode on a Grecian Urn* is not a puzzle. Neither Keats
nor the reader is back where he started when the poem ends, though
the "mystery" of art, to be sure, is deeper for us at the conclusion.
That is why the enigmatic quality of the final lines is, however
frustrating to some rationalistic critics, appropriate to the movement
of the poem. We have been led, as the poet was led by Grecian art,
not rationally to know art better, not to become better connoisseurs,
but to experience more intensely and profoundly the mystery that
is art: that is all we know on earth, and all we need to know.

This is the most intense form of the new kind of experience
which Keats's odes express. But, as I have tried to suggest, we misunderstand its significance if we regard it merely as aesthetic experience, because it embodies a mental leap, an advance in awareness, which may serve as the basis for progress in unaesthetic endeavors. In these odes, as in all of the poems I have discussed, the
poet's underlying assumption is that through art man defines his
special nature and finds a proper and rewarding way of life. Wordsworth, Foscolo, Leopardi, and Keats, each in his own idiom and
according to his own nature, strives to create a new humanism[42]
which will establish the unity of mankind in terms of the vitality
of each man's unique and personal experience.

PART
THREE

Time, Myth, and Total Relatedness:
Essential Poetic Techniques

V ❧ THE TEMPORALIZATION OF SPACE

WORDSWORTH: *Tintern Abbey*

LEOPARDI: *The Infinite*
To the Moon
Sunday Evening

I HAVE suggested that the poets of the early nineteenth century were prophets of a new humanism, and I want now to describe some of the methods by which they sought to realize their visions. In this chapter I shall concentrate on what I call the process of temporalizing space, in the next chapter on what I call the creation of secularized myths, and in Chapter VII on the system of what I call total relatedness. My intent is not to prove a uniformity of practice but to illuminate patterns of purposes and of techniques for attaining those purposes which underlie the diversity of the poetry of an era when poets were not only "original" but also expressed their individuality through a remarkable variety of forms, some new and some as old as the sonnet, the idyll, the meditation, and the narrative.

Tintern Abbey, Wordsworth's principal contribution to the *Lyrical Ballads*, is related to the eighteenth-century tradition of meditative-descriptive poetry which is often called "topographical."[1] I shall not enter into the history of this "local" poetry nor distinguish its varieties, confining myself to the observation that its subject matter is existent natural scenes, so that it is a realistic poetry, in that, however artificial its language, it speaks always of the actual. This distinguishes it from earlier "pastoral" poetry, as does its tendency to treat of large scenes or landscapes. Today we customarily associate the word "landscape" with art, a vista perceived with aesthetic sensibility.[2] Yet a landscape is a natural scene, and we do sometimes use the word without emphasis upon its aesthetic connotations, referring simply to the configuration of terrain. Still,

87

most of us feel a distinction between "landscape" and more generic
terms such as "countryside," a distinction implied by the etymology
of "landscape"—land-form, land-shape. A landscape is not something artificial, like a garden,[3] but, unlike countryside, it possesses
form, and the form, we tend to think, is not so much imposed by
the observer as discovered by him; the form, the aesthetic quality,
is inherent in landscape.

A landscape is not the same as a panorama, but it possesses something of the panorama's spaciousness. Like the panorama, the landscape subordinates detail; its structure is that of large masses. Hence
the primary elements in a landscape are the more obvious and more
permanent elements of the natural world—trees, rivers, mountains.[4]
More than that, landscape implies sky, probably because we can
scarcely be conscious of land formation without some basic element
of contrast. A rural scene may be circumscribed entirely by, say, a
forest, but some appearance of sky is necessary to a landscape, in
which light is always of importance.[5] A landscape is something seen,
so in the landscapes of poetry, sound, smell, and touch are always
subordinate to sight.

Temperament and environment as well as literary tradition helped
Wordsworth to become a landscapist. Sight was his strongest sense—
he more than once complained of the "tyranny" of his eyes. The
bare, open countryside of his native region is a series of "landscapes":
large masses of simple elements, the sky always present, the light and
shade vivid. Indeed, one might almost say that when Wordsworth
speaks of "nature" he means "landscape." It would be surprising if
Tintern Abbey did not owe something to the Neoclassic literary
tradition of landscape poetry, yet the poem is very different from
any of its predecessors, very original.[6]

For one thing, there is little description in *Tintern Abbey*. Only
in the first twenty-two lines does Wordsworth describe the scene, and
even here he makes no attempt to paint with words. The "cliffs . . .
impress/Thoughts of more deep seclusion," and the silent wreaths
of smoke evoke the fancy, not the sight, of a lonely hermit. The brief
description is not unimportant: upon it is founded all else in the
poem, but to Wordsworth the man observing is more important than
what he observes.[7] Wordsworth's subject is his mind, not the natural
scene before him. He differs from his Neoclassic predecessors in that

landscape gives form to his self-expression rather than serving as the subject of his contemplation.[8]

Time precedes sight in *Tintern Abbey*, which begins, "Five years have past." But Wordsworth does not revive one of the old pastoralists' favorite themes: like the Neoclassic descriptive poets he avoids the *carpe diem* motif. Although change plays a significant part in *Tintern Abbey*, in the introductory lines the poet stresses permanence rather than mutability: "again I hear," "I again repose," "Once again I see." Indeed, Wordsworth suggests no mutability in nature, which appears to endure timelessly and without alteration. On the other hand, the temporal relations between the poet as he was, is now, and may be in the future are of an extraordinary complexity totally foreign to any Neoclassic topographical poem. I know of no poem of any kind previous to *Tintern Abbey* which represents so vividly the dynamism of time as it is experienced in individual psychic life. At any rate, it is no serious exaggeration to say that Wordsworth is as much a "time" poet as a "nature" poet,[9] and he may be identified as the first English poet to treat time in all the shifting complexity with which the modern mind regards temporality. Precisely because he is concerned with time in this fashion, he tends to present nature as fixed, as a tangible, enduring structural reference: nature as form.

Tintern Abbey begins with a description that is double: what is seen now is seen "again," the present landscape is coexistent with the landscape seen five years before. Then the poet moves back, considering what "these beauteous forms" meant to him during the five year interval, in what manner—"not . . . As is a landscape to a blind man's eye"[10]— they existed in his mind and what their value then was. They lightened "the weary weight" of an "unintelligible world" and provided a "mood" in which he could "see into the life of things." But then, "with gleams of half-extinguished thought . . . recognitions dim and faint" this "picture of the mind revives again." Now the present scene and the "picture of the mind"—not the previous physical sight—coexist in the poet's mind, and that coexistence produces a prefiguration of the "life" in "this moment" that may nourish "future years." This prefiguration is founded on the poet's recognition that in the course of years he has changed: if the scene before him is the same, his perceiving mind is not what it once was. "Then"—presumably five years before, but perhaps even earlier[11]— "nature to me was all in all." But even that state rested upon an earlier one of "glad animal movements," even as its "aching joys" and "dizzy raptures" have been succeeded by the poet's present more sober, more thoughtful condition of mind in which he hears within the beauteous forms of nature "the still, sad music of humanity." Now he has learned to feel "A presence that disturbs me with the joy/ Of elevated thoughts"; now he is capable of responding not merely to the sensory appearances of things but to that "motion" and "spirit" within appearances "that impels/ All thinking things, all objects of all thought." "Therefore," he asserts, he is "still" a lover of nature; he has changed, but in such a way that, although not "haunted" by the terror and beauty of sensory experiences, he can still recognize in "the language of the sense" a guide and guardian of his "moral being." This is why the two landscapes can coexist in his mind.

Here, at line 111, following a spiral movement typical of many early nineteenth-century poems,[12] Wordsworth has returned to the point first reached at line 48, where he speaks of that mood wherein "we see into the life of things." He has come back to the present but has not yet taken up the future possibilities (raised in lines 64–65). To these he advances with the supposition "Nor perchance/ If I were not thus taught." He is so taught. The subjunctive echoes the earlier uncertainty of lines 49–50, "If this be but a vain belief," because he wants to return to that of which there can be no doubt: the past.[13] Because the present exists now, we can not be certain of it in the way that we can be certain of the past. To hope for the future, to build the future on the present, we must found our idea of the present on our knowledge of the past. This Wordsworth does. Turning to his sister, in whom is expressed "the language of my former heart," who is the embodiment of his past, he finds additional proof that he is building well. She proves he was what he believes he was; in consequence, he probably is what he believes he is; Nature has not betrayed "the heart that loved her." He can, therefore, pray that his sister will become what he now is, that her "mind/ Shall be a mansion for all lovely forms."

From this reassurance derives the final affirmation that in the present moment "there is life and food/ For future years," since even if there should be no future for the poet, the transfusion of his joy to those he loves will make them remember with pleasure this moment—then become the past. Thus the poem closes with "these

steep woods and lofty cliffs,/And this green pastoral landscape" once
more seen in dual existence, as it presently appears and as the poet
prefigures its appearance in his sister's future memory. This final
coexistence not only completes the formal pattern of the poem but
also climaxes the process of temporalizing space which is the dynamic
action of *Tintern Abbey.*

In *Tintern Abbey* the mind working on, and under the influence
of, landscape produces an evocation of what we today can perhaps
most accurately call space-time. The realism of Wordsworth's poem
is entirely different from the realism of eighteenth-century landscape
poetry, though undoubtedly a development of it. The realism of the
earlier poetry resides in its descriptiveness, its representation of what
nature looks like.[14] Wordsworth's poem derives from an actual scene
observed at a specific time, but he treats the natural scene as a formal
entity, a "pastoral landscape," not as a subject to be accurately de-
lineated, because he is more *self*-centered than his predecessors. Much
Neoclassic topographical poetry is indefinite as to where the describing poet stands,[15] and none of it locates its view in personal time,
specifying the place of the view in the detailed chronology of the
poet's life.[16] This Wordsworth does, and it is worthwhile to see how
he does it.

The basic pattern of *Tintern Abbey* is of spiralling repetition, and
this structural characteristic is reflected in the poem's diction. Wordsworth's effort is to bring out the interior potency, the potentiality, of
unextraordinary words and unelaborate, commonplace syntactical
constructions.[17] The first, fifth, and eleventh words of the poem are
"five," and the importance of this repetition is emphasized by the
latter part of line 2: "and *again* I hear." "Again" itself is repeated in
lines 4, 9, and 14, while the "hear" of line 2 links up to the "murmur"
of line 4, which becomes "quiet" in line 8, and, finally, "silence" in
line 18. "Mountain-springs" in line 3 is picked up with the "steep
and lofty cliffs" of line 5. This, also, is the first of many pairs of
adjectives and nouns that are very nearly redundant, "towns and
cities," "Slight or trivial," "the heavy and the weary weight," "dim
and faint," and so forth.[18] The "cliffs" of line 5 become in line 6
"a wild, *secluded* scene," which in line 7 impresses "thoughts of more
deep *seclusion.*"

Line 9 carries the mind *back* through the "Once again/ Do I behold" of lines 4 and 5 to the opening lines. Line 9, "The *day* is come

when *I again repose*," also leads into the "view" of line 10, in which "sycamore" introduces trees: "orchard-tufts" (l. 11); "groves and copses" (l. 14); "trees" (l. 18); "woods" (l. 20). The orchards, "with their *unripe* fruits" (l. 12), are "clad in one green hue" (l. 13) even as the "pastoral farms" (l. 16) are "green to the very door" (l. 17). Throughout these lines there is both simple repetition, "These hedge-rows, hardly hedge-rows," "some Hermit's cave, where . . . The Hermit sits alone," and a less overt reiteration, such as the "vagrant dwellers in the houseless woods," the "uncertain notice" from "among the trees" recalling the "orchard-tufts" that "lose themselves," and so on.

A similar reiterative principle operates throughout the second major portion of the poem, lines 22–49. This section, however, needs less verbal repetition because it catches up ideas, images, and feelings introduced in the opening description. Thus lines 22–25:

> . . . These beauteous forms,
> Through a *long absence,* have not been to me
> As is a *landscape* to a blind man's eye;
> But oft, in *lonely* rooms, . . .

pick up motifs from the earlier section while leading toward later lines' stress on "unremembered pleasure" (l. 31) and "unremembered acts" (l. 34). "Feelings" (l. 30) and the pleasures of the "purer mind" (l. 29), which are "*Felt* in the blood and *felt* along the heart" (l. 28), rather than visual sensations (emphasized in the introductory lines), are at the center of this second section. The "tranquil restoration" (l. 30) produced by the purer feelings, "kindness and . . . love" (l. 35), "that blessed mood" (l. 37), "that serene and blessed mood/ In which the affections gently lead" (ll. 41–42), lightens "The heavy and the weary weight" (l. 39)—compare the "weariness" of l. 27 and the "burthen of the mystery" of l. 38—of this "unintelligible world" (l. 40).

Reason operates on the evidence of physical sensation, and to reason the world is unintelligible. True vision and comprehension result from that "blessed mood" in which spirit supersedes sense. When the "breath of this corporeal frame" (l. 43) and the "motion of our human blood" (l. 44) are "suspended" (l. 45) and "we are laid asleep/ In body" (ll. 45–46) we can "become a living soul" (l. 46). The paradox that life is most manifest when most passive is explained by lines 47–49. "With an eye made quiet"—when, that is, the observer is possessed of a serenity equivalent to the quietness of the original scene—"by the power/ Of harmony, and the deep power of joy/ We see *into* the *life* of *things*." The poet through physical passivity penetrates to the living essence of *things*.[19] He becomes himself like a "thing," which is inert not because it is soulless but because all its "life" is interior, not excursive.

One might continue to trace the pattern of reiterative language, always within a simple, almost formless syntax, through the entire poem, observing how there is progressively less immediate repetition and more repetition of "distant" terms as the poem spirals onward. The progression is most apparent, perhaps, in the concluding lines, "these steep woods and lofty cliffs/ And this green pastoral landscape," where the purposeful exactitude of reiteration is obvious both in itself and in its function. But the analysis above is tedious enough and its point should by now be plain: this system of language is never found in eighteenth-century descriptive poetry. In descriptive verse such reiteration would be unnecessary, since a description to be lively must move from detail to detail, must be linear rather than spiral, elementaristic rather than synthetic.[20] Wordsworth does not describe; he explores the action of his inner consciousness; his poem gradually reveals the significance of a fundamental and complex psychic process.

Wordsworth, however, has often been charged with talking about emotions instead of expressing them, with naming emotions instead of making the reader experience them. *Tintern Abbey* shows us how he names and expresses emotion. Perhaps the crucial sentiment named in the poem is "joy," which is denominated in five different lines:

l. 48: "the deep power of joy" with which "We see into the life of things."
l. 84: the "aching joys" of youth that "are now no more."
l. 94: the "presence" that "disturbs" with the "joy/Of elevated thoughts."
l. 125: the "joy to joy" to which Nature leads us.
l. 145: the "tender joy" with which the poet's sister will remember him "if solitude, or fear, or pain, or grief" should be her lot.

In each context "joy" means something different, yet just as plainly each meaning is related to the others. Likewise, one could show that each "joy" is related to other reiterated terms, especially, "love," "kindness," "blessing," "pleasure." Wordsworth does not rely on the dictionary definition of joy; he is aware that that definition is a generalized, abstract, unexpressive one; his purpose is to create and to express the particularized "meaning" of his specific experience, which would, if one were to discuss it intellectually, be characterized as a joyful one. By the end of the poem we are aware of the nature of Wordsworth's total experience, but if we have read with sensitivity we are also aware that the nature of the total experience cannot be summed up by the particular meaning of any one of the five "joys" named. It is the sum of those five "joys" that creates the unnamed, and abstractly unnamable, joyfulness of the total experience. To Wordsworth and his contemporaries (one thinks of Coleridge's *Dejection* and Keats's *Melancholy*) the naming of an emotion is not a substitute for expressing it but a means to begin expressing it.[21]

Wordsworth believed that it was the poet's function to make the commonplace interesting,[22] and he applied this concept to language. The good poet uses ordinary language because, just as he reveals new insight into familiar objects and events, he can reveal the inner potency of familiar terms and constructions. "Joy" is a familiar term, and joy in a revisited scene is perhaps common, but the "joy" of *Tintern Abbey* as a total experience is unique. The poet's utterance is charged with intense sensibility; it demonstrates the significance in commonplace language and commonplace subjects.

Thus I should argue against the ridicule piled on Wordsworth's theory of language.[23] It is not, it seems to me, extraneous to one of his chief poetic purposes, which, as Professor Basil Willey suggested some time ago,[24] is to create value and interest in a world deprived of mythology, where the poet's "truth" is dependent solely upon the intensity of his personal experience. Wordsworth makes no appeal to any system separable from the immediate experience of which each particular poem is expressive. The validating truth is the experience itself, the revelation of inner energy and beauty within the superficial appearance of trivial things and circumstances. Hence for Wordsworth everything depends upon his truthfulness. This is the price of personalization. When the poet surrenders his fictional privileges, his poetry has validity only insofar as it recreates what his experience actually was. The poet must be certain that what he says he experienced he did in fact experience in just the way he says he did, and this kind of truth, because it relates to no exterior standard, is uncompromising. If the poet lies to himself, disowns or represses his thoughts or feelings, his poetry will be false. The quality of his art will reflect the quality of health, courage, and intelligence which he brings to the understanding of himself.

No wonder Wordsworth thought joy necessary to the creation of poetry,[25] and no wonder that his best nature poetry is more concerned with his private, psychic history than with external phenomena. Psychic truth is an historical truth. It was Freud's chief contribution, perhaps, to develop into a systematic theory the perception that psychic life, like social life, is an historical phenomenon. But Wordsworth understood as well as Freud that what the mind is at any given moment cannot be defined except in terms of what it has been in the past, because psychic life is a life of continuously operating forces and energies. Repression, for example, is not a single, unitary act, like drowning a cat. It is a mental force continuously exerted. To tell the whole truth about one inner experience is to relate that psychic process to all other developing processes of inner life which are always in some manner present and operative. To use Wordsworth's preferred images, inner life is like a breeze or a river, "segments" of which can be isolated only by destroying the reality of the whole.[26]

A "landscape" poem such as *Tintern Abbey* is in fact a process of self-revelation. To know oneself is to know the world in which one lives, since self-understanding always involves understanding of that which is not self. To judge one's own mind is, at least by implication, to judge the place of man in the universe of things.[27] As long as the inner life remains interior it may remain purely idiosyncratic, but once it is revealed it begins to lose its purely personal characteristics, if only because it begins to relate to other things.

Herein lies a key to Wordsworth's "mysticism," well expressed in the famous lines (93–102) of *Tintern Abbey*:

> . . . And I have felt
> A presence that disturbs me with the joy
> Of elevated thoughts; a sense sublime
> Of something far more deeply interfused,
> Whose dwelling is the light of setting suns,
> And the round ocean and the living air,
> And the blue sky, and in the mind of man:
> A motion and a spirit, that impels
> All thinking things, all objects of all thought,
> And rolls through all things.

Here we may observe in a different way what was remarked in an earlier chapter: Wordsworth's conception of the universe is impregnated with a sense of infinity.[28] His universe is not closed and limited, yet, as we have observed in this chapter, the poet's situation, especially psychically, is particularized. In *Tintern Abbey* the minute and the particular coexist with the infinite and the universal. Through particularization the poet reaches the universal; through personalization the poet attains to the level of essential life.

This is Wordsworth's mysticism. The link, the structural relation, between the personal and the universal is the natural world, the landscape. Through intense examination of his fleeting experience of an enduring landscape the poet arrives at a judgment of man's life in the eternal, infinite universe of things. The poet passes *through* personal experience to become the archetype of man and the landscape is transformed from a particular visual scene to a representation of the nature of cosmic order.[29]

Through this intense penetration the poet finds significance and loveliness in a world and a mind deprived of any mythic splendors. The preciousness of the world is not asserted by means of external adornments such as personifications but by the process of entering into its inner life. The poet looks so deeply into himself that he sees through the particular nature of his special personality to the enduring human essence within. Simultaneously he discovers a soul in nature, discovers within the specific appearance of the particular landscape a glimpse of the same essential life. In their essence man and nature share one life.[30]

Thus Wordsworth finds significance in the universe through an act of consciousness, specifically, through becoming aware of the place of consciousness, the distinctive human attribute, in the cosmos. His mystical experience is not that of another world but of a spiritual, an energetic, a vital world within the existent physical world of phenomena. What we call his mysticism must have seemed to him to be total realism.[31]

An analogous mysticism of total realism is found in Leopardi. Consider his poem, *The Infinite,* for example:

Always dear to me has been this lonely hill, and this thicket which on so many sides excludes the far horizon from my sight. But sitting and gazing, I figure in thought beyond that thicket endless spaces, and superhuman silences, and profoundest quiet; wherein my heart is half afraid. And when I hear the wind come storming through these plants, then to that infinite silence I compare this voice: and I recall eternity, the seasons dead, the living present and the sound of it. So in immensity my thought drowns; and sweet to me is shipwreck in this sea.[32]

The first word of the poem, "always," blurs the present moment into an indefinite number of past experiences, but the specificness of the place of these experiences is emphasized by repeated demonstratives, "this lonely hill," "this thicket." The poet's escape from spatial particularity begins with the conjunction "but." At once *this* thicket becomes *that*, something farther from the poet, who "figure[s] in thought . . . endless spaces, and superhuman silences, and profoundest quiet." Then the poet hears "the wind come storming through *these* plants." The sound recalls him to his immediate physical surroundings, and he then compares *"this* voice" to *"that* infinite silence." As Tilgher has observed,[33] comparing is an intellectual activity. The poet compares the sensory phenomenon of the wind's sound to his mental figure of "endless spaces" with their "superhuman silences," which had brought fear to his heart. This comparison brings "eternity" back to his mind. Space has been transformed into time; instead of figuring forth "endless spaces," the poet's imagination now plunges into "the *seasons* dead, the living *present,* and the *sound* of it." The sound of the present is not of course an auditory sensation like that of the wind but an imagined sensation. And in *"this* immensity," the endless spaces temporalized —what we may call space-time—the poet's "thought" is destroyed. But such "shipwreck" is "sweet"; the poet's heart is no longer touched by fear; *"that* infinite silence" has become *"this* sea."

It appears to me self-evident that *"The Infinite* is not an analysis, but a narration . . . of a *process."*[34] De Sanctis observed long ago that Leopardi has no "preconceived idea of infinity" to which he fits his imaginings.[35] Precisely because Leopardi does not begin with an abstract idea, he can arrive at that final paradoxical pleasure "in which thought reacquires its consciousness only to feel itself sweetly annihilated. . . ."[36] This "pleasure is born not of the things contemplated, but of [the process] of contemplation."[37]

The process is the temporalizing of space, which means the penetration of mind into what is external. In *The Infinite* the thought of the "endless spaces" of the cosmos frightens the mind until, through the exercise of its highest potency, the mind, comparing its conception of the silence of infinite space to the finite sensory phenomenon of the wind's sound and adding known time, the memory of past experiences ("always"), creates a new imaginative reality, "this sea" of space-time. Through the synthesis of intellect, sensation, and memory, infinite space becomes—though no less infinite and hence annihilating to thought—no longer alien but related now to the mind's own activity, the personal experience of space-time.

In *To the Moon*, composed about the same time as *The Infinite*, memory plays an even more important role, thus emphasizing some similarities between Leopardi's response to nature and Wordsworth's. Indeed, *To the Moon* might almost be regarded as a pessimistic version of *Tintern Abbey*.

O gracious moon, I remember now that just one year has circled since, full of anguish, I climbed this hill to gaze on you: and you then were poised above this wood, as you are now, filling it with light. But clouded and tremulous your countenance appeared to me, whose eyes were filled with tears because my life was sorrowful: and is, nor changes style, oh my beloved moon. And yet I joy in remembering and counting over the seasons of my grief. Oh, how sweet a thing it is, in the time of youth when still hope's course is long and memory's is brief, to call to mind things past, though they were sad and though the pain endures.

We have observed that Wordsworth in *Tintern Abbey* treats the natural scene as unchanging. In *To the Moon* Leopardi, too, asserts the staticness of nature, illustrating it with the traditional poetic symbol of fickleness, the moon. But the moon's fickleness is illusory, because the moon's changes are repetitions of a cyclic process. The unsophisticated man may regard the moon as always changing, but the learned man recognizes the repetitive pattern of its variations.

In fact, the "dramatic action" of *To the Moon* is created by the moon's cycle cutting across the linear development of the poet's life:[38] as he moves toward death his hopes diminish as his memories increase. The subject of the poem, as is suggested by its original title, *Memories*, is not the moon but the development of the poet's sentiments. To this evolution the circling moon contributes dramatic form—it permits a symbolization of the movement through time of the poet's mind and emotions.

The chief paradox of the poem lies in the poet's "*joy* in remembering and counting over the seasons of my *grief* . . . though the *pain* endures." The *process* of remembering, as distinct from *what* is remembered is pleasurable: the recollection even of anguish may be joyful. What, then, is the process of remembering to Leopardi? Stated crudely, it is the mental recreation of what no longer exists. The roughness of this definition is suggested by the poem, where Leopardi limits the pleasure of remembering to "the time of youth when still hope's course is long and memory's is brief."[39] The joy of remembering depends on the existence of hope. Is the same not true of *Tintern Abbey*? Could Wordsworth treat the past as he does did he not envision the future as he does? We tend to think of our previsions of the future as dependent upon our experience in the past. This is true, and Wordsworth and Leopardi nowhere slight the fact. But they also see the significance of the reverse relationship, the influence of our view of the future upon what we make of the past.

In one way the poets dramatize a commonplace phenomenon, which might be illustrated by the observation that Wordsworth could write *Tintern Abbey* because he and his sister were young and in good health. He could not have written it years later under the tragic circumstances of his sister's mental decay. Hope, as Leopardi never tired of saying, is an illusion, not a fact. It is something we figure forth in our mind, and all too often (always, Leopardi would say) the succeeding reality does not conform to our projected image. As we grow older and hope less, not only because the experience of past reality has taught us the illusoriness of our previsions but also because the limits of our natural existence necessarily enforce themselves upon our consciousness, we lose our power to create illusions. The loss of that power is fatal to the pleasure of remembering, for remembering, too, depends on the power to create illusions. Memory, too, is illusion, since memory is not actual, material fact but a mental fabrication. "Remembering" to Wordsworth and Leopardi is not a mechanical but a creative process.[40] A memory is something created by a particular human mind, and remembering is creative personal experience.

To the Moon as clearly as *Tintern Abbey* distinguishes between the natural, external world of sensation and of mechanical repetition and the human, interior, psychic world of dynamic process. In that separation lies the possibility of sorrow, for unless man brings into existence some quality or force *within* the external world with which the human mind can function harmoniously, man is doomed to isolation. The search for such supranatural harmony is the quest of most early nineteenth-century poets.[41]

This harmony, as we discovered earlier, cannot be simple. In *To the Moon* the moon is called "gracious" and "beloved" by the poet, who is fully aware that the moon moves on in mechanical indifference. This kind of attribution Ruskin condemned with the epithet "pathetic fallacy." What Ruskin overlooked was that poets like Leopardi employed projected pathos (ideally, anyway) in full consciousness of its "fallaciousness," and they condemned such bestowal when made unconsciously.[42] The dramatic effectiveness of "gracious" and "beloved" in *To the Moon* derives from the total poem's presentation of the distinction between the poet's "joy" and "grief" and the impersonal, unemotional majesty of nature.[43]

Deliberate exploitation of the pathetic fallacy is useful to Leopardi, as it often is to Wordsworth,[44] because he portrays nature without distortion or ornamentation. He only simplifies and intensifies; he is confined to the truth of his own experience; he is deprived of the conventional attitudes and traditional fictions of his predecessors' art. The pathetic fallacy, the old "fictional" view of the world, is the antagonist of a new lyric drama in which the poet-protagonist attains an original and deeper truth—the truth of personal imaginative understanding. The old harmony must be superseded by a new and more complex one based on the poet's creative self-assertion.

Leopardi's *Sunday Evening* illustrates the system and significance of this lyric drama.

Sweet and clear is the night and without wind, and quiet stands the moon above the rooftops and the orchards, illuminating in the distance every tranquil mountain shape. O my lady, now every path is silent, and only here and there among the balconies a nocturnal lantern gleams. You sleep, gathered up by gentle slumber in your quiet chamber, and no care gnaws in your mind; you neither know nor guess how deep a wound you have opened in my heart. You sleep; I have come out to salute this sky, whose aspect now seems so benign, and ancient Nature omnipotent, who has shaped my soul for wretchedness. "Hope to you I have denied," she says to me, "even hope; your eyes shall never shine except with tears." This was the holiday: now you rest after its amusements; and perhaps you remember in your dreams how many you pleased, and how many pleased you; I do not recur to your thought, not that I hoped to now. Now I ask how much life remains for me, and fling myself to this ground, and rage, and cry. Oh horrible days of such green age. Alas, I hear a short way down the road the artisan's solitary song, he returning after the games to his poor home; and fiercely does it tear my heart to think how all this world passes, leaving not a trace. Behold, the festal day has fled, and to the holiday the ordinary day succeeds, and so time bears away every human accident. Where now is the clamor of ancient peoples? Where now is the voice of our famous ancestors, and that grand empire which was Rome, and the arms, and the clangor sweeping across the ocean and the earth? All is peace and silence, and all the world rests quietly, and we speak of them no more. In my boyhood, when I had awaited the holiday impatiently, when it was past, I tossed in bed, wakeful and unhappy; and late in the slow night I heard a song among the paths, dying into the distance little by little, that tore my heart—as this does now.

Sunday Evening, despite the assertions, "fiercely does it tear my heart to think how all this world passes, leaving not a trace," and "so time bears away every human accident," is not a lament for mutability in nature.[45] The silent motionlessness of the simple opening creates a sense of the unchanging endurance of nature, a sense reinforced with more emotional poignancy by the conclusion, in which the laborer's song dying in the stillness of the night recalls the similar song and night of so many years before. Mutability is not denied, but it is transposed from its conventional place in nature to a place in the human psyche. In *Sunday Evening* it is man, both as an individual and as a race ("where now is the voice of our famous ancestors"), who changes, and changing suffers, while "ancient Nature omnipotent . . . rests quietly," serenely beyond such transformation.

The transformations wrought by time, because psychic and not physical, can be counterpoised by the human capacity to overcome time with memory. When the poet hears "the artisan's solitary song" it fiercely tears his heart "to think how all this world passes," because the song revives in his mind his experience as a boy. To remember is to relive. Insofar as our mind actively recollects, the past becomes the central experience of the present. The recreative process by which the poet makes the past the present and the distant the near is the moving conclusion of *Sunday Evening.*[46]

It is moving because it is the human capacity to recreate the past imaginatively that renders the flight of time painful. Nature, as it were, is without memory. The natural world is without consciousness of itself, so time is meaningless to it. Hence the poet's sorrow is a tragic affirmation of his painful humanness. His "lady" sleeps tranquilly, unconscious of the wound she has opened in his heart. She, like nature itself, is unaware, and to this degree she contrasts with the poet: she is happier, let us say, because she is less fully human. She may perhaps remember in her dreams how many she pleased, and how many pleased her, but the poet achieves through memory an intensified understanding of the cause and nature of his suffering. In the pathos and loveliness of the final lines there is the completion of a process of realization; they express imaginative awareness of a sad truth.[47] The poet now understands, not rationally but experientially, as he could not understand when as a boy he "tossed in bed wakeful and unhappy," *why* the song "dying into the distance little by little" tore his heart. The remembered song and the present song are the same yet different, because now he feels the significance of that diminishing sound and its sorrowful reverberations in his heart. This process of achieving painfully intensified understanding is the very substance and system of the Leopardian lyric.

Nevertheless it is a mistake, I believe, to emphasize Leopardi's pessimism to the point of entirely separating him from his near-contemporaries.[48] His vision is certainly darker than Wordsworth's, for example, but both poets, as I have tried to show, write similar lyrics of experience. Their presentation of landscape is similar, even though the landscapes themselves are as different as England and Italy. In the lyrics of both, moreover, the central "action" tends to be a penetration by means of creative memory through the particular and momentary to the humanly essential and enduring.

This progress is plain in *Sunday Evening*, in which, as in *Tintern Abbey*, we begin with localization. At first we are confined to the poet's specific experience, and superficially, it is true, we remain with his experience to the end. But as the poem develops from the still serenity of the opening view to the violent outburst of the poet's frustrated passion, culminating in his exclamation, "Oh horrible days of such green age," we are subtly carried through the merely personal toward a broader, more significant realm. In the latter half of the poem the special circumstances and personality of the poet fade without ever entirely vanishing. His personal loss blends with the loss of great civilizations. And his final, pained memory of his boyhood is so represented as to seem a common rather than a unique recollection. Since that memory is at the end linked back to the "artisan's solitary song," the entire experience takes on the character of something we have known ourselves, something that is not the poet's exclusive possession.

The movement beyond the personal is necessary to the dynamic of Leopardi's lyricism, just as it is to Wordsworth's. To deepen and enrich the immediate, "local" sensations of an external natural scene by projecting into them psychic vitality, to add a temporal dimension to what is physical and spatial by subjecting it to the process of creative memory, is to bring into being a new relation between the specific and the universal. Both Wordsworth and Leopardi in describing present a particular scene or object as independent but not isolated, as an aspect of the circumambient world. But they are not really descriptive poets, they are poets of experience, and their genius consists in making particularized, private experiences independent but not isolated aspects of all human experience.

Sunday Evening, for example, is a personal poem which passes through and beyond the personal to humanistic affirmation. Because Leopardi reaches the truly humane through intense contemplation of his personal experience, his lyric has a grandeur that belies its simplicity and brevity. It is fair, I think, to speak of him as a tragic, not a pessimistic, poet.

VI ❧ SECULAR MYTHS

LEOPARDI: *To Silvia / Remembrances*
WORDSWORTH: "Lucy" Poems
Resolution and Independence / Elegiac Stanzas
KEATS: *The Eve of St. Agnes / To Autumn*
FOSCOLO: *To Zante*

POETS who write of personal experience but pass beyond the personal may be expected to represent dramatic characters in an unusual fashion, and in fact, our four poets frequently make mythic figures of their *dramatis personae*. But these tend to be figures of private or what I call secular myths. Their significance is not conventional but self-created and their more-than-natural endowments are not predetermined but emerge dynamically before our eyes. Leopardi's *To Silvia*,[1] the first masterpiece of his poetic "resurrection" in 1828, illustrates this process.

Silvia, do you still remember that season of your mortal life when beauty gleamed in your laughing and shy-glancing eyes, and you, now joyful, now pensive, drew near the threshold of your youth?

The quiet chambers and garden paths re-echoed your perpetual song. Then, sitting intent upon your woman's work, you were happy with the vague and distant future that possessed your mind. It was fragrant May; and thus you passed the time.

I, sometimes leaving my lovely studies and those labored pages in which my better gifts and my best time were being consumed, from the high terrace of my father's house, intent, would listen to your voice and to your rapid hand flying through the laborious woven-work. I gazed into the sky serene, the golden paths and gardens, there the far-off sea, and there the mountain range. No mortal voice can tell what then I felt.

What soothing thoughts, what hopes, what choirs, O Silvia mine! How fair to us appeared all human life and destiny! When memories of such smiling hopes burst forth, a passion bitter and disconsolate oppresses me, and sorrow for my own misfortune seizes me. Oh nature, oh nature, why afterward give nothing that you promised then? Why so deceive your children?

104

You, Silvia, before winter withered all the grass, attacked and conquered by concealed disease, you died, young and gentle one. You saw not the flowering of your years, nor softened your heart at sweet praise of your dark hair or of your shy-glancing and enamoured eyes, nor with your girl friends on holidays went chattering happily of love.

Even as soon perished my fond hopes: the fates also denied to me the years of youth. Alas, how, how you are fled, dear comrade of my dawning age, my lamented hope. Is this that world? These the delights, the love, the tasks, the happenings of which we talked so much together? This the destiny of human life? When truth appeared, you, gentle girl, fell back: and with your hand showed me cold death and a naked tomb from far away.

To Silvia is a single, flowing movement in which the figure of Silvia recedes from the intimacy of "do you remember" to the image of a single hand pointing to "cold death." Simultaneously the poet's imaginative delight increases in intensity until it becomes its opposite, the sorrowful truth of despair, which develops through the fading images of memory until he is left with only the stark reality of "a naked tomb." These movements channel the flow of the poet's past forward and the gradual absorption of his future into his past. At first the future appears bright and joyful; at the end only the past holds happiness. The specific interchange of past and future occurs in the fourth section "when memories of such smiling hopes burst forth, a passion bitter and disconsolate oppresses me." Everything in the lyric appears either in memory or in imaginative prefiguration; the total poem expresses the ever shifting relation of past to future which is our sense of present time.

Silvia is the focus of this evanescent present. Her characteristics, well described by De Sanctis, embody the fluidity, the unformedness of the present. "She has scarcely entered into her youth, at that age in which a girl is being transformed into a woman. What she feels is not yet love: it is something distantly beautiful that makes her pensive but does not disturb her, does not fix her eyes on one object, does not arouse the deep look of desire. Her smile and song express the inner cheerfulness of a life not yet changed from green to the full color of the rose."[2] To this faintly imaged outline of womanhood, circumstances add little specific substantiality: the details of Silvia's work and amusements are generic, they do not particularize her personality. The poet likewise is not individualized, yet there is nothing vague about his relationship to Silvia, which is definite but without specialized character.

This definite-indefiniteness makes one hesitate to call Silvia "real," yet she is no allegory, no abstract representation of youth or beauty or love. Even to describe her as a symbol would seem to deny both the simplicity and the personal poignancy which are the strengths of the lyric. The definite-indefiniteness of Silvia's figure and of the poet-Silvia relation is in itself interesting,[3] but what is more interesting is that Leopardi's contemporaries present people and relationships in the same way.

The ladies to whom Foscolo's odes are addressed exist as Silvia exists. Their reality as individuals is suggested with delicate precision: "I would not see . . . your loving eyes search the doctors' glances for a flattering hope of your former beauty," is all we see of Luigia Pallavicini in her convalescence, yet it reveals enough of that all too human mixture of sorrow and vanity to remove her from the world of pure allegory. Similarly a few realistically described details, while not enough to reduce the poem to naturalistic narrative, are sufficient to make the fatal ride something other than pure symbolism.

Wordsworth's Lucy, perhaps because she appears only in the mode of memory, is portrayed in almost the same fashion as Silvia.[4] Not only is Lucy the focus for the poet's representation of how the illusory desires of "timeless" youth may change to the reality of hopeless remembrance enduring for years, but the impression of Lucy's youth and beauty depends on a dynamic combination of the generic and the specific. "And she I cherished turned her wheel/ Beside an English fire," is concrete but unparticularized. In "and beauty born of murmuring sound/Shall pass into her face," the generalizations "beauty" and "sound" find particularized embodiment in the expression of the girl's features, which, however, we never see. Wordsworth's Lucy possesses a double existence, her actual, historical existence and her idealized existence in the poet's mind. The latter is created out of the former but is neither an abstraction nor a conceptualization, because the idealized Lucy is at least as "concrete" as the actual Lucy. It is the idealized Lucy who is portrayed in vivid similes:

> A violet by a mossy stone
>   Half hidden from the eye!
> —Fair as a star, when only one
>   Is shining in the sky.

The Lucy of the poet's imagination is the actual girl perceived in the full significance of her life's brevity amidst nature's impersonal everlastingness. The actual girl partakes unselfconsciously of nature's beauty and joy; the imagined girl participates blindly in the circling permanence of the entire cosmos. The group of lyrics thus enables us to understand the relation of a singular event of natural joy and beauty to the total, eternal system of the universe, and, therefore, to feel the potential tragedy of all human love.[5]

Lucy is both actual and idealized, but her actuality is relevant only insofar as it signifies her idealization, which, in turn, is valuable only insofar as it makes manifest the significance implicit in the actual girl. The action of these lyrics, then, consists in the dramatic relationing of two modes of being. The final result may be called spiritual insight, if one thinks of the spiritual, as our poets in fact did, as the harmonious relationship between what is physical and natural and what is mental and supranatural.[6]

It is the same spiritual insight which creates the definite-indefiniteness of Leopardi's Silvia. The actual Silvia of the past is incomplete in herself; she is fulfilled by her image in the poet's mind. This image is not a fantasy but an apprehension of the full significance of the real girl, an apprehension of her place, and the place of the poet's feelings toward her, in the total, eternal universe of things. So to apprehend the real is to make it mythic *in itself*, apart from any theological system.

Many of Wordsworth's and Leopardi's poems could be described as myths of memory, but the process of their mythicizing does not require memory. Many of the people in Wordsworth's poetry, Matthew, the Solitary Reaper, and several figures in *The Prelude*, for example, are immediately present. They are to a degree naturalistically individualized, yet their significance does not derive from any detailed realism of characterization. Perhaps the best illustration is the old leech-gatherer of *Resolution and Independence*.[7] Wordsworth's description of the old man, who takes on *for the poet* a symbolic significance, is minute and literal.[8] Yet the specific details appear in a context that makes them suggestive of the cosmic, the mysterious, the suprapersonal; and the effectiveness of the poem *for the reader* lies in the fact that the old leech-gatherer does not become symbolic but remains a unique individual, a "decrepit Man" pursuing an idiosyncratic occupation. The reader appreciates why to the poet

> . . . the whole body of the Man did seem
> Like one whom I had met with in a dream;
> Or like a man from some far region sent,
> To give me human strength, by apt admonishment,

precisely because for the reader the leech-gatherer exists with the solidity of commonplace actuality but is not intricately or complexly characterized.[9] He is an actual human being, but the simplification by which his actuality is presented makes the "spiritual" intimations which he conveys to the poet seem appropriate.[10]

The old leech-gatherer is an envisioned mythic figure, not a remembered one. In this poem there is no temporal separation of elements: the actual old man and the poet's vision of him in mythic proportions coexist simultaneously.[11] But again it is the relationship between the specific physical reality and the specific imagined reality which the poem chiefly expresses. Wordsworth makes us feel the leech-gatherer is both individual and supra-individual, yet somehow self-contained, not a symbolic representation of something other than what he is, which is *both* a simple old man and a living admonishment to fortitude.[12]

It might be argued that all great characters in literature have this double quality. If so, Wordsworth is unusual in forcing us to be conscious of the duality. The leech-gatherer, we recognize, cannot be separated from his ordinary appearance and manner which is so literally described,[13] yet we also recognize that the factual specificness is not complete in itself, that it contains within it another kind of reality, as it were, figured within the form of the old man's physical appearance and actions.[14]

Similar techniques are used by other early nineteenth-century poets not merely in presenting characters but also in organizing descriptive and narrative works. *The Eve of St. Agnes,* for example, is a thoroughly secular myth.[15] Madeline and Porphyro, though fictional beings, are neither allegorical figures nor, in the usual modern sense of the term, symbols. They are a young man and a young woman who attain the consummation of sensual bliss amidst the wintry sterility of nature and the hostility of men,[16] but the loveliness of the consummation springs from the way in which their sensuality never becomes a celebration of the merely natural. Porphyro and Madeline go to bed together; their climactic experience is not a symbol for something else; quite simply, *The Eve of St. Agnes* affirms the beauty of sexual intercourse. But it can affirm that beauty because Porphyro and Madeline are never allowed to become lovers in the later tradition of naturalistic fiction; their reality never becomes the reality of Huxley's lovers "quietly sweating palm to palm."[17]

There are always two levels in *The Eve of St. Agnes*. Madeline first "Hoodwink'd with fairy fancy," then "asleep in lap of legends old," finds her fantasy fulfilled by the actuality of Porphyro's ecstatically sensual adoration. His fullest actuality, however, is to blend into her dream. In the climactic stanza (xxxvi) the reality which fulfills Madeline's imaginings itself passes into a "higher" reality, which is the harmonious unity of the natural and the supranatural.

> Beyond a mortal man impassion'd far
> At these voluptuous accents, he arose,
> Ethereal, flush'd, and like a throbbing star
> Seen 'mid the sapphire heaven's deep repose;
> Into her dream he melted, as the rose
> Blendeth its odour with the violet,—
> Solution sweet: meantime the frost-wind blows
> Like Love's alarum pattering the sharp sleet
> Against the window-panes; St. Agnes' moon hath set.

This transcendence informs with new meaning the complexly developing pattern of contrasts of images—cold against warmth, sound against silence, sculpture and tapestry against the human revelers, the religion of the Beadsman against Porphyro's worship of beauty, Angela's age against Madeline's youth, to name but a few of the elements—which are, as much as the plot, integral to the poem's dramatic action. The sensual bliss of Porphyro and Madeline is not minimized or attenuated, but it is not allowed to remain an end in itself, an ultimate satisfaction. The ultimate satisfaction is what is signified by their physical pleasure. This is why it is not misleading to say that the story of *The Eve of St. Agnes* is not alone the series of events which bring hero and heroine together but is also the developing interrelationship of the images by which those events are represented.[18] There is, in one sense, nothing purely descriptive in the poem, because all its sensory details contribute to the ultimate completion of a suprasensual act which gives order and meaning to those details.

The end of the poem, in fact, shows that the realization of love's dream is a nightmare to the merely sensual.[19] Porphyro and Madeline "glide, like phantoms" from the authentically cold hostility of the castle into the only apparently cold hostility of wintry nature—

> "Hark! 'tis an elfin-storm from faery land,
> Of haggard seeming, but a boon indeed"—

Madeline, ironically, has not been hoodwinked; she has gained a husband. Porphyro, who first appears as a seducer, has claimed a bride. Through Madeline's "dream" they "escape" into reality (including death), leaving behind the "bloated wassailers . . . drown'd all in Rhenish and the sleepy mead . . . in uneasy sprawl" dreaming "of many a woe," with "shade and form/ Of witch, and demon, and large coffin-worm . . . be-nightmar'd." Porphyro's and Madeline's love is founded upon gratification of their senses, but their sensuality is that of true love, sense impregnated with vision. Their love is not the mere lust of the senses, nor is it mere escape from the senses. "And they are gone; ay, ages long ago/ These lovers fled"; death, the ultimate reality of this life, to them will mean something very different from what it means to the Baron and his guests, or the Beadsman, who "after thousand aves told/ For aye unsought for slept among his ashes cold." That "meaning" is not something symbolized so much as it is the completed pattern of contrasting and interpenetrating images by which the passionate love-meeting and its consequences have been figured into suprasensory vision.[20] *The Eve of St. Agnes* remains from beginning to end a romance, but while it begins simply, it ends as a myth of romance.[21]

What I have termed secular myth is an extension of the personal lyricism that goes beyond the merely personal. A myth is a religious story. *The Eve of St. Agnes* is a religious story, but Keats's divinity is not the deity of any orthodox or conventional religion. His divinity is the supranatural vitality which is attained through sensual fulfillment and which sanctifies sensuality by giving it inherent meaning in this world. The vision of Keats's divinity is attained only by intense personal experience of what is most immediately "real"—sensation and emotion.[22]

The secular myth is one of the forms through which early nineteenth-century poetic vision is expressed, but since this vision is at root personal, one cannot delimit the form too rigidly. I shall try simply to illustrate its various aspects by describing four quite different "myths." The first of these, if we take them in chronological order, is Foscolo's sonnet, *To Zante.*

Never again shall I touch your sacred shores where my infant body rested, my Zante, who see yourself mirrored in the waves of the Grecian sea from which virgin Venus rose to life, and made those islands fertile with her first smile, so that your limpid clouds and leafy branches are not passed in silence in the celebrated poem of him who sang the fatal waters and various exile out of which, beautiful with fame and with misfortune, Ulysses came to kiss his stony Ithaca. Nothing else but his song will you have from your son, O my mother earth; to me destiny prescribes an unwept sepulchre.

Here is the same kind of definite-indefiniteness we observed in *To Silvia*, now used to figure forth the Greek island where Foscolo was born and spent the first years of his life. But the definiteness of Foscolo's picture is different from Leopardi's, which is that of authentic memory. One feels that Leopardi records particularized observations, and the evidence of his notebooks proves the feeling to be justified. The details in Foscolo's sonnet are not memories of specific observations. While reading the sonnet we do not feel that we are on the island; we seem to see it from a distance. As Professor Fubini has observed, Zante has a value independent from its place in the poet's memory; it is always the luminous center of a vaster scene.[23]

Yet one cannot ignore the poet's real and personal connection with the island, which, as he tells us in the opening lines, is his motherland. From that personal reality he moves through a kind of animism, the island seeing itself mirrored in the sea, to the traditional myth of Venus rising from the waves. Then he attributes the fame of the island to the loveliness conferred on it by its good fortune in seeing that miraculous birth of divine beauty. The immortality of Zante's beauty, however, appears to derive from its presence in Homer's story of Odysseus' return to "stony Ithaca," a near neighbor of Zante. Odysseus, immortal fictional man, at last carries us back to the poet, now far both in space and time from the period when his young body was washed by Zante's waves. What lies ahead for him is only half of Odysseus' fate, exile without return, the beauty of misfortune but not of fame, an "unwept sepulchre." Yet this sorrow is balanced by something else: Zante will have the poet's song. If fate denies him Odysseus' reward it cannot deny him Homer's. His immortal ancestry—the island that gave him birth—is not refuted, but endures in the poet's art.

Zante thus possesses a double reality, that of its actual being, the place of the poet's birth to which he may not return, and that of its existence in art, a part of the enduring expression of mankind's spirit. Between these two realities lies all of human history. The mythical Zante, which owes its being to the existence of the actual island but which fulfills that material reality, is divine but in no way part of another world. Dante journeys through Hell, Purgatory, and Paradise, and those "places" in some important respects are *not* part of this world. Foscolo does not leave the familiar earth. The slopes of Zante have a corporeal reality which the slopes of Purgatory lack. Foscolo's spiritual reality is secular, humanistic, even scientific in a way that Dante's is not, and in this difference lies much of the complexity and fascination of the art we are studying as well as its relevance to our modern, secular world.

The secularism of these myths is nowhere better illustrated than in the poets' frequent celebrations of works of art, since artistic vision for them is the way of seeing the actual as mythical. Wordsworth's *Elegiac Stanzas* is an unusual example, for the poem concerns the violent death of the poet's brother.[24] The impact of this event was, probably, the principal specific motivation for the poet's turning from a rather nominal Christianity to the profession of an actively orthodox faith. The poem is nowhere confined to the limits of Christian faith, however. Although the last stanza points toward Wordsworth's later quietistic orthodoxy, there is nothing inappropriate to pagan Stoicism or to the philosophy of many modern men who are indifferent to traditional religion.[25]

Indeed, the *Elegiac Stanzas* could scarcely have been written by a man in whose mind Christian doctrine was uppermost,[26] since the poem is without any particularized reference to those elements of the Christian supernatural which would be so obviously relevant to the situation. Instead, the poet stresses that his soul has been "humanised" by his "deep distress." As described in the *Elegiac Stanzas* the process of humanization is sombrely moving and even heroic because it is not sweetened by the reliefs and satisfactions of conventional piety.

As Wordsworth's subtitle tells us, the poem was "suggested by a picture[27] of Peele Castle, in a storm." Yet the poem opens not with a description of the picture but with a description of Wordsworth's actual sight of the castle years before, when for four serene weeks its

"Form was sleeping on a glassy sea. . . . Whene'er I looked, thy
Image still was there,/ It trembled but it never passed away." This
image in memory is the natural reality for which Beaumont's picture,
portraying a "rueful sky" and "pageantry of fear" would seem to be
the dark fulfillment. But this is not quite true. Fulfillment lies not
in the picture in itself but in the poet's response to the picture. Similarly, the "actual" reality is not the castle in itself, nor even its image
in the calm water, but the poet's response to the actual castle and
its image.

This is by no means a hairsplitting distinction. The experience of
art for Wordsworth is a creative experience.[28] To him the aesthetic
object is treated not merely as a faithful copy of nature to be admired
as such (though the imitative element is not totally to be disregarded)
nor solely as a self-contained entity (though to a degree he does so
treat it) but as chiefly valuable for arousing and focussing his own
thoughts and feelings. To Wordsworth art is experience, both for the
artist and for the spectator, so he discusses the work of art in terms
of the feelings it arouses in him, and however controlled by and
related to the art work those feelings may be, their paramount value
lies in their independent coherence as a new creative experience. The
spectator's relation to the work of art is analogous to the artist's
relation to nature—creative not imitative.

We must be wary of reading Wordsworth in the light of later
developments, particularly that of the school of "appreciation."[29] To
Wordsworth the creative experience of art is above all else a humanizing experience. It transports from partial truth to full truth, from
pleasant illusion to sombre reality, from sensory, superficial life to
intense, visionary life, from separateness, "Housed in a dream, at
distance from the kind," to sympathy with and participation in the
grim facts of our fellow-beings' existence, "frequent sights of what
is to be borne."

Of his original sight of the castle, he says:

> Ah! THEN, if mine had been the Painter's hand,
> To express what then I saw, and add the gleam,
> The light that never was, on sea or land,
> The consecration, and the Poet's dream.

Although the "power" of this "fond illusion" has vanished, upon the
memory of its existence is founded the poet's "new control," his

"fortitude," his "patient cheer," his "mind serene," in short his humanized soul braving "This sea in anger, and that dismal shore," which he now recognizes to be an essential element in the totality of life. Beaumont's picture excites his mind to a vision of the true meaning of communion with another man. His brother's death had seemed to destroy that communion, but contemplating the picture, the poet understands that the pain and yet the comfort of such a loss lies in the recognition it compels that the survivor had not been alone, that his spirit *had* mingled with the spirit of the departed.

> The feeling of my loss will ne'er be old;
> This, which I know, I speak with mind serene.

These lines apply equally to "the light that never was" and to the death of the poet's brother. In the loss of a beloved, in the loss of "the Poet's dream," man learns that the illusory "gleam" *is* a "consecration," that love, however fleeting, does sanctify. In the loss of "fond illusion" there is the gain of deeper vision, in death there is the affirmation of love. The fulfillment of youth's dream—

> . . . a world how different from this!
> Beside a sea that could not cease to smile;
> On tranquil land, beneath a sky of bliss—

is the actuality of

> This sea in anger, and that dismal shore.
> .   .   .   .
> That Hulk which labors in the deadly swell,
> This rueful sky, this pageantry of fear!

Yet in this dark fulfillment gleams the assertion of the spirit that is not finally alone, that braves "the lightning, the fierce wind, and trampling waves," that breaks through "the unfeeling armour of old time" to affirm the truth of love. From that supranatural reality, into which the "light that never was" has been transformed, springs the strength to bear "such sights, or worse, as are before me here," and the human faith that "Not without hope we suffer and we mourn."

A somewhat analogous fortitude is implied by Keats's *To Autumn*.[30] In this poem the actual and the mythic are not distinguished, as they are in Wordsworth's. Indeed, the ease with which Keats coalesces the ideal with the real is one of his special gifts.

The first stanza provides a visual, tactile impression of autumnal abundance and ripeness, yet it can scarcely be called descriptive. Pictorial effects are subordinated to the representation of the inward growth, swelling, and ripening of the vegetable world. It is almost as if we were made to touch time—the "Season of mists and mellow fruitfulness"—as an internal, physical pressure toward complete, bursting rotundity, for this sweet, silent enlargement from within, this vegetable perfection, does finally break forth and spill lusciously over with the "o'er-brimmed . . . clammy cells" of the bees, the natural harvesters of copious fruitfulness.

Stanza two dramatizes, through the activities of Autumn personified, the outcome of vegetative ripening. There is a "winnowing wind," a "half-reap'd furrow," a "gleaner," and the "last oozings" of "a cyder-press." Keats's autumnal figure is not, however, like conventional personifications, being at once more human and more vague. The positions of the figure are so various, four in eleven lines, and so quintessentially human, "sitting careless," "steady thy laden head," and so on, that autumn takes on the three-dimensional solidity of sculpture. Yet the sculpture is misty; one cannot even distinguish its sex.

This vague determinateness is appropriate to the second stanza's transitional purpose. Time is no longer a tactile experience of ripening from within; it is seen, as it were, from the outside; it is still represented by plants, but now these are under the threat of another force, that of the harvester, who sleeps on the "half-reap'd furrow" only temporarily sparing "the next swath and all its twined flowers," and who finally watches "the last oozings hours by hours." There is no haste. Autumn sits "careless," or lies "sound asleep," or watches with "patient look." If time is now visible, not a visually imperceptible, swelling inward force, it has so newly emerged that the sense of relentless onward movement does not disturb the mood of mellow completeness created by the first stanza.

The figure of Autumn is the envisioned spirit of what was physically represented in the opening stanza. As the tactile changed to the pictorial in stanza two, in stanza three the pictorial changes to the auditory: in "wailful choir" the "small gnats mourn," "lambs loud bleat," "hedge-crickets sing," "with treble soft/ The red-breast whistles," and "swallows twitter." This autumnal music, a harmony beyond visual personification, is of course introduced by the stanza's opening questions:

> Where are the songs of Spring? Ay, where are they?
> Think not of them, thou hast thy music too.

The interrogative mood and the suggestion of thought are new elements.[31] In stanza one we touched; in two we saw; now we are made to hear—and to think and to question. Our thoughts and questions are directed by the completion of the ripening process begun in the first stanza: the "mellow fruitfulness" of stanza one became the "half-reap'd furrow" in stanza two and now remains only as "the stubble-plains." The day is "soft-dying," the "light wind lives or dies," and the "gathering swallows" suggest the coming of darkness. The fulfillment of the original tactile impression is the sound of life in the midst of death.

Yet the melancholy and the darkness, the sense of time as loss and decay, are restrained because the poet has not emphasized their potentiality within the felt details of the first stanza nor within the envisioned spirit of Autumn in the second. He has no need to because he has so intensely understood the significance of autumn. In the final stanza autumn is not a season nor the spirit of a season but an integral phase in the rhythm of universal life, not the autumn of one year but the "autumn" of a lifetime and the "autumn" of every joyous experience. Hence in the last part of the poem there is no explicit reference to the season and no overt assertion of nightfall. There is simply none of the fecundity stressed at first, no imagined personification, only the recording of unadorned fact:

> Hedge-crickets sing; and now with treble soft
> The red-breast whistles from a garden-croft,
> And gathering swallows twitter in the skies.

We need not be told the meaning of these details, our imagination needs no excitation, for we have been carried to the plane of intensified understanding where the significance of the actual season is manifest.[32] Autumn is *now*, its music is present every moment in the lapsing from completion of each experience; it is our life and the life of our world; it is the sweet but melancholy harmony of every luminous twilight of every season when "gathering swallows twitter in the skies."[33]

The reader may be weary enough of detailed interpretation willingly to forego analysis of Leopardi's *Remembrances*, the last of the myths I wish to discuss.[34] The most interesting feature of the poem is its counterpoint. Actual and mythical reality are not separated entities, as in the *Elegiac Stanzas*, and are not, as in *To Autumn*, coalesced into a continuous process, but are interwoven like distinct yet interdependent melodies. "Now" and "then" do not appear whole, as single units, but alternately rise to view and vanish. This double melody embodies the psychic action of remembering, set into bold relief by the bright, lovely indifference of the natural world. In this poem, however, the poet is not alone with nature: society is present, too, since the poet is surrounded by the horror of beautiful nature's unconcern and by the active hostility and incomprehension of his fellow men. The latter makes specially poignant Leopardi's belief that his true life is his inner life—the life of his imagination. On one hand, in no poem of Leopardi's is the loveliness of nature more vividly set forth. The poet's subjectivity is not permitted to affect the objective beauty of his natural environment. We understand why the poet's sufferings force him to look on nature as he does, but what nature is in itself, distinct from his vision of it, is never obscured. On the other hand, the intensity of his subjective suffering makes us feel that his isolation from his "boorish" townsmen is not misanthropy, that it is not, in other words, the special character of his inner life that alienates the poet but rather the intense vitality of it which isolates him.[35]

Remembering is again simultaneously bitter and sweet, but now more complexly ambivalent. As before, remembering sad events is a joyful experience, because the act of remembering (as distinct from what is remembered) is inherently pleasurable, but when the poet remembers Nerina even the sweetness of the act of remembering is embittered by the profound painfulness of his loss. Yet, paradoxically, the memory of Nerina is so sweet that the pain of loss is mollified.

When the poet was with Nerina he did not think of suicide, as he had when alone, even when his mind was animated by illusions. He does not suggest that Nerina's attractiveness was illusory; Nerina participates in actuality in a way that Silvia does not. Silvia appears as the most intense of the poet's youthful illusions, but Nerina is more than this.[36] If her attractiveness is illusory, it is so intense and so complete that it becomes a higher reality,[37] in fact, the embodiment of the "actual" inner vitality which separates the poet from his boorish townsmen. This is why Nerina's death is so painful to the poet: to lose her is more serious than to lose his youthful dreams.

The poem's conclusion, then, forces us to feel the inseparability of joy and anguish as the condition of the most intense personal experience. What makes us human beings is our capacity to create illusions, and this exposes us to one level of suffering. Love, too, may begin as illusion, but it is so intense that it transcends itself, becomes a supranatural actuality. To love, then, is to feel the highest delight, to be creative, but to love is also to become vulnerable to a loss that is not the mere loss of illusion.[38] The subjectivity which sets the poet apart from his fellows marks him as more thoroughly human than they and, therefore, as certain to suffer more profoundly.

His suffering is not the result of a specific action or character development. It is the condition of simply existing as a man. Hence Leopardi, like Hamlet, cannot reject or escape his suffering. He must grasp the bitter joy of fully conscious life. This reveals an important strength of the form I have called secular myth. It is well suited to the expression of the inherent tragedy of fully conscious life. This tragedy is Leopardi's preoccupation, and its lucid, fearless dramatization his glory. However much we recognize to be narrow and idiosyncratic in Leopardi, we never doubt that he suffers in the profoundly exquisite fashion which distinguishes man from all other suffering creatures. No voice in literature is so simply a human voice as his.

The success of the secular myth depends on this human quality. The form serves to celebrate powers that are uniquely man's, and whether its subject be a man's dealings with the natural world, his fellows, or his own past, the secular myth exalts, in a sense deifies, that which is quintessentially human. Hence these are tragic myths, consecrations not of the formal, the perfect, and the immutable, but of the personal, the problematic, and the transitory.[39]

This new kind of myth, I believe, signals the birth of a new kind of life. It is not the utopian life envisaged by the political revolutionaries of the late eighteenth century, since it is uncertain, complex, tragic. It is, in fact, genuinely new and therefore filled with potencies and possibilities, confusions and hazards, that could not have been predicted. That which is most filled with life is most surprising, most marvelous. To the poets of the early nineteenth century the beginnings of this intensified vitality were irresistible, and a new vision, even when it made them suffer, became the substance and spirit of their art.

Yet their prophetic vision concentrated not on the novel but on the familiar, not on the future but on the past.[40] They did not look beyond this world but within it. They achieved, therefore, a re-awakening of interest in the commonplace and a re-creation of themes and ideas which had become aesthetically sterile. I want now to turn to the problems and successes of their re-creative enterprise, calling attention first to their perception of the total relatedness of phenomena as a basis upon which to found their vision of a new life.

VII ⚘ AN ART OF LIFE

LEOPARDI: *The Village Saturday*
Night Song of a Wandering Asiatic Shepherd

WORDSWORTH: *The Old Cumberland Beggar*

Leopardi's "new vision" of familiar things is best illustrated by his "idylls," which are, literally, revitalizations of an old literary form.[1] One of the best is *The Village Saturday*.

The peasant girl comes from the fields at sunset carrying a sheaf of hay and clasping in her hand a bunch of violets and roses, as is her custom, to decorate her bosom and her hair for tomorrow's holiday, toward which her thoughts have turned already. The old woman, seated among her neighbors on the steps, spinning, faced toward the failing daylight, tells stories of her happy past, when she bedecked herself for festive days, of how, slim and lively then, she used to dance the whole night through with all those well-remembered comrades of her lovely youth. Now the air darkens, the far sky turns a deeper blue, and shadows fall from roof tops and from hills beneath the whiteness of the newly risen moon. Now the bell proclaims the coming holiday as if its sound could comfort every heart. The troop of boys, shouting in the village square and jumping back and forth, sets up a cheerful noise, while the field-worker, whistling softly, comes home to his frugal meal and thinks of his approaching day of rest.

Afterward, when every other light has been extinguished, and all around is silent, hear the hammer tapping, hear the rasping saw, as the carpenter labors by lamplight in his shuttered shop, straining to complete his work before the whitening of the dawn.

This of the seven is the most cherished day, full of hope and joy; tomorrow will bring back tedium and sadness dragging from hour to hour, as each within his thought returns to his accustomed labor.

Playful little boy, this—your flowering age—is like a day filled up with happiness, a day serene and bright, heralding the festival of life. Enjoy yourself, my little brother;[2] yours is a happy state, a joyful season. I'll not tell you more; but if your festival seems somewhat slow in coming, do not grieve for that.

The organizing principle of this poem is to be found in the final bitter judgment, not in the opening description, which is so ordered as to make the judgment effective. One must not confound, as many Italian critics have done, Leopardi's "idylls" with earlier, more purely descriptive idylls, for Leopardi does not imitate the old form, he

120

recreates it.[3] He is more concerned to dramatize his subject's value than to describe it, but Leopardi's judgment of value is embodied in his subject, the preciousness of which is, in fact, its inner life. The vital interior energy which makes the subject valuable to the poet is best understood, I believe, as analogous to the pattern of forces which holds together a molecule. The inner vitality, the value, is inseparable from the physical, sensorily perceptible form within which it is contained. Hence Leopardi, like Wordsworth, *up to a point* is a descriptive poet—but it is beyond this point that the organizing center and chief significance of his poetry lie.

The first two parts of *The Village Saturday* are an objective description of the villagers' behavior. The third part, however, reveals the villagers' actions to be founded on an illusion. What had been emotionally neutral becomes permeated with sorrow as in the final part we penetrate into the realm of interior life. At this point the boy's particular anticipations take on universal significance (hence my translation "little brother"): they represent the essential character, not of this society alone, but of all human existence. The opening description had seemed to be a transcription of the archetypal rituals of the simple life in a rural village, but at the conclusion of the poem we understand the description to be the external shape, the material form which manifests the interplay of inner, invisible forces that are the fundamental processes of human life.[4]

The visual impressions are embodiments of life's energies. The figures and activities dramatized are archetypal precisely because they are not elements in a portrait of life in Recanati. Here, as in all of Leopardi's best idylls, the poet forces us "to see into the life of things," and the inner energy we are made to see is important not because it is transcendental or sacred but because it is so mundane. It is important for the same reason that gravity is important.

Life's inner energy, however, is in one way more important than gravity, for it is not explicable on the level of physics any more than the principles of biological evolution are explicable by the laws of chemistry.[5] To Leopardi life's inner energy is fully manifested only in man's activities. The archetypal situations and actions of the descriptive portion of *The Village Saturday* are human archetypes. To see into the life of things is to see as a man, and to see most deeply into life is to perceive that supreme vitality which is only latent in the fall of a boulder or the spring of a tiger but which can be realized in the smallest gesture of a man.

Thus it would be wrong to disregard the specificness of the scene in *The Village Saturday*, since its particularity possesses a preciousness in its own right. The inner vitality Leopardi celebrates can only manifest itself in the specific because it is a particularizing energy. All human beings are alike because they share in conscious life, but the possession of consciousness makes possible, and beneficial, an individualization not attainable by lower forms of life nor by inanimate matter.[6]

It is by dramatizing this principle of human life that Leopardi exalts the simple and the humble without sentimentalizing or distorting it. He leads us to see the commonplace in all its ordinariness as manifesting a powerful and enduring vitality which is not from God and is not the expression of the natural laws of physics.[7] To do this he must show what is common within what is individual, he must show diversity in similitude. In *The Village Saturday* he accomplishes this by separating himself from the villagers. The poet's subject matter, the scene he describes, is created by the simple, even trivial, action of undistinguished Italian peasants, but the poet perceives the inner system of that action, of which the actors themselves are not aware. The poet and the villagers are unalike, just as, on a simpler level, the villagers differ from one another. Yet what the poet perceives, the inner system of human life, he shares with the villagers. In his isolation, which enables him to describe objectively at first, he discovers a bond of "commonalty": the "little boy" becomes his "little brother." His understanding of the villagers is an understanding of himself. The boy does not actually hear the poet speak, yet the poet does speak to a child—the child that lives within each adult reader.

Leopardi's last idyll, given in translation here, is his best, in a sense even transcending the idyll form.[8]

Night Song of a Wandering Asiatic Shepherd

What are you doing, oh moon, there in the sky? Tell me, what is your purpose, mysteriously silent moon? You rise at evening, and move on, contemplating the desert, then set. Are you not yet weary of travelling that eternal road? Are you not yet bored, do you still desire to gaze upon these valleys? Like to your life is the shepherd's. He rises in the twilight of the dawn, moves his flock across the plain, and sees herds, and springs, and grass; exhausted, he rests himself when evening falls: he hopes for nothing more. Tell me, oh moon, of what value to the shepherd is his life, your life to you? Tell me: where leads this brief wandering of mine and your immortal course?

A withered man, white-haired and weak, barefooted and half-naked, with a heavy bundle on his shoulders, over mountains and through valleys, over sharp stones and through deep sands and underbrush, in wind, in storm, in blazing seasons and in the icy months that follow, runs on, runs panting on, struggling through rivers, swamps, falling, staggering up, more and more in haste, without pause or rest, lacerated, bloody; finally arriving where his path and all his weary efforts end: a ghastly and immense abyss into which he plunges headlong, forgetting all. Virgin moon, such is mortal life.

Man is born in pain and in his birth risks death. He first learns agony; and from the beginning his mother and father try to comfort him for being born. As he grows they help him, little by little with acts and words striving to encourage him and to comfort him for his human state; no kinder duty of parents to their children. But why give to the light, why sustain, a child who must be comforted for life? If life be unfortunate, why must we endure it? Unblemished moon, such is the mortal state. But you are not mortal, and perhaps care little for my words.

Yet you, lonely, eternal traveller, seeming so thoughtful, you perhaps understand the purpose of this terrestrial life, our sufferings and lamentations; what death may be, that final vanishing of color from the countenance, and disappearance from the earth, and loss of loving and familiar comradeship. Certainly you comprehend the why of things, and see the fruit of morning and of evening, and of the silent, endless going on of time. You surely know, to what sweet love of hers Spring smiles, for whom the warm days come, and what seeks Winter with his frosts. A thousand things you know and can discover a thousand more that are hidden from a simple shepherd. Often when I look at you, standing thus mute above the desert plain, whose far circle the sky alone confines, or following pace by pace my flock and me, or when I see the stars burning in the sky; I say to myself, wondering: to what purpose so many lights? the infinite air, and that fathomless serenity of sky? what meaning to this solitude immense? and what am I? Thus I muse about myself and of this proud, immeasurable earth and its innumerable tribes; then of all the workings and the movements of all celestial and all earthly things, revolving without pause, returning always to their starting point; no purpose, no use, can I search out. But you surely, immortal maiden, understand it all. This I know and feel, that these eternal circlings and my fragile being may bring some good or happiness to others; to me life is evil.

Oh my resting flock, oh blessed, I believe, not to know your misery! How much I envy you! Not only because you are almost free from sorrow, because every hardship, every privation, every chilling fear you forget at once; but more because you know no tedium. When you rest in the shade upon the grass, you are tranquil and content; and the year's greater part you pass thus without anxiety. But when I sit upon the grass, within the shade, at once a discontent attacks my mind, and a spur so pricks me that, in repose, I am even farther from finding a place of rest or peace. Yet I desire nothing nor have cause for restlessness. What it is that gives you pleasure, or how much, I cannot say; yet you are blessed. Little gives me pleasure, oh my flock, yet not of that alone do I complain. If you could speak, I would question you: why, lying at his ease, is every beast contented with his laziness, while if I lie at rest, tedium seizes me?

Perhaps had I wings to fly above the clouds and number one by one the stars, or like the thunder roam from peak to peak, I might be happier, my gentle flock, I might be happier, bright moon. Or perhaps my thoughts wander from the truth in looking at the destinies of others. Perhaps in whatever form, in whatever condition it be, in cradle or in lair, the day of birth to all that's born is fatal.

The *Night Song* is more plainly "invented" than are the earlier idylls—without being fantastic or in any way improbable it is not autobiographical.[9] The speaker is a dramatic character. It is a mistake, I believe, to dismiss this fact by observing that the shepherd is a transparent disguise for Leopardi himself, because for our poets of personal experience such disguise was difficult,[10] but they usually did come to it late in their careers. Even as they passed through the personal to the essentially human in their autobiographical poems, so as they matured they tended to prefer more objective forms of expression.[11]

The *Night Song*, furthermore, is intensely simplified.[12] There is nothing in the poem but an old man and his sheep on a bare plain beneath a brilliant moon: starkness could scarcely be carried further. Yet the shepherd is a complete man. He is not fragmented. His condition forbids any psychological or sociological elaboration; he is simply a man, but not in any way a partial man. Hence the paradox of many of Leopardi's earlier poems here is raised in bolder relief: man is but a tiny part of the universe, yet he confronts cosmic enormousness on equal terms. Nothing could be more humble than the shepherd, yet the entire cosmos serves as a background for his sufferings and questionings. Both the objectification and the simplification of the *Night Song* sharpen the fundamental Leopardian drama.

The questions with which the poem begins are of course never answered. Leopardi wishes to show that answers are to be found only in an understanding of why such queries arise. The questions also fallaciously endow the moon with a life like man's, though simultaneously the obviousness of the fallacy dramatizes the difference between man and the mindless bodies of the celestial universe. The comparison of the shepherd's life to the moon's round leads to the final question which sums up this likeness in dissimilarity: "where leads this brief wandering of mine and your immortal course?"

Part two intensifies the difference between the shepherd and the "virgin moon." The picture of the "withered man" who struggles through a course of sufferings only to plunge into an "immense abyss" is not a literal description of the shepherd's life. It is, rather, his imaginative conception of man's life. The poem is concerned with the relation of such a conception to the functioning of the material universe: the "facts" of the shepherd's life are never as significant as what he makes of them.

Part three emphasizes the meaninglessness of the suffering journey imaged in part two. From that meaninglessness rises the implication of a human spirit which binds humans together and sets them apart from all else in the cosmos. In this bond of separateness, and there alone, is to be found any meaning that suffering may have.

Part four locates the origin of man's suffering in his engagement with the cycles of time, embodied in days, seasons, and heavenly bodies. Individual man participates in these cycles yet not harmoniously, since he moves straight to death, and it is precisely his awareness of this incompleteness upon which is founded the shepherd's judgment: "to me life is evil." Because the individual participates in the cyclic harmony of the natural universe yet is aware that he is not entirely comprehended by that mechanical order, he can judge it, and he can judge it to be insufficient to him—to be evil.[13]

In part five the shepherd turns from the moon to his flock, apparently nearer to him in condition, although, just because of this superficial propinquity, illustrative of the uniqueness of man's consciousness. This consciousness is the cause not of joy but of special suffering, a suffering more painful than the physical anguish caused by "sharp stones" and "icy months." The suffering which strikes hardest when man is physically at ease is *noia*.

Noia—tedium, boredom, unfocussed dissatisfaction—is the disease of an *active* mind. It is the discontent which besets a mind capable of conceiving things different from what they are, of envisioning the impossible, as the shepherd does at the beginning of part six. *Noia* is a specifically human disease, one that might be called self-created, since it results from the inner energy of the mind. It expresses the profound disharmony between man and the natural universe: it appears most forcefully when a man is physically at ease: "if I lie at rest tedium seizes me."

The distinction between the pain inflicted by nature and that inflicted by man's consciousness shapes the indefiniteness of the poem's final sentence: "*Perhaps* . . . the day of birth to all that's born is fatal." As regards natural creatures the statement needs no qualification. Nothing can die that has not been born; to be born is to become vulnerable to death. The doubt is only whether this grim logic applies in a special way to man's special condition. Possibly a man's "day of birth" is doubly "fatal," since on that day is born not only a physical being but also a consciousness inevitably susceptible to *noia*.

Nevertheless, the most significant characteristic of the *Night Song* is not its grimness but its tentativeness, present throughout in the shepherd's modesty and self-confessed ignorance.[14] Its tone is one of doubt and questioning. Its effectiveness lies not in its "message of despair" but in its dramatization of man's problematic condition.[15]

Through the shepherd Leopardi defines the limits of man's comprehension. For all his stylization, the shepherd impresses us as deeply and essentially human because what he does is fundamental to human activity.[16] He perceives the confines of his existence and he asks why those confines exist. So to see and so to ask is to be a man.[17]

Temporary participation in the mechanical round of the natural universe is not satisfactory to the shepherd. He lacks the Neoclassic humility which finds self-abnegating satisfaction in the harmonious perfection of natural systems. Nor is the shepherd resigned to the meaninglessness of his life—the nihilists and oriental mystics[18] who claim Leopardi for their own are wrong. The *Night Song* might almost have been written as an explicit refutation of Nietzsche's assertion that man will worship nothing rather than have nothing to worship. The shepherd is, in fact, a humble exponent of what Keats called "negative capability."

But the shepherd is only part of the poem; his "negative capability" is one half of a dramatic dialectic. There are only two elements in the *Night Song*: the unconscious matter of the universe and the shepherd's mind. The "action" of the poem consists in the interaction of mind and matter, and what results—that is, the total poem—is something neither purely mental nor purely material but a dramatization of the interplay of these elements. It may fairly be termed a representation of what human life quintessentially is, insofar at least as human life is to be regarded as the interaction of mind and matter. The poets of Leopardi's era, I believe, strove so to define human life.[19] That is why they so frequently portray intermediate conditions (dreams and the like), why their transcendentalism and their realism are seldom absolute, why they so often are satisfied to present men and their actions as dubious and uncertain, as potentialities rather than realizations, and why they tend to regard art as an intermediate creation that links the mental to the physical, the particular to the universal, the present to the past, sensation to vision.

Wordsworth's representation of human life as an interaction of mind and matter is well demonstrated in a poem written at the height of his powers and when his liberalism was still ardent, *The Old Cumberland Beggar*. Wordsworth's polemic is directed against legislation aimed to eliminate begging by establishing workhouses for the aged indigent. He maintains the almost Dickensian position that "progressive" legislation is abominable because it denies to the indigent their essential humanity. But Wordsworth, unlike Dickens, represents his beggar's essential humanity as an historical phenomenon. The "history" of the old beggar is not part of the poet's experience alone—

> Him from my childhood have I known; and then
> He was so old, he seems not older now—

but also that of the rural population among whom the old man begs.

> . . . While from door to door,
> This old Man creeps, the villagers in him
> Behold a record which together binds
> Past deeds and offices of charity,
> Else unremembered, and so keeps alive
> The kindly mood in hearts which lapse of years,
> And that half-wisdom half-experience gives,
> Make slow to feel, and by sure steps resign
> To selfishness and cold oblivious cares.

Wordsworth takes care to let us see the beggar as infirm, of dull intelligence, unoccupied, useless by ordinary standards. So the old man might be seen by a casual passerby. It is only when we know the old man's history, and when we know the complete story of his life and of the effect of his repeated circuits of the countryside, that we appreciate what service he renders, wherein consists his moral dignity.

The preciousness of the old beggar is found not in his existence at any one moment but in the total continuity of his life. The beggar's worth is determined by the interplay through time of psychic activities and material circumstances. The interplay, of course, is not perceptible in a single view: it must be imaginatively experienced.

No one denies that the emergence of an historical awareness is one of the principal intellectual events of the late eighteenth and early nineteenth centuries, but the nature of this sense of history is misunderstood, I believe, if we look for it only in novelists like Scott and Manzoni or in professional historians. *The Old Cumberland Beggar* shows this sense of history to be an awareness of the power and logic of interior forces. Wordsworth says of the beggar, "he appears/ To breathe and live but for himself." But the poet demonstrates that the appearance is misleading. What the old man accomplishes for the villagers, and what they are because of his "invisible" influence exerted over the course of many years, is not apparent to immediate observation: it can only be deduced by study of the operation of hidden patterns working through time. Such study of grander phenomena is the task of modern history. Modern historians examine the inner life of men's societies; focussing upon the interior life of events, they deduce the pattern of invisible forces of economics, ideologies, customs, and so forth, which are not visible at any one instant or at any single place but can be perceived only by finding the logic or coherence which binds together many separate phenomena. The modern historian thus differs from the classical historian who believes that simply by ordering his facts he can represent what "really" happened, that is, the meaning of historical events. The modern historian marshals his facts so as to reveal the forces which are not the facts themselves but their hidden relationships, and in this relationship he finds meaning. Like the medieval historian, the modern one seeks for the invisible pattern within the complex of phenomena. But of course most modern historians are scientifically rather than theologically oriented; the interior pattern, the meaning they discover, is a pattern and meaning of this world in itself not referable to a theological system. Both the purpose and the method of the modern historical procedure appear in miniature in *The Old Cumberland Beggar*.

But Wordsworth is not an historian. "History" in *The Old Cumberland Beggar* serves to exalt the humble by forcing us to see in it a revelation of something like cosmic order.[20] Like Leopardi's villagers, Wordsworth's old beggar is simultaneously a specific individual, with all the value of individuality, and an archetype, a precious proof "that we have all of us one human heart." We are shown the local effect created by the unique person, but at the same time we are made to see that effect as expressive of the permanent principle of humane existence.

> Where'er the aged Beggar takes his rounds,
> The mild necessity of use compels
> To acts of love; and habit does the work
> Of reason; yet prepares that after-joy
> Which reason cherishes. And thus the soul,
> By that sweet taste of pleasure unpursued,
> Doth find herself insensibly disposed
> To virtue and true goodness.

Wordsworth, like Leopardi, simplifies. He focusses intensely on a specific person in a particular locale.[21] The integrity of the old beggar as an individual, that is, the integrity of his history which has made him what he is now and has made him an influence upon his community, is the unity of his life. The error of the statesmen who set up workhouses that shut out "the natural silence of old age" is precisely that of seeing the beggar not as a total historical entity but as a fragment, as a life separate from other lives, even his own past life. He is now an indigent nuisance, they say: anybody seeing him on the road can recognize that. No, answers the poet, to treat him as if what he is at this moment were *all* he is would be to deny that a man's life is a coherent totality. What a man is at any given instant and what his influence for good or ill may be, must be judged in terms of his whole history as a complete process. To base social action *only* on immediate appearance is to deny that human existence is a continuous process within which any one event can be truly understood only as it relates to the whole of which it is a part. To repeat, in different words, the analogy applied to *The Village Saturday*, it would be absurd to treat oxygen separated from water as if that oxygen illustrated the nature of H_2O. Yet English reformers, like French revolutionists, treat not molecules but humans in just such a partial, analytic way. To Wordsworth they are terribly mistaken.

Like the *Night Song*, *The Old Cumberland Beggar* illustrates the characteristic attempt of early nineteenth-century poets to represent human life as a synthesized whole. To Wordsworth and his contemporaries the truth about man could not be arrived at by partial methods. Because the method of political economy, or that of sociology, or that of psychology, is confessedly partial these methods inevitably distort the full truth about man. Only poetry can utter the full truth. Above all, the partial methods falsify the truth about the right relations between man and man. These can be understood, a good relationship distinguished from a bad, only if each man is regarded not as a thing, an economic unit (consumer, say), a psychological unit (psychotic), a social unit (middle class), but as a complete man. A man's wholeness constitutes his identity[22] and makes possible complete and valuable relations with other men and active, creative participation in the life of the universe (see lines 67–87).

Like all of Wordsworth's best poems, *The Old Cumberland Beggar* shows how a poet perceives and what he perceives. By "seeing into" phenomena the poet perceives a vital unity invisible to ordinary sight and unintelligible to the merely rational, that is, analytic, intellect, and the interior synthetic unity constitutes the value of the phenomenon perceived. To the ordinary rational observer the old beggar is "obviously" a useless nuisance. Poetic vision alone reveals his preciousness.

This poetic vision, like that of Leopardi's poems, is not a special gift. It is the way all men can and should see.[23] Analogously, what poetic vision perceives is not something superficially spectacular but is, instead, the inner vitality of the commonplace. The poet does not discover the extraordinary so much as he reveals the full significance of the ordinary. He does not seek unusual experience and does not delight in novelty so much as he finds value in typical experience and revived pleasure in what is familiar.[24] One might say that our poets do not need sensational subjects, because their aim is to reveal the total relatedness of the objects or phenomena they encounter, and the revelation of how things and events interrelate is in itself most wonderful.

Our poets are original not because they seek for novelty but because they are personal. Wordsworth and Leopardi are at their personal best writing of common experiences of ordinary life, and Keats and Foscolo are often at their personal best reworking familiar

literary traditions. For these four poets poetry is a created intermediary between unique experience and the generality of human
life which all men share. Thus each of their poems is a specific,
independent intensification of the harmony which is the life of
the universe, at its most marvelous and significant a reflective life,
the life of man.

To illustrate this understanding of the nature and the goal of
poetry, we must examine the deliberately literary work of these
poets, because the total relatedness they reveal includes not alone
the physical dimensions of the natural world but also the cultural
dimensions of religious, philosophic, and literary traditions. We
must, as implied above, turn from Wordsworth and Leopardi to
Foscolo and Keats. The oddness of this pairing deserves a moment's
attention, since it cuts across the pattern of age as well as of nationality, for Wordsworth and Foscolo were near contemporaries,
a generation older than Keats and Leopardi. Wordsworth and
Leopardi, however, were in their different ways solitary men, men
open to a limited range of experience upon which they brooded.
As compared to them, Keats and Foscolo were worldly. Possessed
of strong inner resources, they nonetheless liked and were stimulated
by the rub and press of social intercourse.

One must not push the contrast too far, yet there is reason for
calling attention to it. Keats and Foscolo are also the more fanciful
and less realistic artists. Wordsworth and Leopardi are at root
naturalists: they probe deep, to the core of what they have actually
seen and felt; both lack inventiveness; neither is especially literary;
their best poetry is surprisingly free from influence. Keats and
Foscolo are extraordinarily literary poets. Their verse is filled with
echoes of other poets' work, and their subject matter, too, is often
detached from immediate reality: *Hyperion* and *The Graces* were
written during the Napoleonic era. Yet Keats and Foscolo were not
escapist dreamers, nor were they, in the usual sense, learned writers.

In his celebrated book, *The Seventeenth Century Background,*
Basil Willey observes that

. . . one is struck by the absence, in Pope's poem [the *Essay on Man*] of any
sort of mythological machinery. . . . It would have been unthinkable in Pope's
time that a serious poet should have used any such machinery, . . . Mythologies, including the Christian, were now felt to be exploded; . . . But though
Pope and his contemporaries were debarred by their intellectual climate from

using any great system of commonly-accepted symbols, as Dante and Milton could, they could still employ mythological material for other purposes . . . for technical convenience and for purposes of "delight." It is in this manner that the mythologies of the ancient world are generally used by eighteenth century poets.[25]

This eighteenth-century heritage, Professor Willey shows, put Wordsworth in a difficult position, "left alone, seeking the visible world."

. . . his debt to tradition, unlike Dante's, was a negative one; he owed to it his *deprivation* of mythology. . . . Centuries of intellectual development had now brought matters to this, that if poetry were still to be made, it must be made by the sheer unaided power of the individual poet.[26]

What Professor Willey says about Wordsworth's position is, I believe, undeniable. But what, then, are we to make of poets like Keats and Foscolo, who devote so much energy to exploded mythologies? Professor Willey, whose interest is in Wordsworth, barely touches the problem.

The new poet must therefore either make poetry out of the direct dealings of his mind and heart with the visible universe, or he must fabricate a genuine new mythology of his own (not necessarily rejecting all old material in so doing). Keats and Shelley often follow the second of these methods.[27]

No one seems to have picked up the trail of difficulties raised by Willey's observation. The fact is that Keats and Shelley and Foscolo, far from "rejecting all old material" employ little but "old material." If they "fabricate a genuine new mythology of their own," they fabricate it out of the stories and figures of the most familiar mythology, that of ancient Greece. They are not Swedenborgians or proto-Blavatskians.

The Hellenism of the early nineteenth-century poets is a specific and specialized manifestation of the general literary effort of the time to reveal the preciousness of the familiar and forgotten. Wordsworth's Michael, Scott's seventeenth-century Covenanters, and Keats's Hyperion have nothing in common but their creators' desire that we should recognize their heroes to be worthy, each in his own way, of the attention of sophisticated and serious-minded men.

Greek mythology held a special position in the movement which endeavored to assert the value of what had been forgotten, or had become too familiar, or had been despised as trivial. The gods and goddesses of ancient Hellas were familiar because they had been the subject matter of some of the finest art in the world, and Keats and Foscolo were attracted to the mythology of Greece not as mythology per se but as the substance of admirable art. Yet they conceived of admirable art as creation and not imitation, so their return to the subjects of classical literature did not involve them in copying its forms. *Hyperion,* for instance, is in one way at least a more original poem than Pope's *Essay on Man,* Dryden's *Absalom and Achitophel,* or Milton's *Paradise Lost,* all of which adhere more closely than does Keats's poem to established models of structure and decorum. *The Graces* likewise is without any formal prototype. Keats and Foscolo, in fact, were attracted to Renaissance and classical writers because they believed, however erroneously, that these earlier writers had practiced a more creative art than had the later Neoclassicists. In using as subject matter part of the old mythology Keats and Foscolo associated themselves with what they believed to be the best part of the literary tradition of Western Europe, that part which, in their view, had flourished when art was both socially important and possessed of spiritual vitality.

Relevant at this point is the "double life" of our poets, who were also critics.[28] I have paid scant attention to their criticism, and there is no need now to become engaged with the rich diversity of their comments and doctrines. But I must point out that each wrote significant criticism. The criticism of some, Wordsworth for example, and like him Shelley, found expression in what may be called manifestos. Some—Foscolo, and, in England, Coleridge—wrote critical essays and delivered formal lectures. Most interesting of all are Keats and Leopardi, whose insights and principles were for the most part expressed privately, Keats's in his letters, Leopardi's in his journals. The forms of early nineteenth-century criticism by poets are various, but the method and manner are everywhere alike: the method is personal, the manner dedicated.

These poets are never littérateurs. They never chat about books. To them art is of transcendent importance: it is human life at its most intense, so their criticism, even when it is casual and private, is passionate. Surprisingly, little of their critical effort goes into polemics against their adversaries. They are convinced of the truth of their vision, and they are eager to demolish what they believe to be false theories of art, but they are not interested in belletristic debating. Literature is too important for that, and, besides, they all adhere, in one fashion or another, to a premise which renders literary polemics secondary, namely, that good criticism is at root the expression of one's personal experience of a particular work of art.

It follows that their criticism treats of principles of artistic endeavor and of imaginative activity, but seldom formulates stylistic rules. Hence, unlike Neoclassic critics, they devote little space to the enumeration of defects, and usually they strive to express the spirit of a great work of art. In short, they are not really descriptive critics. Historians of criticism often condemn them as unsystematic and contradictory.[29] To these poet-critics one work of art serves as the subject matter, not the formal model, of another work of art. This makes for some inspired if unsystematic criticism; it also results in some valuable poetry—including *Hyperion* and *The Graces*, the subjects of the next two chapters.

FOUR

The Envisioned Ideal:
Organic Relation of
Future to Past

VIII ❧ COMMEMORATIVE PROPHECY

KEATS: *Hyperion*
The Fall of Hyperion

YPERION and *The Graces* are "criticisms" of classical art, in that they reveal their authors' experience of the most sublime art of the Western world, the spirit of which they recreate for us to experience afresh. By fabricating a genuine new mythology out of old materials, Keats and Foscolo simultaneously affirm the unity of the human spirit and the diversity in which it expresses itself. They are original and experiential while celebrating the most enduring and fundamental truths of human life.

Let us begin with Keats's poem, first trying to answer the question which, I suspect, underlies most of the objections to *Hyperion*: can a sophisticated reader care about Apollo and Hyperion? I think much of Keats's art is directed to making a virtue out of this apparent difficulty. Because we do not care about Apollo and Hyperion per se, we are free to respond to their situation with an appropriate ambivalence. This freedom is not available, for example, to readers of *Paradise Lost*. The meaning of the conflict between the Olympians and the Titans must be dramatically created by the poet, who cannot rely on his readers' allegiance to traditional attitudes toward the antagonists. The significance of his poem must be self-established,[1] but he is protected against mere idiosyncrasy by the fact that his subject matter derives from our oldest and most viable literary tradition.

Whether or not *Hyperion* is to be called an epic, its particular characteristics may be defined by contrast with our epic tradition, which began, it seems safe to say, in the humanizing of what had been narratives about divinities—myths.[2] Much of the power in epics such as *Gilgamesh* and the *Iliad* derives from the way in which their human protagonists emerge, under our eyes so to speak, from purely magical and religious contexts in which gods, not men, dominate all activity. Achilles' manhood is impressive because he stands so close to the gods. In *Hyperion* man reassumes divine proportions; epic re-approaches myth. The Titans and the Gods are, if the word may be divested of pejorative associations, supermen. Keats's monumental figures, so enormously sensual, express spiritual actions and attitudes. So their strength is curiously similar to that of Achilles or Gilgamesh. Though complex, self-conscious, and aesthetic as their "primitive" forebears were not, Keats's protagonists, like the earlier heroes, have their being in a realm that is not earth, not heaven, but inseparable from both.

Hyperion narrates the birth of a new kind of divinity. Keats is not literarily archaistic; he does not ask us to admire the ancient Greek god Apollo; he asks us to see Apollo as a manifestation of the evolutionary principle which gives dynamic order and meaning to the universe. Thus the remoteness of the Titanomachia also serves Keats's central purpose.

For this reason the mythic, rather than symbolic, nature of the personae of *Hyperion* is appropriate. Apollo does not stand for something other than himself, yet he is not merely the old Apollo. He is not a literary reconstruction of a dead mythological figure, yet he is not fully separable from the ancient mythological figure. Keats's Apollo manifests a beauty that surpasses his individuality. He is *a* god. He is not a symbol of unchanging divinity nor is he a timeless object of adoration. Apollo must be one of many gods, not merely because there are other Olympians, but because there have been and will be other kinds of gods, other dazzling manifestations of developing beauty.

To Keats beauty is harmony, and there can be progress from simple to complex harmony. Such progress is dramatized by *Hyperion*, which moves from the description of Saturn, wherein sensory particularities are subdued to the harmony of a single mood of tranced sadness, to the narrative of Apollo's dying into godhead, which unifies in vital concord contrasting sensations, feelings, and thoughts. The Olympians, as Oceanus says, surpass the Titans in "might" because the Olympians are "first in beauty." Titanic beauty is little more than mechanical unity; Olympian beauty is an organic unity which reconciles contraries and diversities.

But *Hyperion* is more than story, it is history—the early history of the universe.[3] The progress from Titanic to Olympian beauty reveals our cosmos to be a developing historical entity, as subject to,

and a theater for, evolutionary processes. Keatsian evolution, however, differs from Darwinian. Keats thinks in purely aesthetic terms;
he does not anticipate the later scientific concept. Darwin applies
the theory of evolution horizontally, to one level of being at a time.
Keats concentrates upon the thresholds of being. The scientific evo-
lutionist seeks to connect man with the animals and the physical
world, but Keats seeks to connect man with the gods and a supranatural world.

Nevertheless, the "system" of *Hyperion* is evolutionary;[4] in this
respect Keats labors in direct opposition to Milton, and, indeed, to
the entire classical-Renaissance literary tradition upon which so
much of *Hyperion* depends.[5] What principally characterizes Keats's
poem, in fact, is the intensity with which a commemorative, tradi-
tionalistic impulse interacts with a prophetic, progressive impulse.
Keats fabricates a new personal mythology out of old religion and
traditional literature.

Hyperion progresses from simple harmony to complex. The marvelous opening lines portray a scene in which all the details are
of a piece, each contributing to a mood of sad silence appropriate
to Saturn's fallen divinity (the italics are mine):

> *Deep* in the *shady sadness* of a vale
> *Far sunken* from the healthy breath of morn,
> *Far* from the fiery noon, and eve's one star,
> Sat *gray-hair'd* Saturn, *quiet as a stone,*
> *Still* as the *silence* round about his lair;
> Forest on forest hung about his head
> Like *cloud on cloud. No stir* of air was there
> *Not* so much life as on a summer's day
> Robs *not* one light seed from the feather'd grass,
> But where the *dead leaf fell,* there did it *rest.*
> A stream went *voiceless* by, *still deadened more*
> By reason of his *fallen* divinity
> Spreading a *shade:* the Naiad 'mid her reeds
> Press'd her *cold* finger closer to her lips.
>
>   Along the margin-sand large foot-marks went,
> *No further* than to where his feet had stray'd,
> And *slept* there since. Upon the *sodden* ground
> His *old* right hand *lay nerveless, listless, dead,*
> *Unsceptred;* and his *realmless* eyes were *closed;*
> While his *bow'd* head *seem'd list'ning* to the Earth,
> His *ancient* mother, for *some comfort* yet.
> (I, 1–21)

Saturn listens to the Earth for comfort. To Hyperion words of comfort are spoken by Coelus, who is "but a voice," whose "life is but the life of winds and tides," yet who speaks "from the universal space." Coelus is more "heavenly" than Earth, and Hyperion's superiority to his fellow Titans derives from his association with the sky. He is "earth-born/ And sky-engendered." One must admire Keats's narrative strategy: Apollo and Hyperion are more equally matched than any other pair of God-Titan opponents and their clash ought to be the climax of an evolutionary movement in which "supranatural" gods are born out of the agony of "natural" deities. Apollo, though "Celestial," is not detached from the earth. Not only is he born on Delos but his assumption of divinity occurs under the aegis of Mnemosyne,

> ". . . an ancient Power
> Who hath forsaken old and sacred thrones
> For prophecies of thee, and for the sake
> Of loveliness new born."
> (III, 76–79)

The new celestial must encompass within his progressive divinity the memory of earthly powers. The old is not to be obliterated but absorbed into a more complicated and comprehensive unity, just as *Hyperion* is meant to absorb previous literary traditions into a new unity.

To understand Apollo's dying into life, therefore, we must understand Hyperion's living into death, which is the climactic representation of all the Titans' tragedy. Unlike Saturn, who is old and gray and surrounded by silence and inertness, Hyperion "flares" along, "full of wrath," in a blaze of crystalline and golden opulence to the sound of "slow-breathed melodies" from "solemn tubes." The entrance to his palace, unlike the tranced woods in which Saturn sleeps, is described with the dynamic richness of full Keatsian synaesthesia.[6]

> And like a rose in vermeil tint and shape,
> In fragrance soft, and coolness to the eye,
> That inlet to severe magnificence
> Stood full blown, for the God to enter in.
> (I, 209–12)

Yet one notices that "this haven" of Hyperion's "rest" and "this cradle" of his "glory," a structure of pure light, seems now strangely alien from the earth.[7] The beauties of the earthly world appear in reference to Hyperion's palace only in metaphors and similes. The palace, full of "the blaze, the splendour, and the symmetry" of artifice, suffers "death and darkness" when elements of the natural world intrude. The Titans have fallen. Natural phenomena appear to Hyperion as "effigies of pain," as "spectres," and as "phantoms," and this is the effect of the Olympian triumph. Hyperion is a Titan, an earth god, and he swears "by Tellus and her briny robes!"[8] Yet earthly nature enters his "lucent empire" as a threat, in its least attractive guise, as something sinister and suggestive of death: the "cold, cold gloom" of "black-weeded pools" and the "mist" of a "scummy marsh." Hyperion's impotence, when he finds himself unable to utter his "heavier threat" is imaged by a serpentine power usurping his supramundane godhead.

> . . . through all his bulk an agony
> Crept gradual, from the feet unto the crown,
> Like a lithe serpent vast and muscular
> Making slow way, with head and neck convuls'd
> From over-strained might.
> (I, 259–63)

Hyperion, "releas'd," in desperation attempts to disrupt the order of nature; he bids "the day begin . . . six dewy hours/ Before the dawn in season due should blush." Hyperion is "a Primeval God," but "the sacred seasons might not be disturbed." The Titans, more primitive divinities than the Olympians, are identified with purely natural processes; Hyperion's actions reveal how shaken is his divinity. The Olympians are not to be identified, however, with the antinatural. Rather they represent nature advanced to a new level. Hence the conflict of the poem is not between good and evil but between one kind of truth and beauty and a superior kind of truth and beauty. The inert lifelessness of the opening scene where all the animation of the natural surroundings is deadened by Saturn's presence symbolizes the limitation of the primeval gods: they do not represent the progress and fulfillment of natural life. Their successors will be more "godlike" because they will carry forward and more nearly fulfill the developing natural processes of earthly life. Implicit here is the idea that increased consciousness fulfills, does not thwart "nature": man's supranatural life is the proper evolutionary successor to unreflective biological existence.

Hyperion, "by hard compulsion bent," no longer strides and stamps and flares.

> And all along a dismal rack of clouds,
> Upon the boundaries of day and night,
> He stretch'd himself in grief and radiance faint.
> (I, 302–4)

He is approaching the gray passivity of Saturn; he has reached the boundaries of day and night moving toward darkness. Apollo at the same moment, as we learn in Book III, has also reached "the boundaries of day and night," but the Olympian is moving toward light. He appears in a dim, quiet solitude analogous to that of Saturn ("I have sat alone/ In cool midforest") that is as much a psychological condition as a physical situation:

> ". . . For me, dark, dark,
> And painful vile oblivion seals my eyes:
> I strive to search wherefore I am so sad,
> Until a melancholy numbs my limbs."
> (III, 86–89)

But, contrary to Hyperion, Apollo begs that Mnemosyne may "point forth some unknown thing." The new and unknown attracts and draws forth his godhead instead of strangling it.[9] He does not stretch himself in grief and radiance faint but aspires toward the natural lights of the heavens, the inanimate "brilliance" and "splendour" of which he desires to fill with the passion of life.

> ". . . There is the sun, the sun!
> And the most patient brilliance of the moon!
> And stars by the thousands! Point me out the way
> To any one particular beauteous star,
> And I will flit into it with my lyre,
> And make its silvery splendour pant with bliss."
> (III, 97–102)

We travel from Hyperion to Apollo by way of the council of the Titans, which is held in a cavern far from the life and light of surface earth.[10] The most important speech in this deliberation is that of Oceanus,[11] who advises acceptance of the truth that the Titans have been overpowered by a "fresh perfection" and "a power more strong in beauty." Although Oceanus speaks the truth, the "comfort" and "consolation" he offers is bleak. "Receive the truth, and let it be your balm," he says, asserting that

". . . to bear all naked truths,
And to envisage circumstance, all calm,
That is the top of sovereignty."
(II, 203–5)

This stoicism is the "top of sovereignty" for the Titans. It is not
the top of sovereignty for Apollo. Every Titan who speaks regrets
that he, and his world, is no longer "all calm." The passivity of
Saturn in defeat, ironically, reveals the limits of the life he ordered
in triumph. Oceanus preaches stoicism because the characteristic
quality of Titanic rule was placidity. Even fiery Enceladus urges
renewed war to regain "the days of peace and slumberous calm."

Apollo, representative of the Olympians, does not seek "days of
peace and slumberous calm." He hates his idleness, he wishes to
make the stars "pant with bliss," he is exhilarated to godhead by
the knowledge of "dire events, rebellions . . . Creations and destroyings." The life over which Apollo will preside is to be active,
violent, aspiring.

Evolution, as described by Oceanus, is a process of rising and
lifting, a process of increasing movement and activity, a process
by which more and more vitality emerges and gives meaning to
inert, disorganized matter. "From Chaos and parental Darkness
came/Light," he says. The "sullen ferment" of chaotic darkness
"for wondrous ends/Was ripening in itself," and when "the ripe
hour came" light was born.

". . . Light, engendering
Upon its own producer, forthwith touch'd
The whole enormous matter into Life."
(II, 195–97)

First chaos, then light, an ordering of inanimate matter, finally
life, a further ordering of light. The Titans came into being with
the appearance of life. They are now to be superseded, not because
life is to vanish, but because a more intense kind of life is being
born out of the old life, just as the old life (a more intense kind of
"light") was born out of the older light, which, in turn, had emerged
from darkness.

The new life that is being born, the life of which the Olympians
are the highest representatives, is a life of increased intelligence,
and, since the universe now includes life, increased consciousness of
life, increased consciousness of self. "Knowledge enormous makes

a God of me," cries Apollo. He is aware of becoming a god: his godhead is in large measure his self-awareness.

The intensity of Apollo's self-awareness is impossible for Oceanus. He is aware of the god who replaces him and he knows the new god is somehow superior to him, but in what this superiority consists he does not know. Were he capable of the "knowledge enormous" which fills Apollo's mind Oceanus would be an Olympian. He is not capable of that knowledge, and, because he is the wisest of his kind, he does not try for it. He retires stoically.

Clymene, not so wise, experiences the anguish of not being able to comprehend. She suffers what Oceanus would have suffered had he not possessed the wisdom to recognize his limits. In so suffering, however, Clymene prepares the reader for Apollo's apotheosis. *Hyperion* opens with a scene of complete deadness and silence, one without consciousness, for Saturn sleeps and his divine sleep trances his surroundings. When Hyperion himself appears we have action, but arrested action, awareness (Hyperion recognizes the stifling of his divinity), but arrested awareness. In the cavern we have more activity, the arrival of Saturn, the debate, and finally the appearance of Hyperion. But this activity is cramped, self-lacerating, incon-clusive, and the same adjectives might be applied to the awareness developed by the arguments.[12] Oceanus' opening plea for stoical endurance is finally answered by Enceladus' hopeless fulminations.[13] But the Titans' struggle into self-defeat is the matrix of agony out of which the Olympians are born, and in the unfinished third book we move upward and outward from the cavern to reach, finally, the ecstatic sufferings of Apollo dying into a more intense and har-monious life, a life fully conscious of its own power and capable, therefore, of reconciling the potent diversities of a wonderful and ever developing cosmos. Apollo's ecstasy and its significance is adumbrated by Clymene, whose plaintive speech links Oceanus' stoicism to Enceladus' rage.

Clymene dramatizes the truth of what Oceanus has said, while emphasizing the painfulness of his truth. Her story reveals how unfit are the Titans to control the new life that pervades the universe.

> "I stood upon a shore, a pleasant shore,
> Where a sweet clime was breathed from a land
> Of fragrance, quietness, and trees, and flowers.
> Full of calm joy it was, as I of grief;

> Too full of joy and soft delicious warmth;
> So that I felt a movement in my heart
> To chide, and to reproach that solitude
> With songs of misery, music of our woes."
> (II, 262–69)

Clymene could only *reproach* the joy and warmth of nature with "songs of misery." It is not in the Titans' power to *reconcile* contraries, as it is in the Olympians' power, as is shown by the music which destroys Clymene's sad melody murmured into "a mouthed shell." "That new blissful golden melody" was, for Clymene, "a living death" which, she relates, made her "sick/ Of joy and grief at once." What sickens her and is for her "a living death" is the new harmony which enables Apollo "with fierce convulse" to "die into life."

The apotheosis of Apollo which concludes the fragmentary third book is, as one might guess from Clymene's story, the exact opposite of Saturn's trance at the opening of the poem. Saturn sleeps in silence, dimness, and inertness.[14] The apotheosis of Apollo is a birth full of sound, movement, and the radiant anguish of emerging consciousness. The contrast between the two passages is best told in the concluding images. Saturn, like a sculptured figure, is long bowed to the earth for comfort, whereas from Apollo's "limbs Celestial" some yet undefined power is forever about to emanate. But the contrast is not merely that Saturn retreats toward familiar consolation and Apollo yearns toward new and painful wonder. The difference between the two divinities lies in the different harmonies which unify the contrasting passages. The description of Saturn is harmonious in that nothing contrary to the mood of tranced stillness intrudes. The narrative of Apollo's apotheosis reconciles contraries. For instance, Apollo's ecstatic words contrast to Mnemosyne's "silent face," as the "wild commotions . . . of his limbs" contrast to her rigid pose, "upheld/ Her arms as one who prophesied."[15] Likewise *dire* events . . . pour" into his brain like "some *blithe* wine"; his "level glance . . . steadfast kept/ Trembling with light." Virtually every word in this narrative of "Creations and destroyings" is matched by a contrary, so that the Dionysiac fury of the event is controlled by an Apollonian symmetry of form.

The harmony of the Saturn passage is substantive, that of the Apollo passage compositional, a total order imposed upon diverse sensations, feelings, and ideas. The beauty born with Apollo is the beauty of complex design. The particularities retain their integrity: pain remains pain, it does not become pleasure; death and life remain distinct conditions; creations and destroyings remain opposed processes. But pain and pleasure, life and death, creations and destroyings interlock in a design that reconciles them.[16] Apollo's birth is meant to transform the value, the meaning, of each of these particular elements, because the god's birth is the birth of understanding of the place of each particularity and its opposite within the scheme of cosmological history.

The comprehension of this scheme, the dying out of incomplete life into total life, should not merely change the value of the parts but should also increase it, because the formal symmetry of the whole event will reflect back upon each particle more energy than it alone can generate. Once the encompassing design is conceived, each element within it will be seen to contribute not alone to its own existence but to the ordering, the significance, of all existences together. The final contrast between Apollo and Hyperion is probably that life become conscious of its system of vitality is more intense and precious and enduring, more fully supranatural, self-transcending, divine, than unreflective life, life unaware of its own potency.[17]

One must speak tentatively because Keats did not finish *Hyperion*. We can only speculate as to why he was dissatisfied with it, but his own "explanations" suggest that he was more troubled by stylistic problems than by his subject matter. Perhaps he did not control the style necessary to represent the Olympian life, a style which ought to transcend that of the first books. The logical culmination of the Keatsian Titanomachia ought to be the triumph of Apollo over Hyperion. Oceanus' stoical retirement before Neptune is not a reconcilement of contraries, not an absorption of an old, incomplete beauty into a new, more complete beauty. This reconcilement and absorption are necessary to authenticate Olympian divinity, and they should be fashioned in a manner suggested by but not fully realized in the narrative of Apollo's apotheosis.

At least partial realization of this new manner is found, perhaps, in the early portion of *The Fall of Hyperion: A Dream*, Keats's recasting of the original poem.[18] *The Fall* is certainly a more personal poem than *Hyperion*, and it might be argued that it is also more literary,[19] that it includes a wider range of literary references and incorporates a more intense appreciation of its mythological and poetic sources.[20] The key to this double development seems to me to lie in Keats's recognition that the life of full consciousness, including of course consciousness of self, must be deeply involved with visions or dreams.

Consciousness, after all, is more than mere perception. A mind fully aware is not satisfied by appearances, it strives to comprehend more than meets the eye. Consciousness is also something more than common sense. A mind fully aware is sensitive to causes and motives which lie beyond the reach of workaday rationalism. No one could deny that scientific activity of the past one hundred and fifty years has advanced man's awareness of the workings of his universe and of his own being. And the modern understanding of the natural universe is founded, as A. N. Whitehead pointed out, upon a willingness to accept as truth explanations that seem to controvert "common sense." Most important work in the physical sciences today concerns phenomena which simply cannot be observed by the naked eye. Psychoanalysis of course, is founded upon the study of what appears to be irrational, particularly upon the study of the "truth" of dreams.

Keats was neither a proto-Freud nor a proto-Einstein. He knew little about science and contributed nothing directly to its development. In some respects he looked backward, toward Socrates, who examined life with the most intense rationality, who constantly sought self-awareness, and whose climactic utterances passed beyond dialectic into stories of visions. But Keats also looked forward. In *The Fall of Hyperion* he suggests a conception of poetic truth as visionary truth which foreshadows our contemporary interest in extraordinary mental conditions and in new systems of logical enquiry and organization. This is perhaps why *The Fall of Hyperion* is so complex, and why, specifically, even more than the earlier version it speaks in two voices, one commemorative, one prophetic.

The Fall of Hyperion is above all else what Keats himself called it: a dream. In the first eighteen lines of the fragment the word "dream" appears five times.

> Fanatics have their dreams, wherewith they weave
> A paradise for a sect; the savage, too,
> From forth the loftiest fashion of his sleep
> Guesses at Heaven; pity these have not
> Trac'd upon vellum or wild Indian leaf
> The shadows of melodious utterance.

> But bare of laurel they live, dream, and die;
> For Poesy alone can tell her dreams,
> With the fine spell of words alone can save
> Imagination from the sable charm
> And dumb enchantment. Who alive can say,
> "Thou art no Poet—may'st not tell thy dreams"?
> Since every man whose soul is not a clod
> Hath visions, and would speak, if he had lov'd
> And been well nurtured in his mother tongue.
> Whether the dream now purpos'd to rehearse
> Be Poet's or Fanatic's will be known
> When this warm scribe, my hand, is in the grave.
> (I, 1–18)

The distinction drawn here appears to be intended as the foundation for everything else in *The Fall*.[21] Keats distinguishes between the poet on the one hand and, on the other, the fanatic, the savage, and the "man whose soul is not a clod" but who has not "been well nurtured in his mother tongue." These latter differ from the poet only in that they do not or cannot effectively tell their dreams, so their dreams die with them. The poet is like them in that he, too, dreams. But his melodious utterance lives on after his death. "Every man," Keats says, "hath visions and would speak"—if he could. The fanatic differs from "every man" and the savage in that he does speak. The fanatic can "weave/ A paradise for a sect." The poet, also, differs from the savage and "every man" in that he can speak; with his "fine *spell* of words" he escapes their "dumb enchantment." He differs from the fanatic in that he speaks better, and so escapes the "sable charm," achieves something precious not for a "sect" but for all men.[22]

All men, including poets, are dreamers. The poet alone can effectively tell his dreams. Hence the poet can be certainly recognized only after his death. If what he has told results only in "a paradise for a sect" he is to be identified as a fanatic. If his melodious utterance does more than delude a few, does more than create a fantasy world of escape, and bodies forth, instead, heretofore unrecognized truth, he is to be identified as a poet.

This differentiation is not possible until the Apollo of *Hyperion* has died into life. Until life has evolved to the point where it not only exists but is conscious of its existence, the problem of "dreaming" cannot arise. As long as we are unconscious of ourselves we cannot be mistaken about ourselves. But as soon as we attain self-consciousness we are open to self-misunderstanding and self-delusion.

That Keats was interested in this problem is implied, I believe, in his dramatic strategy of presenting his story as a vision within a vision within a dream. His first words after the introduction are: "Methought I stood where trees of every clime." He is "purpos'd to rehearse" a dream, and the suprareality of that dream is accentuated by its setting, an idyllic garden where, contrary to nature's practice, every species of tree flourishes. In this paradisial setting Keats drinks a "transparent juice" which he describes as "parent of my theme," because it induces a "swoon" from which he wakes, not in the garden, but in "an old sanctuary," an "eternal domed monument." There he encounters Moneta, who transports him, first, to "the shady sadness of a vale" where he can observe Saturn and Thea, because

> . . . there grew
> A power within me of enormous ken,
> To see as a God sees, and take the depth
> Of things as nimbly as the outward eye
> Can size and shape pervade,
> (I, 302–6)

and later to Hyperion's palace where he observes in the same god-like fashion.

By presenting inspired perceptions within a vision of which he dreamed, Keats makes his form functional, that is, representative of the nature and worth of that awareness which transcends ordinary observation and ordinary reason. The truth he seeks to establish, after all, is extraordinary. Ultimately it is the manner of the dream's presentation that must convince us of its substantive value, and Keats seems to want his literary dream, in one way at least, to be like an actual dream, in which style is literally substance. Dreams differ from waking thoughts in that form or manner of apparition is decisive in dreams. One can rephrase an argument but not a dream; a dream can recur only by repeating its form.

Keats also discusses dreamers with Moneta, and about that discussion have gathered most of the critical controversies concerning *The Fall of Hyperion*.[23] There is too little evidence for anyone to explain with assurance Keats's meaning and intentions, but I should like to suggest some ways in which my understanding of the direction of his thinking relates to the major problems of the poem. If we accept *The Fall* in the most nearly finished form Keats achieved, that is, with the twenty-three lines beginning "Majestic shadow, tell me" (the cancelled passage comprising lines 187–210 of Canto I) excised, Keats's argument is not inherently difficult, for it does not become fully engaged with the dreamer-poet distinction.[24] Keats asks by what right he has been allowed to attain the altar, and is told:

> . . . "Thou hast felt
> What 'tis to die and live again before
> Thy fated hour, . . .
>
> .   .   .   .
>
> None can usurp this height . . .
> But those to whom the miseries of the world
> Are misery, and will not let them rest.
> All else who find a haven in the world,
> Where they may thoughtless sleep away their days,
>
> .   .   .   .
>
> Rot on the pavement where thou rotted'st half."
> (I, 141–53)

Keats then asks why he is alone, since

> "Are there not thousands in the world . . .
>
> .   .   .   .
>
> Who love their fellows even to the death
> Who feel the giant agony of the world;
> And more, like slaves to poor humanity,
> Labour for mortal good?"
> (I, 154–59)

These humanitarians are like Keats in that the miseries of the world will not let them rest. They are, however, more than he:

> . . . "they are no dreamers weak,
> They seek no wonder but the human face,
> No music but a happy-noted voice—
> They come not here, they have no thought to come—
> And thou art here, for thou art less than they."
> (I, 162–66)

We may overestimate Keats's praise of busy do-gooders. He certainly credits them with virtue, but perhaps he subtly implies their limitations, too, by having Moneta—one must remember that her wisdom is not complete, for she is not a true Olympian but "the pale Omega of a wither'd race"—praise the humanitarians in terms which recall those "who find a haven in the world." The humanitarians find their satisfaction and fulfillment, their "haven," in the world. True, they "feel the giant agony" of the world, but in a fashion that might be meant to recall the giant agony of the Titans, who were unable in *Hyperion* to sustain the feeling, as Apollo could, of pain and joy together. If so, from one point of view Keats is indeed "less" than the humanitarians, as the Olympians give the impression of being physically less than the Titans in *Hyperion*, but from another point of view he is more: he can bear "more woe than all his sins deserve," and can be "admitted oft" to paradise-like gardens.

Then in a passage which Keats (according to his good friend and careful scribe Woodhouse) meant to strike from *The Fall*, the discussion is carried from the poet-humanitarian contrast to the poet-dreamer contrast. Keats proposes that poets are not "useless," that their "melodies" do good, though he does not yet claim himself to be such a poet, a "physician to all men." Moneta replies with the query: "Art thou not of the dreamer tribe?" And she asserts:

> "The poet and the dreamer are distinct,
> Diverse, sheer opposite, antipodes.
> The one pours out a balm upon the world,
> The other vexes it."
> (I, 199–202)

In the introductory lines Keats states plainly that the poet is a dreamer. The difference between poet and fanatic lies in the effectiveness of their expressions, but both tell their dreams. Possibly Moneta's distinction is meant to assist in refining the earlier definition. According to her the poet-dreamer pours out a balm upon the world while the fanatic-dreamer vexes it. Both, as it were, offer potions: that of the poet-dreamer heals, that of the fanatic-dreamer poisons.

At any rate, Moneta's words bring forth an angry exclamation from Keats, his first violent outburst:

> "Apollo! faded, farflown Apollo!
> Where is thy misty pestilence to creep
> Into the dwellings, thro' the door crannies,
> Of all mock lyrists, large self-worshippers,
> And careless Hectorers in proud bad verse."
> (I, 204–8)

This is the first mention of Apollo in *The Fall*, and, in keeping with the pattern of imagery introduced by the word "physician" at the opening of the cancelled passage, he is invoked, not as the god of poetry, but as the god of pestilence.[25] But Keats skillfully links the god's two functions: Apollo is called upon to destroy not dreamers but bad poets, "mock lyrists," and "careless Hectorers in proud bad verse." This returns us to the problem of Moneta's words. In the introduction Keats defines the fanatic as less than the poet but not as evil. Now he condemns those who tell their dreams without genuine poetic gifts as vexatious poisoners of the world. He who weaves "a paradise for a sect" is now identified as a "self-worshipper"—not a worshipper of Apollo's suprapersonal truth—who ought to be destroyed.

> "Tho' I breathe death with them it will be life
> To see them sprawl before me into graves."
> (I, 209–10)

It may be that the harmless fanatic is now seen to be the poisonous dreamer because Keats has reached the point where he is able to invoke Apollo; that is, he has passed the first tests of his initiation into genuine poethood. It is certain that this Apollo is not the new-born god of *Hyperion*. He is "faded" and "farflown." It appears to be the bad poets, the fanatic dreamers, who have exiled him. As remarked above, the effectiveness of a dream depends entirely upon its style. A badly told dream is a falsification, a distortion of the dream's truth. The "large self-worshippers" destroy the truth of Apollo, not because they dream, but because they recount their dreams badly. The poet recounts his dreams well and thus makes manifest the truth of his vision;[26] by his art he invokes Apollo the healer who "pours out a balm upon the world." Keats, not claiming to be a poet yet, is nonetheless dedicated to the "objective" truth of vision. Thus it will be "life" to him, even though he must personally suffer extinction in the process, to see the proud falsifiers of vision destroyed.

I do not wish to insist dogmatically on the correctness of this reading, and I propose it principally because it suggests that at the end of his career Keats may be reaffirming his faith in the truth expressed by Apollo's apotheosis in *Hyperion*. But if so Keats does not merely repeat his earlier celebration of evolutionary consciousness. He recognizes that increased consciousness leads inevitably beyond ordinary rationality to the exploration of the truth of dreams and visions.[27] And he recognizes that the best authentication of such visionary consciousness lies in the manner of its expression. The moral, then, would be that in the modern world the evil man is he who falsifies his dream or vision by telling it badly. This is no minor, aesthetic sin. It is blasphemy, the distortion of the highest truth. The genuine poet must be a good and useful man—"a sage, a humanist, a physician to all men"—for his well-told dream will embody the truth that surpasses the limited truth of sensory observation and rational discourse.[28] The dedicated poet expresses the one truth fully appropriate to modern man's capacity for conscious life.

Whatever the problems and uncertainties of *The Fall of Hyperion* may be, this faith in his art, this confidence in the worth of his poetry as something more than ornamental and entertaining sustains all Keats's finest work.[29] In this belief, moreover, Keats is typical of his era, not unique.[30] His contemporaries share his passionate conviction that in uttering beautifully their private visions they contribute to a better, a more fully human life for all men—that they in fact help to bring to birth the new life falsely promised by political revolutionists and social reformers, fanatic-dreamers who are not poets.[31]

IX ❧ THE GRACES OF CIVILITY

FOSCOLO: *The Graces*

THE GRACES, though not an "evolutionary" poem like *Hyperion*, celebrates a civilizing process, for Foscolo's poem develops a fundamental motif of *Jacopo Ortis*: men need principles for transmuting their violent, primitive passions into finer, more enduring emotions. We should not try to disavow our most basic impulses but instead should render them what Foscolo calls "modest" or "discreet." Foscolo does not wish us to attenuate our emotions nor to back away from sensory experience. On the contrary, he wishes us to recognize that only a civilized man is capable of experiencing the most intense sensations and powerful emotions.

To understand *The Graces* one needs to know something of its curious history. Foscolo first conceived the idea of the poem in 1803, that is, well before he began *The Sepulchres*, but after his main work on *Jacopo Ortis* and after writing his most famous odes and sonnets.[1] He labored at *The Graces* off and on for twenty years, his most concentrated effort coming in 1812–13, shortly before he exiled himself from Italy,[2] but he never completed the poem.

The Graces is not, however, unfinished in the sense that *Hyperion* is unfinished, nor can *The Graces* properly be called a fragmentary poem, for, as Barbi says, each apparently separable lyric part in fact contributes to a total and unified conception.[3] Yet Foscolo never found an organization for the poem which entirely satisfied him. The main structure is firm; not all of the parts fit perfectly into it. This failure in perfect fit probably kept Foscolo from publishing his most ambitious work. He printed only a few excerpts, and the poem as a whole was unknown until the middle of the nineteenth century. Then Orlandini, in the *Le Monnier* edition of Foscolo's works, published what he called *The Graces*, consisting of parts of the many verses Foscolo had collected under that title. What Orlandini published, unfortunately, falsified Foscolo's total plan and purpose, but for many years Orlandini's edition was the only authority for the poem. As a result a critical tradition became established, made almost irresistible by De Sanctis' concurring opinion, that *The Graces* was a failure, and that in laboring over the poem Foscolo had mistaken the true bent of his genius. "Poor Foscolo," said De Sanctis.[4]

Toward the end of the century more responsible editors than Orlandini turned their attention to *The Graces*. Chiarini and then Ferrari published texts that, whatever their limitations, reliably represented a substantial part of what Foscolo had written and went a long way toward reconstructing his order. These texts gradually transformed critical opinion of *The Graces*. By 1930 it was recognized as an important poem in its own right and as representative of a central tendency in Foscolo's genius, and today it is perhaps more admired than *The Sepulchres*, while Italian literary scholars are unanimous in asserting the supreme importance of *The Graces* in any comprehensive judgment of Foscolo and his era. Unfortunately, no definitive text has yet been established, and until this is done any general critique of the poem must be tentative.

Foscolo's introduction to *The Graces* speaks of the three hymns composing the poem as if they were a temple.

To the immortal Graces, the triplet daughters of Venus and the sisters of Love, the temple is sacred; born the day that Jove granted beauty, wisdom, and virtue to mortals, the goddesses serve to keep always enduring and always renewed those three celestial gifts, ever more modest as they are more praised. Enter and worship.[5]
(Introduction, ll. 1–9)

Throughout *The Graces* one art form is made to express itself through a sister form,[6] but there is no confusion and Foscolo's style is never "operatic." Singing, instrumental music, painting, sculpture, architecture, poetry, and the dance each makes its unique contribution to an ideal harmony of beauty, wisdom, and virtue which it is the purpose of *The Graces* as a whole to embody for our admiration and inspiration. The unity of *The Graces*, then, is created out of intricate diversity. The goddesses hymned are the graces of this life, not the grace of eternal life. They are the unified but diversified spirit of art, not in the narrow aesthetic sense but in the sense of civilization, the supranatural as opposed to the natural. They represent man's continual aspiration to achieve ever more intense and lasting beauty and wisdom and virtue.

In his invocation to the first hymn, to Venus, Foscolo prays to the Graces for the inspiration of their mysterious harmony so that he may depict their beauty. But his desire for the inner music which inspires beautiful figures is not an end in itself, is not the desire for mere self-expression. He wants his utterance to rejoice his country, Italy, afflicted by the tyranny of foreign oppressors. To Foscolo all true poetry is political poetry, because it inspires men to be free,[7] and in his earlier verse Foscolo's politics tend to be specific and more or less practical. In *The Graces* he absorbs the particular tragedy of early nineteenth-century Italy into a more metaphysical schema. He does not minimize Italian difficulties and he is as resolute an opponent of tyranny as ever, but he now sees his country's travail as one moment in man's perpetual struggle to be free, to be civilized, to be wholly human. Foscolo's withdrawal from direct political polemic is an inevitable distancing which accompanies the deepening of his philosophic vision.[8]

The first hymn tells of the birth of the Graces and of the early progress of mankind into civilization. The setting is the legendary land- and seascapes of prehistoric Greece. Foscolo's conception of mankind's earliest history derives from Vico, but in some important respects also contradicts Vico, since Foscolo sees human history as a single, unitary evolution: with the birth of the Graces civilization was born—a unique event, the most important in human history.

Before there were the Graces, man was ruled by instinct, competing with his fellow men as with animals for a place in the sun. Divinity was the power residing within natural phenomena: Jove personified lightning; Poseidon, earthquakes; Venus, the attraction of the sexes. As Foscolo says, these early gods kept themselves at a distance. They might have created some of earth's agonies; they did not further participate in the world. Knowledge of these gods scarcely constituted religious experience. At last Venus took pity on man and appeared one day out of the waves of the Ionian sea surrounded by the Graces, who brought to man an understanding of civility—in love, in religion, and in social intercourse. And the several arts were taught to man by the Graces to preserve civility.[9]

An understanding of art is inseparable from an awareness of its artifice, its envisioned and created qualities which distinguish it from that which is purely natural. The heightened consciousness and sensibility demanded by art is central to Foscolo's conception of what constitutes civilization. The scheme of his conception may be summarized as follows: Venus, to whom the first hymn of *The Graces* is dedicated, is the spirit, the interior force, of the natural universe; it is she who brings the Graces to mankind. In other words, the arts and graces of civilized life arise in nature, for Venus is love and the sexual urge, she comes to man from the sea, from the very heart and womb of the natural world. In his vision of humane man Foscolo equates the growth of sexual attraction into transforming love—Venus—with the growth of the arts and civilities of society —the Graces. The parallel clarifies his conception of civilization emerging once for all time in human history. Many biologists today believe that the emergence of vital force from inert matter—the beginning of life—was a single and unique event. This accomplished, diversification and spread followed as irreversible and inevitable consequences of the original, unitary impulse. What biologists postulate as the history of living matter, Foscolo postulates as the history of civilization. His faith and belief are that once love and art and civility are experienced there can be no turning back to primitiveness, that the elaboration of civilization becomes inevitable.

Thus Foscolo can be at the same time historical, tracing the progress of civilization from Greece to Rome to Renaissance Italy, and suprahistorical, portraying what the direction and goal of civilization's evolution will be.[10] He sees civilization as a succession of discrete historical phenomena, and, simultaneously, as a single, unitary impulse or aspiration. Hence the arts are the supreme expression of civilization. Each work of art is a unique historical representative of the ideal, achieved through the artist's skilled, civilized handling of finite sensory particularities, which constitutes a creation transcending the temporal and the material.[11]

The second hymn of *The Graces*, to Vesta, who represents the crafts and skills of civil life, celebrates the transfer of the center of civilization from Greece to Italy, with special attention to the achievement of Italian poets from Dante to Tasso, concluding with verses complimentary to the wife of a Milanese leader of Foscolo's own day. Thus the subject of the first hymn is prehistory and the appearance of the Graces, and the subject of the second is human history up to the moment of writing. The third hymn carries us out of history to a metaphysical realm. This last hymn, to Minerva, who represents wisdom and spiritual tranquillity, while more idealized and philosophical than its predecessors, is at the same time more personal and more specific.[12] Here Foscolo is free to give full play to his projection of what the Graces might accomplish; hence the idealizations of the third hymn are not abstractions but concrete embodiments of his supranatural aspirations.

In his exordium of the final hymn, Foscolo prays for inspiration from the art of Amphion (with whom he associated the Homeric hymns), Pindar, and Catullus: "Sacred poets, give me your art, to me the spirit of your languages, and following in the Tuscan mode I shall more burningly embellish the celebrated stories." Only Foscolo's "mode" is new; his subject matter is old. Old and diverse materials shaped into an original unity of form, this is the essence of his poetry. The "celebrated stories" are in fact the spirit of the older poets speaking to him from the sepulchre of the past, "illuminating with Elysian light the lonely fields where wandering Imagination led me to discern the truth." No passage in *The Graces* better illustrates the way in which Foscolo transforms the Neoclassic ideal of imitation of the ancients into a new ideal of inspiration from the ancients.[13] Imagination is the key to this transformation. Imagination it is which enables the poet to create the new out of the old, to reanimate the spirit which binds all men in a union of diversities, and to annihilate the time and space barriers of the natural world.

The third hymn opens with the flight of the Graces to Minerva, when they are frightened by the fierce delirium of the god of Love. Minerva comforts them and promises to protect them, which she does by having a veil woven for them on the lost continent of Atlantis. But the story of Tiresias, who saw Athena bathing and was punished by blindness, intervenes before the description of the weaving of the veil. The story is apparently a fragment of what Foscolo intended as a long section describing the journey of the Graces to Atlantis. But the point of the Tiresias story is plain: "Alas, man may not see celestial beauty without tears." One recalls *The Fall of Hyperion*. Keats and Foscolo each knew the cost of imaginative vision: increased knowledge of man's littleness and vulnerability. We misunderstand these poets if we fail to recognize that their aspiration is inseparable from their humility.[14]

The climax of the third hymn is the weaving of the veil for the Graces, which takes place on Atlantis, an island

in the midst of the ocean where the earth curves nearest to the stars; an immense land, according to antique lore, once the blessed nurse of immortal harvests and immortal men. In vain today the navigator searches the waves for it, now steering by our stars, now by those of the Southern hemisphere; if, deceived by desire, he sees its mountains whiten in the distance, he begs the winds to hasten him and by ancient report calls it Atlantis. (III, 85–94)

Here Minerva rules the minor deities, who are instructed by her in every gracious art; here are "chaste dances and pure songs, the flowers undecaying, the lawns green, the day always golden, and clear and starry the nights." Minerva calls the goddesses around her, and together they weave the magic veil promised to the shy Graces. Iris rains iridescent colors from the winds of heaven which Flora figures into new shapes on the cloth as it is woven, the warp controlled by naked Hours and the woof by the purple-robed Fates. Psyche combs the cloth, sadly murmuring, "Alas, how many joys Love promised and left only grief," while, to cheer her, Thalia plays the lyre, Terpsichore circles in dance around the work, and Erato's song keeps pace with Flora's embroidering needle.

What she embroiders on the veil are archetypal scenes of human life. First, "ardent Youth, singing and dancing amidst the chorus of her hopes: Time strikes with rapid touches his ancient lyre, and the dancer descends the slope none reascends." This first scene, like the later ones embroidered on the veil, follows a pattern which begins with the picturing of an idealized state, is penetrated by the sorrows of actual life, but concludes with a reaffirmation of the vitality of the ideal. Thus the first episode concludes: "The Graces wake flowers at her feet to adorn her garlands; and when your blond locks shall have vanished, and your name is lost, those flowers shall live, O Youth, and they shall breathe fragrance around the funeral urn." This reiterates the theme of *The Sepulchres* in condensed and idealized form.

Next Flora depicts the shy joy and beauty of conjugal love. Then, in one of the most complexly moving passages of the poem, we are shown compassion arising in a soldier on guard at a prison, who dreams of his parents, at home far away praying for him. He awakes and sees his prisoners, and sighs.[15] Next appears a festal banquet,

where "Hospitality presents the cups of honor to exiles." Here candid
Praise and merry Criticism reign, while to one side "beautiful Silence
sits, discreet of countenance." A different quiet dominates the final
scene, which portrays maternal tenderness.

A mother keeps single vigil amid darkness and silences, nourishing a lamp by
the cradle, fearing that the cries of her first child may foretell death; and in
that delusion she sends up to all the gods of heaven her lament. Blessed! still
not to know how fortunate for children the eternal sleep, and that those cries
foretell a life of sorrow.
(III, 188–96)

The veil completed, Hebe drenches it in ambrosia, making it
eternal, and the Graces are clothed in it, "untouched amidst the
flames of love, they go to rejoice the earth; and thus veiled the virgins
appear naked as before." The image of veiled nakedness is dear to
Foscolo, and the image of the magic veil is to be found in the poetry
of many of his contemporaries. But it is what Foscolo expresses by
means of the veil of the Graces, not his use of a characteristic conceit,
that matters.

The veil of the Graces is imaginative creation. Depicting reality, it
celebrates ideal loveliness. Protecting, preserving, itself figured with
designs, it is yet transparent, revealing in all its inherent beauty the
naked truth which it enfolds. The veil is woven of the stuff of dream
and illusion and vision, but its insubstantial fabric is immortal, preserving as perpetual inspiration the beauty of life's inner vitality. So
the veil, itself a creation of art, keeps free and effective the joyful
inspirers of all the arts of civilized life, the Graces, who are the
"daughters of Venus and the sisters of Love." Art cannot be dis-
associated from love, and love is a divine gift, a creative force. It is
found in the sexual urge and the attraction to physical beauty, but
it may surpass its beginnings, its goal being supranatural beauty and
supranatural truth. This truth, like beauty, has its beginnings as
physical truth, truth in nature. Through love this simple truth becomes "spiritualized," a process which is not outside nature but
within nature, and supranatural truth, like supranatural beauty, is
the fulfillment of natural truth, a fulfillment which transcends its
origin.

The Graces descend, clothed in their magic veil, upon poet, painter,
and sculptor to inspire and illuminate them. But then,

The veil of the Goddesses suddenly sends forth a sound, like that of a distant harp, running softly on the wings of Zephyr; as an unknown harmony came among the islets from the Aegean, when the delirious Bacchantes tied to the severed head and fair hair of Orpheus the wonderful lyre, hurling it into the waves; and, sighing with nearby Ionia, the sacred Aegean sustained that harmony, and the islets, astonished, heard it, and the continents.
(III, 231–41)

This sound is produced by the veil itself, not by the Graces whom it enfolds. To Foscolo the veil possesses autonomous "intermediate" reality and vitality. Between the divine being of the Graces and the natural being of the artist floats the insubstantial but eternal harmony of art. The gods inspire man to make art, but its more-than-mortal beauty is man's creation. It is not accident that what Flora embroiders on the veil are scenes of ordinary human life, because art is natural reality made divine by human vision. The Bacchantes destroy Orpheus, but his song, sustained by the life of nature which he brought to intense fulfillment, lives on to touch with wonder the earth from which it emerged and which it now makes more beautiful, more delightful, more fit for creatures who may aspire to more than natural existence.

It may be illuminating to trace the process by which Foscolo arrives at his celebration of art. Let us look first at one of the most famous passages in *The Graces*.

> I from my hill
> When the winds fall silent among the towers
> Of lovely Firenze hear a Pan,
> A guest unknown to the silent eremites
> Of nearby Olivet: he at noon
> Makes a thicket his home, and with a reed's sound
> Calls his sheep to the spring.
> He calls two dark girls in the evening,
> Nor do they seem to me to bend the grass dancing.
> He guides the dance.
> (II, 395–404)

In this passage in the second hymn Foscolo is turning from praise of Dante and Petrarch to Boccaccio. His transition, as so often in *The Graces*, is simultaneously abrupt and indirect. The lines above seem not to emerge out of those immediately preceding, and only in succeeding lines do we discover that Foscolo is characterizing Boccaccio's art by means of the "nymphs" with whom Boccaccio peopled the hills and valleys surrounding Florence.

The enchantment of the passage, so rightfully admired by Italian critics,[16] is appropriate to its mood, which is that of the entrancement of the hot stillness of a Mediterranean noon. And the sight of Pan is a magical experience. Yet within the magic lies historical actuality: the modern poet narrates the appearance of a primitive classical deity in surroundings which recall the Christian Middle Ages and the Renaissance.

The key to the passage is the first person narration: "*I* from *my* hill." The movement of the lines is away from the strong awareness of personal identity and "possession" to a more complex awareness: "nor do they seem to me." Self-awareness is not obliterated; this remains an intensely personal experience, not shared, for example, by the hermits. But what is at first only personal is enlarged to the suprapersonal. At the same time the poet's, and the reader's, attention is narrowed and concentrated. At the conclusion Florence and Olivet have faded and we and the poet see only the dancers. Our sense of place diminishes as the vision of the dancers sharpens. Music and dance blend; there is no color, only the purposely vague *dark*; all is mystery, movement, and the "unheard melody" of ancient panpipes.

The conception from which the passage emerged occurs in the letter of September 8 in the 1798 version of *Jacopo Ortis*. Jacopo there tells how, out walking early one morning,

I saw five little springs that hurried to unite in a clear lake. How fresh were those waters shaded by dense willows . . . agitated by the continuous cascades of the springs. I wanted to undress and plunge into the pond that seemed to welcome me voluptuously. My heart sang a hymn to nature, and my fantasy deceived itself invoking the nymphs who are the amiable guardians of the springs. *Illusions,* cries the philosopher. And is not all illusion? All! Blessed the ancients who believed themselves worthy of the kisses of Venus, who worshipped beauty and the graces, who diffused the splendor of divinity through the imperfections of man, and who found the beautiful and the true by cherishing the idols of their imagination. The Greek and Roman religion educated artists and heroes, and to this we owe the masterpieces fate has snatched from the hostility of the centuries. Thus I reflected while splashing in the water. . . . I returned to pass the rest of the morning in company with my Plutarch.

Here illusion is negative. The writer permits himself to toy with a fancy because he finds the world and his life tedious and useless. The praise of ancient religion is conventional, the retreat to Plutarch an escape. And this first Jacopo is a rather simple youth: the water is inviting, he bathes, and while splashing he idly considers that the ancients were not foolish. The tone reinforces the triviality of the episode.

That it was not trivial to Foscolo is apparent when we read it in the light of the passage from the Graces. But long before he began *Io dal mio poggio* he had reshaped the episode. In the 1802 version of *Jacopo Ortis* it no longer appears in the introduction but much later, after the episode of the kiss. Not surprisingly, the tone is significantly altered.

After that kiss I have become divine. My ideas are more sublime and smiling, my appearance gayer, my heart more compassionate. Everything appears more beautiful to my gaze, the complaints of the little birds, the whispering of the breezes among the leaves are today softer than ever; the plants grow more fertile, the flowers at my feet take on color; I shall no longer flee mankind; all nature seems to be mine. My soul is all beauty and harmony. If I could paint or sculpture that beauty I would disdain all earthly models and find them instead in my imagination. O love, the fine arts are your children; you first brought sacred poetry to the earth, the only nourishment of generous souls who can transmit from their solitude their superhuman songs to distant generations, spurring them with words and thoughts of godly inspiration to the highest ideals; you refire in our breasts the single virtue useful to mortals, that piety which sometimes brings smiles to the lips of the unhappy condemned to sighs; and always through you revives the fruitful pleasure without which all would be chaos and death.

Deliciously enraptured I see before me naked nymphs, dancing, garlanded with roses, and in their company I invoke the muses and love; and beyond the banks where cascades sound and spume I see the rising bosoms, the shining hair tangled over shimmering shoulders and the laughing eyes of Naiads, amiable guardians of fountains. *Illusions!* cries the philosopher: and is not all illusion? All! Blessed the ancients who believed themselves worthy of immortal goddesses' kisses, who sacrificed to beauty and to the graces, who diffused the splendor of their divinity through the imperfections of men, and who discovered BEAUTY and TRUTH by cherishing the idols of their imagination. *Illusions!* but meanwhile without these I should feel life only in sorrow, or what frightens me more, only in a rigid and weary passivity; and when this heart shall feel no longer, I will tear it from my breast with my own hands, and fling it away like an unfaithful servant.

The passage adumbrates much of the essential spirit of *The Graces* and makes a much more positive affirmation of the value of art than does the 1798 version. Jacopo has dropped his conventional sophistication and become almost a poet. He is now less literal, yet his vision is supported by the naturalism of his account. Vision is becoming actuality: "I see before me." The equivalent passage from *The Graces*, however, is superior because in it symbolization is complete: the poetry *is* what it is about. Between the prose and the verse it is the verse which is objective, clear, and concentrated. The prose is somewhat strained; Jacopo insists on the strength of his feelings and the truth of his vision, but in *The Graces* there is no insistence, there is neither description nor comment. The poet simply narrates his vision. Our feelings are aroused, as they are not in the novel, because Foscolo no longer insists or argues; like Keats in *To Autumn* he states the facts. But—and this is the point we must not lose sight of—his "facts" are of personal, visionary experience. His objectivity enables us to share what is subjective and creative. If one wishes to use the conventional terminology of literary history, one has to say, I suppose, that the progress of Foscolo's art is toward a more "classical" manner of expressing an ever less "classical" matter.

Let us look now at part of an early draft of the poetic passage.

> I see supple nymphs descending
> Through the woods of Fiesole in the evening
> To dance on the lawn and to bathe themselves
> All naked in the river . . .[17]

In the final version these four lines become three words, "two dark girls." Foscolo completes the transformation by bringing in Pan, who objectifies art within the vision of the poet. In the draft "supple nymphs" come down "to dance"; in the final version two dark girls move in formal beauty to the music of the pipes of Pan. The vision has become expressive form, emotionalized design, self-sustaining energy and harmony.

Possibly we tend to forget today that Pan is a god,[18] that insofar as he embodies "natural forces" he endows them with beauty, immortality, divinity. The poet's experience is not of something natural but of something supranatural.[19] In *Jacopo Ortis* we feel that Jacopo has projected into a natural scene figures derived from classical art and religion, but in *The Graces* we feel that Pan and the two dark girls are actually present. They are no longer erudite memories but living figures. They seem "real" and "lifelike" because they no longer represent, as they do in the novel, the "spirit" of the natural scene, the mood of the situation. Rather they express what the poet becomes when his imagination reshapes his natural environment. They embody the active power of the mind *creating experience.*

Going on now to another passage in the second hymn, we find a different expression of Foscolo's belief in the creative, shaping power of the imagination.

Already with her foot and finger and searching genius, and with her eyes intent upon the strings, she, inspired, calls forth the notes that paint how harmony gave motion to the stars, the sea of air, and to the earth coming forth from the ocean, and how it shattered the uniform creation into thousands of aspects of light and shade and reunited them in one, and gave sounds to the wind and colors to the sun, and changingly continuous purpose to restless fortune and to time; so that together dissonant things might express the union of divine harmony and lift minds beyond earth. As when the wind Eurus at dawn merrily stirs the quiet of Lake Como, and the helmsman sings to that rustling, and nearby lutes rejoice, and the flute softly laments for love-sick youths and nymphs in wandering gondolas; and from the banks the shepherd answers with his pipe; from the hills' depth resound horns that terrify the deer, while, rhythmically from Lecco, the hammer, mastering bronze, thunders from fiery caverns; astonished, the fisherman lets fall his net, and listens. So does the harp's harmony wander through our long valley; and while the player pauses, the hills still listen.
(II, 107–35)

This passage is perhaps most remarkable for what it is not. As Luigi Russo says, "Notwithstanding the lutes, and the soft flute and the bagpipe of the shepherd and afterwards the horns of the hunters, this landscape evoked by Foscolo is in no way arcadian or romantically conventional."[20] Russo is right, yet Foscolo's presentation is nothing if not literary. As Russo says later in the note from which I have just quoted, "Virgil and Poliziano and Tasso are within this passage, but its soul is new and modern." Perhaps we can define in what way the "soul" of the passage "is new and modern," in what way Foscolo's treatment of his subject is like that of his contemporaries and different from that of his predecessors. First, the "picture" of the lake scene is painted with sounds, and sounds as compared to sights are fleeting.[21] Our vivid sense of the scene's timelessness is in fact created by the unity of many details of transitory sensations. The artistry of Foscolo is to harmonize into archetypal unity a variety of evanescent impressions, and his contemporaries, too, order unique

ideas, images, and experiences into wholes which are generic and
archetypal. What Fubini says of Foscolo's poetry—"it comes to a
climax in the creation of a myth which the poet has borne within
himself all his life"[22]—could be applied to most early nineteenth-
century poets.

But the scene at Como is only a part of the whole passage, which
evokes the music of a harp. To understand the whole passage we
must turn back to the description in *Jacopo Ortis* of Teresa playing
the harp. In the prose Jacopo says "all, all was harmony," but harmony is not dramatized. In the poetry the scene is the embodiment
of harmony and is symbolic in the Coleridgean sense of partaking
"of the reality which it renders intelligible." While enunciating the
whole, the scene "abides itself as a living part in that unity of which
it is the representative." The poetry is sensually more concrete than
the prose, yet at the same time more abstract; that is, the poetry
extends the particular insight of the passage in the novel to a vision
of the universal order of all experience. In the novel the central
insight is limited by the actual circumstances of the event. In the
poetry there is less superficial naturalism, since the descriptive details
are also literary allusions, which are valuable not for their allusive-
ness but for the support they give to the poet's shaping of the natural
world. Foscolo does not surrender his belief in the supreme worth
of personal experience; he asserts with increased dramatic effectiveness that in artifice—what man makes of his environment—not in
the natural world per se is to be found the most intense and significant *human* experience.

The scene at Como is plainly marked off ("as when") as an
extended simile, but one does not, I think, feel it to be separate from
what has gone before. It impresses one as part of the universal harmony hymned before, precisely because it does not conceal its artifice
or pretend to be naturalistic. It is less a natural description than an
ekphrasis,[23] the elaborated description of a work of art. It is not so
much a view of Lake Como as an original recombination of what
other artists, "Virgil and Poliziano and Tasso" and Homer and
Catullus, too, have made of similar natural scenes. The harmony
which rules man's world is nature-into-art, what the human imagination has made and can make of nature.

Foscolo locates essential harmony in the inner dynamics of phenomena, and he believes man should use his imagination to penetrate

material appearances. Foscolo does not ask us to reject nature, for he returns us from the *ekphrasis* to actual nature: "so does the harp's symphony wander through our hollow vale; and while the player rests, the hills still listen." Thus by discovering the intensified life within nature man's imagination endows the natural world with enhanced beauty and preciousness.

The harpist "calls forth" notes that depict how harmony "*gave motion* to the stars . . . and to the earth *coming forth* from the ocean." This harmony of birth and motion is not the mere mechanism of biological existence. Harmony "shattered the uniform creation into a thousand aspects of light and shade and reunited them into one . . . so that dissonant things together might express the union of divine harmony and lift minds beyond earth." It is this process which the artist reënacts when he creates. As Coleridge said, he "dissolves, diffuses, dissipates, in order to recreate." The artist does not escape from his personal experience, but he shapes that experience: he does not simply undergo it. His power so to shape is supported by the shaping experiences of other men, but with literary tradition as with nature, the artist must make for himself. He must not repeat, imitate others, but must refashion their work into a new synthesis, and in so doing he will extend and invigorate conscious, artificial, civilized life. The Graces are the spirit of civilization, and they may penetrate and illuminate even our most intimate experiences if we invoke them by exercising that creative power which enables us to be, if something less than divinities, something more than natural creatures.

X ↷ REVIEW AND CONCLUSION

WORDSWORTH: *Intimations of Immortality*

A REVIEW of some points made in this study may fittingly be organized around a commentary on a single poem—Wordsworth's *Immortality* ode—since I have used this method throughout earlier chapters. The method seems appropriate to the character of early nineteenth-century literature, in which the uniqueness of each work is evidence of its participation in a new style. I have tried to capitalize on this circumstance, working inductively and selectively to present an unusual and illuminating perspective of early nineteenth-century literature. The following discussion of the *Immortality* ode, therefore, aims not merely to review previous judgments but also to dramatize the value of seeing a well-known work from a new viewpoint. I shall not, then, so much offer a new interpretation of a much-interpreted poem as try to convey something of the pleasure and understanding I have gained from studying this landmark of English literature in relation to other works by Wordsworth, Foscolo, Keats, and Leopardi.

The *Immortality* ode, like *The Prelude* and *Jacopo Ortis*, arises from a practical crisis in the artist's life. But the ode is not politically inspired; the crisis it speaks of is at once more personal and more universal than the French Revolution. The ode used to be described as Wordsworth's lament for his failing poetic power. Lionel Trilling,[1] however, has argued persuasively against reading the poem simply as a lament, and Gilbert Highet, in a less celebrated essay, has argued as persuasively that the greatness of the ode lies in its expression of the anxieties and discouragements which occur to most men in their early and middle thirties.[2] Wordsworth does regret a loss of visionary power, and, since he regarded himself as above all else a poet, he must regret the loss of poetic strength. But Wordsworth believed that a poet speaks to men profoundly and humanly. If this is so, the poet's crisis should be relevant and important to other men.

168

The ode is like *The Prelude* and *Jacopo Ortis* in that its autobiographical content is not an end in itself. The ode is not mere self-expression. It passes through the personal to reveal a pattern of all human experience, and this surely is the foundation of the poem's appeal. The opening stanza speaks so directly to what we all know that we almost forget its first-person form.

> There was a time when meadow, grove and stream,
>   The earth, and every common sight
>   To me did seem
>   Apparelled in celestial light,
> The glory and the freshness of a dream.
> It is not now as it hath been of yore;—
>   Turn wheresoe'er I may,
>   By night or day,
> The things which I have seen I now can see no more.

The ode is also like *Jacopo Ortis* and *The Prelude* and *The Broom* in affirming that through loss and suffering we learn to value the spirit of humanity which binds us to our kind. We learn not merely through rational comprehension but through intense sensual-spiritual experience; so, like the longer works, the ode suggests an appropriate pattern for all human life, from youth to maturity, which will do justice to the necessarily changing relationship between man and the natural world. The key to this pattern is the poet's desire to be a creative participant in the vital energy which seems to him both to animate and to order every part of the universe.

> I hear the Echoes through the mountains throng,
> The Winds come to me from the fields of sleep,
>   And all the earth is gay;
>   Land and sea
>   Give themselves up to jollity,
>   And with the heart of May
>   Doth every Beast keep holiday.
> (ll. 27–33)

The ode springs from the fundamental motive which makes Wordsworth, Foscolo, Leopardi, and Keats the poets they are—the desire to contribute actively to the harmony they regard as the central principle of life.[3] So to contribute is a poet's—a man's—supreme achievement, and any doubt of this capacity is specially unnerving.

> Ye blessèd Creatures, I have heard the call
>   Ye to each other make; I see
> The heavens laugh with you in your jubilee;
>   My heart is at your festival,
>   My head hath its coronal,
> The fulness of your bliss, I feel—I feel it all.
>   (ll. 36–41)

The uneasiness implied by the insistence of these lines—especially by the repetition in the last—springs from doubt of self, and awareness of a possible psychic insufficiency. Typically, there is no external threat; on the contrary, the world around the poet is unselfconsciously happy. Recovery, renewed confidence, must be achieved by the poet himself, alone. He must save himself by discovering a new way of seeing and feeling which will not be an escape but a penetration into a more intense reality.

Hence the unique form of the ode also marks it as typical of its time, when poets dramatized the essentially human in poems of personal experience. Nor is it surprising to find in the *Immortality* ode the same mixing of the simple and experiential with the complex and the literary which we have observed in many lyrics. The ode is artistically wrought and it utilizes traditional imagery and allusions, yet its form is original and irregular and it never departs from specific sights and sounds and particularized feelings experienced by William Wordsworth. In no other poem, perhaps, is Wordsworth more successful in translating the traditional into the personal, and so permitting us to see and to feel commmonplace and conventional sights and emotions with renewed sharpness and poignancy.

> The Rainbow comes and goes,
> And lovely is the Rose,
> The Moon doth with delight
> Look round her when the heavens are bare,
> Waters on a starry night
> Are beautiful and fair;
>   The sunshine is a glorious birth;
>   But yet I know, where'er I go,
> That there hath past away a glory from the earth.
>   (ll. 10–18)

The transformation of the conventional into the original is the source of much of our poets' complexity. Their subject matter is often commonplace. That is, the scenes they describe, the events they narrate, the emotions they evoke, the ideas they consider tend to be familiar scenes, events, emotions, and ideas. Keats is not the first poet to speak of the pleasures of melancholy, nor is Foscolo the first to contemplate tombs. Leopardi viewing the ruins of past civilizations and Wordsworth surveying his vanished youth are engaged in conventional poetic occupations. But the poets bring to bear on the commonplace intensely personal imaginative power, so their poems reveal the mysterious energy which exists latently within the ordinary and the familiar. The *Immortality* ode, specifically, illuminates the special human potency concealed within the processes of natural decline, biological loss.

The ode combines intellectual questioning, sensory evocation, and emotional conflict into an imaginative representation of the first principles of human growth and development. Hence the ode includes one of Plato's most compelling myths, imagery derived from St. Augustine (see ll. 162–68), reminiscences of Wordsworth's particular, idiosyncratic experiences as a youth (see ll. 142–46 and Wordsworth's comment on them in his Fenwick note), and imagery drawn from specific, personal observations. In the ode, then, as in so many of the poems already discussed, we are made to feel in a variety of dimensions the individual man's lonely littleness simultaneously with an increased awareness of the potential grandeur and extended community open to him by virtue of his imagination. The ode is another expression of our concurrent strength and weakness as creatures both naturally and supranaturally endowed: it is "the *meanest* flower that blows" which brings "thoughts that do often lie too deep for tears," that is, beyond natural sorrow.

The ode is not crudely optimistic, yet—again typically—it is affirmative. It says that man is eroded and frustrated by natural processes but that he may conquer the merely natural and physical, albeit at the cost of suffering and tragedy, and that the inner human potency is adequate so to shape experience as to attain to a supranatural, suprapersonal mode of being. Hence the poem is visionary, though it is a vision of this world humanly transfigured.

> The Clouds that gather round the setting sun
> Do take a sober colouring from an eye
> That hath kept watch o'er man's mortality.
> (ll. 197–99)

It is appropriate for Wordsworth to turn to Plato's myth, which so powerfully expresses one of mankind's most consistent aspirations, because he strives through self-analysis and self-assertion to create a new and organic, not a conventional and mechanical, relation between the individual and the traditions of his civilization. Wordsworth does not passively accept Plato's myth, he reworks it for his own purpose, forces it into active combination with his private experience. He mythicizes his experience in itself by dramatizing its "total relatedness," its relationship not only to the processes of the natural world but also to the processes of the developing human imagination. The ode is a new, secular myth—Plato's "notion" is usable because it has "sufficient foundation in *humanity*," says Wordsworth[4]—which expresses an advance in man's consciousness of his special function: the continual discovery and creation of new reality.

The relation of the *Immortality* ode to the odes of the seventeenth and eighteenth centuries, therefore, is rather like that of *Tintern Abbey* to earlier topographical poetry. Both of Wordsworth's poems derive from the respective traditions but creatively transform them. *Tintern Abbey*, like Leopardi's *The Infinite*, is immediately impressive because the method by which the change is accomplished—the temporalization of space I have called it—is the central action of the poem. The *Immortality* ode illustrates the connection between "threshold" poems such as *Tintern Abbey* and *The Infinite* and Leopardi's later idylls, Keats's great odes, and Foscolo's *The Graces*, wherein we are not shown the process by which space and time are united but are at once and throughout presented with their unification.

In the *Immortality* ode Wordsworth conveys an impression of the natural world as timeless and unchanging. Meaningful change occurs only within man and through the exercise of his imagination. So the ode is concerned with the development of the poet's mind; the mode once more is that of memory. The older man does not despair, because he remembers, recreates the significance of his youthful experience. And youth is enlightened by the activating memory of pre-existence—which is to Wordsworth, I believe, less Plato's pre-existence than the earliest expression of man's inborn shaping spirit, his inherent capacity to participate in something other than purely natural life.

Thanks to the human heart by which we live,
Thanks to its tenderness, its joys, and fears,
To me the meanest flower that blows can give
Thoughts that do often lie too deep for tears.
(ll. 201–4)

Yet, as the strength found in a memory of a memory itself suggests, the ode is not simply optimistic: what it celebrates lies on the far side of tragedy. The core of Wordsworth's experience is the problematic character of man's being. The "thoughts that do often lie too deep for tears" are, indeed, precisely the thoughts which our four poets most often enshrine in their secular myths. For they celebrate the possibility of mankind's advance into a new realm, the realm of fully conscious life.

What I have called their "humanism" is a humanism of intensely developed awareness. The *Immortality* ode is a representation in miniature of man's life, as are Leopardi's idylls. But, like Leopardi's poems and Foscolo's *The Graces* and Keats's *Hyperion*, the ode does not merely report what our life is but also envisions what it might be, what its possibilities are. Most of the poems discussed in this book are poems of vision where regularly "The Winds come . . . from the fields of sleep" and we often move "about in worlds not realized." The "recovery" dramatized by the ode is founded on Wordsworth's understanding that in man alone exists the power to make effective the mysterious interior energy of life. This makes possible a mature, creative participation in nature,

I love the Brooks which down their channels fret,
Even more than when I tripped lightly as they,
(ll. 193–94)

and the ideal of a humanized existence not without pain but not confined within the mechanism of physical and biological processes:

We will grieve not, rather find
Strength in what remains behind;
In the primal sympathy
Which having been must ever be;
In the soothing thoughts that spring
Out of human suffering;
In the faith that looks through death,
In years that bring the philosophic mind.
(ll. 180–87)

The *Immortality* ode, then, illustrates how often we encounter in the work of our poets the same underlying pattern. Their poems celebrate conscious life, a life of full awareness, a life available to no living creature but man, yet not detached from the processes of nature. It is life at its most essential and intense, life at its highest potential of vitalness. Such life does not escape sorrow and evil, but it does provide a kind of immortality through creative, individual contributions to the extension of civilization. So these poets must in part look back. They validate their faith in a specifically human life by proving that civilizational work of earlier men, above all their art, still lives. They glorify poetry and assert its organically paradoxical nature. Poetry is the most intense and enduring expression of humane, civilized life. Mediating dynamically between the natural and the supranatural, between envisioned ideals and intractable reality, poetry embodies man's aspiration to experience as an individual that which is suprapersonal and through this embodiment to endow with preciousness all in the existent cosmos which otherwise must be alien, hostile, meaningless.

I am led to the conclusion, then, that the play of forces which creates the special character of early nineteenth-century literature is more intricate than has sometimes been suggested. Examination of the four poets together suggests that there exists what I should like to call a "Mediterranean" impulse in early nineteenth-century poetry. The Mediterranean (as opposed to a "Germanic") impulse is toward form (new and dynamic form, to be sure) rather than toward fragmentariness, toward Hellenic rather than Medieval ideals, toward the ode and idyll rather than the ballad, toward meaning rather than melody, toward increased civility rather than a return to the primitive, toward spiritual democracy rather than self-assertive anarchy, toward intuitions of the bright clarity of Apollo rather than the misty weirdness of Wotan.[5]

By no means do I wish to deny the "Germanic" side of poetry of this era. Indeed, my point is that if we are to understand the style of early nineteenth-century literature, we must give full weight to *both* of two opposed forces whose interaction defines it. I have tried here to characterize the one of these forces which appears to have been somewhat underestimated. We have too often forgotten, I believe, that early nineteenth-century poets are at least as much concerned with articulating a new understanding of the proper relation of the individual to the world of *civilization* as with articulating a new understanding of the proper relation of the individual to the *natural* world.

This leads to an interesting, though admittedly speculative, conclusion. At the beginning of the nineteenth century, Europe became simultaneously more separatist and diverse (nationalism, for example) and more unified (improved transportation and communication, for example). The poetry studied in this book appears to prophesy the ultimate meaning of this double movement which, it seems plain today, leads in the direction of a single, worldwide culture. This poetry suggests that within the single culture a new, more specialized diversity may develop—just as the domination of biological life by a single species, man, permitted a new, specialized kind of diversity, cultural diversity, to appear on earth.

Wordsworth's, Foscolo's, Keats's, and Leopardi's poems are as diverse as they are similar. The likenesses I have suggested are not misleading, yet the uniqueness of each poet's art within the patterns of similitude must not be underestimated. We see in the first years of the nineteenth century, then, not merely a change from one style to another, but instead the emergence of a new kind of literary style.

Before the end of the eighteenth century a literary style, any style, was a pattern of relatively simple coherence. More contemporary styles possess more complex coherence. The individual artist of the last two centuries is less directly controlled by a suprapersonal pattern. He chooses more freely than his predecessors, hence the pattern which he helps to establish is more intricate and fluid. It is a different kind of pattern from that of earlier styles because its organizing principle is different. The older style might be compared to the constellations of the night sky, where we see the bear or the scorpion composed of stars of diverse magnitudes and colors and in diverse spatial relations to one another but all of them lights, all of them similar elements. The modern style might be compared to the pattern on the earth which we see from an airplane. This view, even from great heights, is not fixed. Its shifting aspect, caused by the movement of the plane, symbolizes, as it were, the more subtle movements within the scene which are, though literally invisible, essential to its character. For it is a scene of mountains and rivers but also of fields and cities and highways. Here elements differ in kind as well as degree and one is fascinated by a sense of implied though unapparent unity and of inherent principle elusive of simple definition.

Perhaps the difference indicates only that earlier literary styles were more geographically confined and were not founded upon a developed historical consciousness. But my study of these poets, who simultaneously dramatize their unique, individual experiences and affirm the preciousness of an all-encompassing civility, suggests that the early nineteenth century was a time of even more radical change than we have yet recognized. Then, I think, was born a new vision, a vision of a single, worldwide civilization which would make possible more intense personal fulfillment for every individual than can be achieved from a diversity of civilizations. Possibly, therefore, the past century and a half has been convulsed by the birth pangs of a new kind of human life, a metacultural life, of which the poets I have studied are the first prophets.

Appendix ❧ *Notes* ❧ *Index*

Translations:

FOSCOLO: *The Sepulchres*

LEOPARDI: *The Broom*
Remembrances

THE first two translations which follow are presented for the convenience of readers unfamiliar with *The Sepulchres* and *The Broom* who may wish to read through the poems in their entirety, uninterrupted by my critical commentaries. The translation of *Remembrances* is given because my comments, in Chapter VI, on this long and important poem do not include any direct quotations.

The Sepulchres

Beneath the shade of cypresses and within urns comforted by tears is death's sleep perhaps less desolate? When for me the sun will no more make fruitful earth's lovely family of plants and animals, when future hours will not dance before me the beauty of their deceiving flatteries, when I shall hear no more, sweet friend, your poetry and the nostalgic harmony which orders it, nor in my heart will the spirit speak of the gracious Muses and of love, single inspiration of my wandering life, then what recompense for lost days will be one stone distinguishing my bones from the infinite number death sows on land and sea? It is too true, Pindemonte! Even Hope, the last goddess, flees our sepulchres; oblivion confuses all things in its night; and a relentless force transforms them from one movement into another; and time transfigures the last relics of man and his tombs and the features of the earth and sky.

But why, anticipating time, will man deny himself the illusion which halts him, though dead, at the threshold of the underworld? Does he not perhaps live even underground, when for him day's harmony is stilled, if with soft anxieties he can awaken that harmony in the memory of his friends? Divine is this correspondence of loving senses; a divine gift within men; and through it we often live with a dead friend and he, dead, lives with us, if reverently the earth which cradled and nourished him as a child, offers him a final refuge in her maternal lap, protecting his sacred relics from insulting storms and the profane feet of the multitude, and if a stone preserves his name, and a kindly tree, fragrant with flowers, consoles his ashes with their soft shade.

Only he who leaves no heritage of affections takes little joy in urns; and if he looks beyond his funeral rites he sees his spirit wandering amidst the lamentations of Acherontian temples or hiding under the great wings of God's pardon; but he leaves his dust among the nettles of a wasteland where no loving woman prays, no lonely wayfarer hears the sigh nature breathes to us from the tomb.

Nevertheless today a strange law enjoins sepulchres from our pitying gaze and denies the dead their name. And without a tomb lies your priest, O Thalia, who singing to you in his wretched hovel with constant love reared a laurel and hung it with wreaths to you; and your smile enriched his songs which lashed the Lombard Sardanapalus, whose only joy is the bellowing of steers among the Abduan and Ticinian hollows, blessed promise of slothful feasting. O lovely Muse, where are you? I do not feel your ambrosial breath, fragrance of your divinity, among these trees where I sit longing for my mother's home. And you would come and smile on him under that linden whose downcast leafy fronds now tremble because, O Goddess, they do not cover the urn of the old man to whom once they were generous of calm and shade. Perhaps, drifting among common graves, you seek where sleeps the sacred head of your Parini? To him this city, licentious nourisher of emasculated singers, gave no shade within its walls, no stone, no epitaph, and perhaps the mutilated head of a thief, parted from his crimes upon the scaffold, now bloodies Parini's bones. You hear among the rubble and the tangled brush a vagrant bitch scraping in the burial pits and howling hungrily; and flitting from a skull where it fled the moon, an owl fluttering among crosses scattered across the dreary waste and defiling with protesting sobs the rays which the pitying stars cast on long-forgotten graves. In vain do you pray, O Goddess, for dews upon your poet from this squalid night. Alas! no flower rises over the dead unless it is honored by human praise and tears of love.

From the day that marriages and courts of law and altars made human beasts feel compassion for themselves and others, the living protected from corrupting airs and wild animals those pathetic remains which Nature in her eternal changefulness destines for other purposes. Tombs were the testimony of high enterprise and the altars for sons, and from them came forth the answers of the household gods, and an oath sworn by the ashes of ancestors was sacred; this religion, mingling in diverse forms civic and familial love, preserved intact through the long succession of years. Not always did sepulchral stones pave temples; nor the stench of corpses wreathed in incense contaminate worshippers; nor were our cities darkened with pictured skeletons: mothers spring from terrified sleep and stretch bare arms over the beloved heads of their cherished babies, fearful that they be wakened by the ceaseless moaning of one dead begging his descendants for the sanctuary's venal prayers. But cypresses

and cedars impregnating the breeze with their pure fragrance stretched their
evergreen branches over urns perpetually remembered, and precious vases received votive tears. Friends stole a spark from the sun to illuminate the subterranean night, because the eyes of a dying man seek the sun; and all breathe
their last sigh for the fading light. Fountains pouring lustral water nourished
amaranths and violets on the turf of the grave; and whoever sat there to pour
out libations of milk and to share his sorrows with the cherished dead, sensed
about him a fragrance like the air of blessed Elysian fields. Compassionate
illusion, that makes dear to British maidens the gardens of suburban cemeteries, whither they are led by love for a departed mother, where they prayed
the merciful Gods to return the hero who hewed his coffin from the tallest
mast of a conquered ship. But where the fervor for famous deeds sleeps, and
the ministers of civil life are opulence and fear, marble blocks and monuments
rise in futile pompousness as inauspicious images of death. Already the
pedantic and the rich and the riffraff nobles, the honor and wisdom of our
beautiful Italian kingdom, have buried themselves still alive in sycophantic
courts, with their family crests their only glory. For us let death prepare a
quiet home, where at last fortune ceases her persecutions, and friends enjoy not
an inheritance of treasure but of warm emotions and the example of liberal
song.

Heroic souls are fired to noble actions by the urns of heroes, O Pindemonte;
and for the pilgrim they make beautiful and holy the earth that has received
them. When I saw the monument where rests the body of that great man, who,
seeming to temper the sceptre of princes, tore off its laurels and revealed to
mankind how stained it is with tears and blood; and the arch of that one who
raised in Rome a new Olympus to the Deities; and that of him who saw more
worlds revolve within the ethereal vault, and the sun, motionless, illuminating
them, thus first clearing the ways of the firmament for the Englishman who
there soared so loftily; you are blessed, I cried aloud, for your happy breezes
pregnant with life and for your streams that the Apennines pour down to you
from their crests! The moon, rejoicing in your air, mantles with clearest light
your hills, exulting in their wine harvest, and your sloping valleys, clustered
with homes and olive groves, pour forth to the sky the incense of a thousand
flowers; and you first, Firenze, heard the song that lightened the anger of the
fugitive Ghibelline, and you gave family and language to the sweet-lipped
favorite of Calliope who, adorning love—naked in Greece and naked in Rome
—in a veil of transparent purity, restored her to the bosom of Celestial Venus;
but still more blessed because you gather in a single temple the glories of Italy,
her only glories, perhaps, since the ill-defended Alps and the shifting omnipo-
tence of human fortune have despoiled you of arms, treasures, altars, native
land—all, except memory. So when hopes of glory shall blaze in daring minds
and within Italy, from you we shall draw good auguries. And to these marble
monuments Vittorio came often for inspiration. Angered with his country's
gods, he would wander silently where the Arno is most barren, gazing long-
ingly at fields and sky, and when no living appearance softened his anguish,
here the austere man rested; and on his face lay the pallor of death and hope.

With these great he abides eternally; and his bones tremble with love for his fatherland. Ah, yes, from that religious peace a God speaks; and nourished Greek valor and anger against the Persians at Marathon, where Athens consecrated tombs to her heroes. The sailor coasting that sea under Euboea saw through the vast darkness sparks flashing from helmets and clashing swords, fiery smoke fuming from pyres, saw spectral warriors glaring with steely arms seeking the battle; and through the horror of night's silences the tumult of phalanxes reverberates across the plain, and the trumpets' sound, and a charge of rushing cavalry, trampling the helmets of the dying, and lamentation, and hymns, and the song of the Fates.

You are happy, Ippolito, to have travelled the spacious kingdom of the winds in your green years. And if the helmsman directed the tiller beyond the Aegean Isles, surely you heard the shores of the Hellespont resound with ancient deeds, and the sea roaring as it carried Achilles' armor to the Retean shore where lay the bones of Ajax; to the great-hearted, death is a just arbiter of glory; neither cunning wisdom nor the favor of kings could keep the Ithacan's hard-won spoils, for the sea, incited by the infernal gods, stole them from his wandering ship.

And let me, whom the times and my desire for honor cause to be a fugitive among different peoples, let me be summoned to make the heroes live again by the Muses, inspirers of human thought. They are enthroned as guardians of sepulchres, and when time with his cold wings has brushed away even their ruins, the Muses gladden the deserts with their song, and harmony conquers the silence of a thousand centuries. And today in the untilled Troad one place shines immortal to pilgrims, immortal through the Nymph to whom Jove was husband, and to Jove she gave a son, Dardanus, from whom sprang Troy, Assaracus, the fifty bridal beds, and the empire of the Julian race. For when Electra heard Destiny calling her from day's living breezes to the courts of Elysium, to Jove she offered this final prayer: And if, she said, my tresses and face have been dear to you, and our sweet wakeful nights, and if the will of the fates does not permit me a better reward, at least look down from heaven on your dead friend so that the fame of your Electra survive. And the Olympian groaned; and, bowing his immortal head, rained ambrosia from his locks upon the nymph and consecrated that body and her tomb. Here lay Erichtonius and here slept the just ashes of Ilus; here the Ilachan women unloosed their tresses, alas, in vain crying out against their husbands' impending doom; here Cassandra came, when the God in her breast forced her to prophesy Troy's fatal day; and she sang a song of love to these spirits, and guided here their grandsons and taught the youths the loving lament. And she spoke, sighing: Oh, if ever heaven permits you to return from Argos where you will serve the horses of Tydeus' and Laertes' son, in vain will you search for your fatherland. The walls built by Phoebus shall smoke beneath their ruins. But the Penates of Troy shall dwell in these tombs, because it is the gift of Gods to preserve their proud name in misfortune. And you, palms and cypresses, which Priam's daughters plant, and which will grow, alas so soon nourished by widows' tears, protect my ancestors; and whoever with reverence shall restrain his axe from these consecrated branches shall suffer less from internecine strife, and shall with holiness touch the altar. Protect my ancestors. One day you shall see a blind beggar groping under your ancient shadows, and, muttering, penetrate the burial vaults, and embrace the urns, and question them. The secret recesses shall groan, and the tombs tell all, Ilium razed twice and twice rerisen magnificently above its silent roads to make finer the final trophy of the fatal sons of Peleus. The holy bard, calming those tormented souls with his song, shall make immortal the Argive princes through all lands embraced by the great father Oceanus. And you, Hector, shall be honored by tears wherever men lament and hold sacred blood poured out for a fatherland, and as long as the sun shall shine on the calamities of man.

The Broom, or The Flower of the Wasteland

Here on the arid spine of this fearful mountain, Vesuvius the destroyer, which no other tree nor flower gladdens, you scatter your solitary tufts, fragrant broom, contented with the wasteland. Thus I have seen your shoots make lovely the barren fields round that city that was once mistress of mankind, by your grave and silent aspect testifying to her vanished empire. Now I encounter you again in this soil, lover of sad places and of those abandoned by the world, faithful comrade of afflicted fortune. These fields—strewn with unfecund ashes, buried by lava, petrified, echoing beneath the wanderer's steps, where the snake lurks and coils in the sun, where the rabbit retreats within his hollow hiding-place—were once farms and homesteads, gold with grain, resounding with the lowing of herds, were once gardens and palaces, grateful retreats for the leisure of the mighty, were once famous cities which the haughty mountain, pouring fiery torrents from its burning throat, obliterated together with their residents. Now a single ruin buries all. In this you root yourself, O gentle flower, as if in pity for the doom of others, flinging toward the sky your sweet perfume to console the wasteland. To these slopes let him come who exalts with flattery our mortal state, let him see how loving Nature cares for humankind, and let him justly estimate our strength, when our hard nurse, when least we fear, can with her slightest movement wipe out part and can, with motions scarcely greater, at once annihilate us all. Depicted on these slopes is man's *magnificent and progressive destiny.*

Gaze here and see yourself, proud and stupid century, you who have abandoned the path marked out for you before by reawakened thought, you who have turned back your steps, vaunting your retreat as progress. All the great minds, who are by evil fate your sons, flatter your childish babbling, though within themselves they scorn you. I shall not sink into my grave bearing such obloquy; rather, I shall exhibit openly the contempt that tightens in my breast, though I know well oblivion threatens anyone who dares attack his age. Hereafter I shall laugh at that evil, which you and I will share. You dream of liberty while you enslave once more that thought through which alone we revivified, in part, from barbarism, through which alone our civilization grows, and through which alone the public destiny is guided on toward better things. The truth displeased you by displaying the low condition and the bitter fate that nature gives to us. To this you show your back, like a coward, turning from the light that illuminates the truth: and, fugitive, you call vile the one who follows it, and great-souled only him who, deceiver or deceived, clever or mad, extols man's state beyond the stars.

A man impoverished and weak of body but of generous and of lofty soul does not esteem himself, nor claim to be, rich in health and gold, nor make himself ridiculous by splendid living or by shows of strength, but without shame allows the weakness of his fortune and his force to appear, admits this openly and judges his condition according to the truth. Nor do I think a creature great of soul, but stupid, rather, who, born to die, reared in pain, says: "I was made for pleasure"; and out of festered pride scrawls reams promising lofty destinies and new delights, of which this globe and heaven itself know nothing, to peoples whom one wave of the plunging sea, one breath of air diseased, one tremor of the earth destroys so that even the memory of them will scarce survive. A noble soul is he who burns to lift his mortal eyes against our common doom, and who with open speech, detracting nothing from the truth, confesses the evil lot assigned to us by fate and our depressed and frail condition; he who is strong and enduring in his suffering nor will add fraternal hate and wrath—the worst of evils—to his other miseries by blaming mankind for his sorrow, but casts the blame upon the truly guilty one, the power that is our mother by our birth, in will our stepmother. Her he calls enemy, and thus believing that, as is the truth, the human company was from the first united and arrayed against her, he esteems all men confederated, embraces all men with truest love, offering and expecting prompt and effective aid in the dangers and vicissitudes of the common war. To take up arms against his fellow man, to ambush, to impede his neighbor seems to him as foolish as if one in a camp beleaguered 'round by enemies, at the height of their assaults, forgot the foe, stirred up harsh strife among his friends, and with his sword spread panic and destruction through his ranks. When thoughts like these shall be, as once they were, made manifest to people everywhere, that horror which first forced mortals into social fellowship, joined against pitiless nature, shall be in part restored by knowledge of the truth, the honest, upright intercourse of citizens, justice and piety, shall root themselves in other soil than the madnesses of pride, founded on which the people's honor stands as firm as all that roots itself in falsity.

Often on these desolated slopes, which the hardened flood has clothed in black, still seeming to move undulating on, I sit at night, and above the melancholy slope in the deepest blue I see the flaming stars, which the distant sea mirrors, and the whole world shining with wheeling scintillations through the empty vault of heaven. And when I fix my sight upon those lights, seeming but points, which are, in truth, immense, so vast that to them this earth and sea are but a point—to which, indeed, not man alone but this whole globe, whereon mankind is nothing, is entirely unknown; and when I see, beyond these, still infinitely more remote, those knots of stars which to us appear like clouds, wherefrom not only man, nor earth alone, but this universe of stars, infinite in number and in mass, our golden sun but one among them all, is unknown or seems, as they seem to the earth, a mere point of doubtful light; to my thought then what do you seem, O son of man? And remembering your lowly state, of which the soil I tread bears testimony, and that you—in contrast —think yourself the ruler, the final purpose of the Whole, and that you have often pleased yourself with fabling how to this obscure grain of sand named earth the authors of the universe of things descended, for your good, often chatting pleasantly with you, and how this present age, that in knowledge and civility seems most advanced, insults the wise by reviving these derided dreams; what feeling then, unhappy mortal children, what final thought assails my heart? I do not know if laughter or if pity then prevails.

As a little apple, falling late in autumn from the tree, which its ripeness and no other force brings down, smashes and buries instantly the beloved homes of a race of ants, tunnelled laboriously through soft loam, laying waste their riches and their works, which, zealously gathering, the industrious colony with lengthy toil throughout the summer had amassed foresightedly; even so, falling from above, hurled from the mountain's roaring womb through the deep sky, a cloud of ashes, pumice, rock, blackness and ruin, combined with boiling lava torrents bursting furiously through the mountain's flank, pouring its incandescent mass of molten metal and burning sand in a raging flood, bore down and overwhelmed and covered up in instants those cities washed on the shore of that very sea. Wherefore above them now the goat is pastured, and on the other side new cities rise whose roots are in their sepulchre, and the ferocious mountain seems to spurn their prostrate walls. Nature cares not nor values more the seed of man than that of ants; and if one is massacred less frequently, there is no cause but that man breeds not quite as fast.

A full eighteen hundred years have passed since disappeared, overwhelmed by blazing fury, these thronged cities, and the poor farmer, tending carefully his little vines, which the scorched, dead soil of these sad fields scarce nourishes, still raises suspicious glances toward the fatal peak, which, no more kindly now, still looms terribly, still menaces disaster for himself, his children, and his impoverished farm. And often the poor man, on the roof of his miserable hut, lying sleepless all the night in the wayward wind, many times leaps up, watches the course of the fearful boiling flood, that still pours out of the unexhausted womb over the sandy ridge and shines from sea-girt Capri across Naples' Bay to Mergellina. And if he sees it nearing, or if in the depths of his household well he hears the water seethe and gurgle, he wakes his children, wakes his wife in haste, flees with whatever they can snatch, and sees from far off his cherished home, his little field—their sole guard against famine—prey to the ruinous flood which, crackling, overwhelms it, spreads inexorably and everlastingly above it all. Returns to daylight from an old oblivion extinct Pompeii, like a buried skeleton which piety, or greed, draws from the earth to show publicly. From the deserted forum amidst the ranks of upright broken columns, the traveller contemplates the distant cloven summit and smoking plume still hanging in menace above the shattered ruins. And in the awfulness of secret night, through the emptied theaters, through the mutilated temples, and through the blasted houses where the bat conceals its young, like a baleful torch flickering darkly among abandoned palaces, runs the shimmer of the ghastly lava that distantly through shadows reddens all the ruins. So, ignorant of man and the ages he calls ancient and the succession of generation after generation, nature stays forever young, or, rather, follows a course so long she seems forever young. Meanwhile empires crash, languages and peoples pass away: she sees them not: and man presumes to vaunt his immortality.

And you, supple broom, who with fragrant shoots make beautiful these despoiled fields, you, also, will soon succumb to the cruel power of subterraneous fire returning to familiar haunts, extending its greedy edge over your gentle tufts. And you will bow your innocent head under the burden of mortality, not stubbornly, but not until that time bowing in vain and cowardly supplication before your future conqueror, and not rearing in mad pride against the stars nor against the wasteland—your birthplace and your home by fortune, not by choice; wiser and less weak than man in not believing your frail race to be given immortality by destiny or by yourself.

Remembrances

Beautiful stars of the Bear, I did not believe I should return after so long to my custom of contemplating you, shining over my father's garden, and conversing with you from the windows of this house where I lived as a child and which saw the end of my joys. How many imaginings once and how many fantasies from your aspect and from that of the lights of your companions, I created in my mind. It was then that, silent, seated on the green turf, I used to pass the greater part of many evenings, looking at the sky and listening to the song of the frogs scattered about the distant countryside! And the firefly wandered about the hedges and the flower-beds and the wind murmured through the fragrant pathways and among the cypress in those woods; and within my father's house sounded voices from time to time, the servants at their tranquil work. And what immense thoughts, what sweet dreams were inspired in me by the sight of that far-off sea, those purple mountains that are discovered from here, and that I thought some day to cross with difficulty, what secret worlds, what secret happiness I imagined for my life. Ignorant of my destiny and of how many times I willingly should have changed this, my sad, bare life, with death.

Nor did my heart tell me that my green age would be condemned to consume itself in this savage place of my birth, among a people boorish, vile, to whom learning and knowledge are foreign names, and often the subject for smiles and jokes; who hate and flee me, not even for envy, since they do not consider me superior to themselves, but because they think in my heart I so esteem myself, although to no one have I ever given sign of it. Here I pass the years, abandoned to myself, obscure, without love, without life; and against my will amongst the crowd of ill-wishers I become bitter; here I am despoiled of kindness and manliness, and I am forced to hate mankind by being crushed among this herd; and meanwhile the dear time of youth flies; more dear than fame and laurel, than the clear light of day, and breath: I lose you without a single delight, uselessly, in this inhuman habitation, among my griefs, O single flower of barren life.

The wind comes carrying the sound of the hour from the village belfry. It was a comfort, this sound, I remember, to my nights, when a boy, in the dark room, a prey to continuous terrors, I lay awake, sighing for morning. In this place there is nothing I see or hear which does not bring back an imagination and arouse a sweet remembrance. Sweet in itself, but the thought of the present with sorrow usurps its place, and empty desire for the past, even though sad, and the recognition: I have been. That veranda over there, faced toward the last glimmers of the day; these frescoed walls, those figured beasts, and the Sun that rises over the lonely fields, to my listlessness brought thousands of delights then, when powerful illusion was my companion wherever I was. In these ancient rooms, the snow glittering outside, the wind whispering around these spacious windows, my voice re-echoed, cheerful, filled with pleasure, during that time when the bitter, unworthy mystery of things displays itself full of sweetness; the ingenuous boy, like an inexperienced lover, joyously contemplates his deceitful life, innocent and untested, and imagines it a divine beauty to marvel at.

O hopes, hopes; smiling deceptions of my first age! always, in speaking, I return to you; because through the going on of time, through the changing of affections and thoughts I do not know how to obliterate you from my soul. Phantoms, I know, are glory and honor; delights and goods mere desire; life has but one fruit, useless misery. And although my years are empty, although deserted and obscure my mortal condition, little, I see clearly, has fortune taken from me. Alas, but how often, O my ancient hopes, do I think back to you and to that dear imagining of my prime; at once I contemplate my life so vile and so sorrowful with death all that remains to me today of those so grand hopes; I feel my heart constrict, I feel then I do not know how to resign myself to my destiny. And when finally invoked death shall be beside me, and the end of my misfortune shall be reached; when the earth shall be a strange valley, and the future shall flee my gaze; of you, my dreams, surely memories shall rise up in me; and that image shall still make me sigh, shall make my futile life bitter to me and temper the sweetness of that fatal day with grief.

And already in the first juvenile tumults of happiness, anguish, and desire, I called on death many times, and long I sat there by the fountain, thinking of bringing to an end within those waters my life and sorrow. Afterward, my life brought into danger by blind disease, I wept my beautiful youth, and the flower of my poor days that dropped so much before their time; and often in the late hours, seated on my familiar bed, sadly to the failing night-light making verses, I lamented with silences of the night my fleeing spirit, and I sang to my failing self a funeral song.

Oh, who can remember without sighs the beginnings of youth, O days of grace inexpressible, when to the rapt mortal for the first time the girls smile; everything around smiles in competition; envy is silent, not awakened yet or still benign; and (astonishing marvel) the world almost puts forth its right hand in aid, excuses his errors, celebrates the newness of his coming into life, and, bowing, acclaims him for a master—oh fleeting days. Like a flash you are extinguished. And what mortal can be ignorant of his bad fortune, if that beautiful season is already past for him, if his good time, if youth, alas, youth, is exhausted.

O Nerina, do I not hear these places speak of you? Have you fallen from my thought? Where have you turned, my sweet, that here I find of you only a memory? Your native countryside sees you no longer; that window from which you used to chatter to me, and which sadly reflects the glitter of the stars, is deserted. Where are you, that I no longer hear the sound of your voice, as one day I did, when every distant accent of your lips that reached me made me pale. Another time. Your days are past, my sweet love. You have passed. To others is given passage through this land today and dwelling in these fragrant hills. But swiftly you passed; and like a dream was your life. You went dancing forth, joy shone in your face, in the carefree imaginings in your eyes, that light of youth, when suddenly fate extinguished them and laid you low. Alas, Nerina, the old love rules in my heart. If sometime I go to a festival, if I move among a cheerful crowd, within myself I say: you no longer adorn yourself, you no longer move among crowds. When May returns and the lovers bring flowering branches and songs to the girls, I say, my Nerina, for you spring will never return, nor will love return. Every serene day, every flowery slope that I see, every enjoyment that I feel, I say: Nerina now feels pleasure no more; no longer sees the fields, the sky. Alas, you have passed, my eternal regret: you have passed; and have made companion of all my lovely imaginings, of all my tender feelings, the sad and precious movements of my heart, bitter remembrance.

❧ NOTES

INTRODUCTION

1　Limitations of space have forced me to omit some important works. I particularly regret that I am not able to discuss Keats's *Endymion*, Wordsworth's *Excursion*, and Leopardi's *Operette Morali*, but each of these
would require a chapter (see the final note to Chapter II). For the sake
of brevity, also, I seldom make reference to early nineteenth-century poets
other than the four with whom I am concerned.

2　Readers who know no Italian can learn a great deal about Leopardi
through four excellent books: Iris Origo, *Leopardi* (London, 1953), a most
readable biography; J. H. Whitfield, *Giacomo Leopardi* (Oxford, 1954),
a thoughtful, scholarly study of the poet's art and thought; John Heath-
Stubbs, *Poems from Giacomo Leopardi* (London, 1946), a superb poetic
translation of Leopardi's best poems. G. L. Bickersteth's complete edition
of Leopardi's poems (Cambridge, 1923) has a scholarly introduction and
thorough notes. The translations, however, reproduce Leopardi's meters
and rhyme schemes at the expense of meaning. J. H. Whitfield's careful
translations in *Leopardi's Canti* (Naples, 1962) now provide the best
scholarly text for English readers. Foscolo is not so well served. The only
brief introductions are Ernesto Grillo's *I Sepolcri* (London and Glasgow,
1928), which includes a translation of Foscolo's most famous poem, and
E. R. Vincent's *The Commemoration of the Dead* (Cambridge, 1936).
Vincent's *Ugo Foscolo: An Italian Exile in Regency England* (Cambridge,
1953) is a splendid study of Foscolo's later career with particular emphasis on his relations with English literary men and patrons of literature.
There is no available translation of Foscolo's novel nor of *The Graces*.
The Penguin Book of Italian Verse, introduced and edited by George R.
Kay (Harmondsworth, 1958), includes a good selection of the poetry.

3　Morse Peckham, *Beyond the Tragic Vision* (New York, 1962), p. 97.

4　Chesterton's book, *Robert Browning*, was first published in 1903. My quotations are taken from the London edition of 1926, pp. 168–70. See also
Chesterton's suggestion as to how a modern would rewrite the *Odyssey*
(p. 172) and his discussion of the relationship of the new poetry to the
idea of "free speech" (p. 173).

5　All my quotations from Meyer H. Abrams, *The Mirror and the Lamp*
(New York, 1953), are from pp. 22–23, a passage that summarizes well
Abrams' central concern. But the book does not lend itself to summary;
it is impossible to quote briefly from it without distorting the detailed
subtlety of its arguments.

6　A. O. Lovejoy, "On the Discrimination of Romanticisms," *Essays in the
History of Ideas* (Baltimore, 1948), pp. 228–53. The article was first pub-

lished in 1924, however, and has had to be considered by all serious students of Romantic literature since that time.

7 Peckham, *Beyond the Tragic Vision,* p. 92.

8 *Ibid.,* p. 97.

9 Both of these quotations are from the second of the articles cited in the text, p. xiv.

10 Earl R. Wasserman, *The Subtler Language* (Baltimore, 1959), p. 11.

11 *Ibid.,* p. 186.

12 My most glaring omission is that of René Wellek. Wellek has written so much on this subject that any brief exposition of his opinions is almost sure to be seriously misleading. This is particularly true because his major contribution, in my opinion, has been his insistence, never merely conventional, on the continuity of literary and critical tradition. No modern scholar is more adept at delineating the *history* of literature, the relationship between developing patterns both of aesthetic theory and of expression. I hope that my debt to Wellek, Gérard, Langbaum, Fogle, Stallknecht, Whitehead, and others who have contributed to the modern definition of Romanticism will be sufficiently indicated by notes in following chapters.

CHAPTER I

1 There were in fact three editions of the novel during Foscolo's lifetime, in 1798 (Part One only), in 1802, and in 1817. These are collected in *Opere di Ugo Foscolo,* Vol. IV, Edizione Nazionale (Florence, 1955), well edited by Giovanni Gambarin, who describes the complexities of the various publications and some of the associated textual problems. All references in this chapter are to this volume, some of the shortcomings of which are pointed out by C. F. Goffis, *Nuovi studi foscoliani* (Florence, 1958), pp. 113–40.

2 See Chapter VIII. This subject has been a focal point for studies of Foscolo, a most thorough and intelligent review of which is to be found in Walter Binni, *Foscolo e la critica* (Florence, 1957). Three works in particular should be cited: Mario Fubini, *Lettura dell' "Ortis,"* (Milan, 1949), the author being the finest of all Foscolo scholars; Carlo Grabher, *Interpretazioni foscoliane* (Florence, 1948), especially good on the relation of *Jacopo Ortis* to *The Graces* and on the changes between the first and second versions of the novel; E. Bottasso, *Foscolo e Rousseau* (Turin, 1941), which covers much more than the title indicates. Probably the basis for all modern studies of Foscolo is Eugenio Donadoni's monumental *Ugo Foscolo, pensatore, critico, poeta* (Palermo, 1910), but at least as important is Mario Fubini's *Ugo Foscolo,* first published in 1928, reissued with a bibliography in 1931, and again reissued in 1962 (Florence) with a complete revision and recasting of the notes and bibliographical references. Although I usually refer to Fubini's later publications, Fubini's central critical position is clearly set forth in this early work—on *Jacopo Ortis* see pp. 1–32 and 287–92.

3 Another thoroughly discussed subject. Besides the works cited above, Bona-

ventura Zumbini's "Il Werther e il Jacopo Ortis," *Studi di Letteratura Comparata* (Bologna, 1931), pp. 87–131, though a reprint of an article written in the first years of this century, is still worth attention; see esp. pp. 94, 95, 105, and 109. Probably the best study of Foscolo's originality is Carlo Dapelo, "Il *Werther* e *L'Ortis*," *Lettere italiane*, V (1953), 176–86, for example: ". . . esiste pure una fondamentale differenza tra i due romanzi proprio nella mozione degli affetti; nel sentimento della natura; nella condotta dell'azione; nelle reazione dei protagonisti allo sviluppo degli avvenimenti e, soprattutto, di fronte alla morte" (p. 178).

4 Page references are to the 1802 version in Gambarin's edition, cited in note 1 above, which includes the useful feature of systematic cross-reference with the first version of *Jacopo Ortis*.

5 Odoardo, the shadowiest character in the novel, might have been developed as the traditional rationalistic antagonist of a sentimental hero. That he is not so developed is undoubtedly revealing of Foscolo's purposes. See Grabher, *Interpretazione foscoliane*, pp. 5–31, esp. p. 7.

6 Teresa's unhappiness springs from her father's determination to marry her to the unfeeling Odoardo against her own inclination and that of her mother, who has separated from her husband in objection to the match. Jacopo judges Teresa's father to be a good man, an honest man, but a tyrant, if only a domestic one. The judgment is important, since it quietly challenges the ideal of the enlightened despot. To Foscolo despotism is despicable no matter how enlightened, and he doubts that genuine decency can flourish in a society which permits any form of tyranny.

7 See E. Raimondi, "Un episodio dell'*Ortis* e 'Lo bello stile,'" *Giornale Storico della letteratura italiana*, CXXX (1953), 351–67.

8 Jacopo (and Foscolo) do not object to the rich and powerful because they are rich and powerful but because they tend to forget that sorrow and suffering are the human lot. Jacopo repudiates the point of view that the poor and humble are less in need of honor than are the prominent and wealthy. The rich man tends to forget that he is a man. He thinks of man's natural condition as happy, and his misconception leads him into the evil of acting inhumanly. Jacopo asks, "To love virtue must one live in sorrow?" His own answer is yes, but this does not commit him to the "proletarian fallacy"—that only the lives of the poor are "real," that only the sordid is "genuine." The Foscolo-Jacopo view is typical of all major Romantic poets but is usually misconceived by modern critics.

9 An interesting discussion of associated literary and artistic "syndromes" is to be found in Wylie Sypher, *From Rococo to Cubism* (New York, 1960), pp. 3–59.

10 It is surprising how often this idea turns up in early nineteenth-century literature. Probably its best expression in English is Thomas Hood's *The Last Man*.

11 See Fubini, *Lettura dell' "Ortis,"* pp. 85–90, for a discussion of the early and later versions of this scene, pp. 90–102 for a general discussion of the significance of the 1817 version; and see Chapter VIII of this book.

12 Compare Wordsworth's *Elegiac Stanzas* ("Peele Castle").

13 See Zumbini, in *Studi di Letteratura Comparata*, p. 109; Fubini's *Lettura dell' "Ortis,"* is organized to explain Foscolo's development. See also R. Ramat, *Itinerario ritmico foscoliano* (Città di Castello, 1946) where the emphasis is on *Jacopo Ortis* as Foscolo's first effort to establish his own "poetic myth."

14 For both Wordsworth and Foscolo privations though important are not decisive because "the rights of others" are positive rather than negative, are less a matter of economic well-being than a matter of achieving imaginative-spiritual fulfillment.

15 Today we think of rebels as violent extremists sacrificing others to their utopian dreams. To Foscolo the true rebel is one who, having passions to curb, does restrain them; he sacrifices himself, not others. Significantly, Jacopo's departure is hastened by an intensification of the reactionary Venetian persecutions. The practical expedience of Teresa's father, raised to the level of civic policy, produces the police state. Italian critics, it seems to me, have been unduly reluctant to recognize the significance of the family-state parallel which runs throughout *Jacopo Ortis*.

16 Here, as in many places in the novel, Foscolo's debt to Alfieri needs to be assessed carefully. The best discussion I know is in Fubini, *Lettura dell' "Ortis,"* pp. 15–39. Fubini calls the novel "l'unica tragedia della scuola alfieriana non indegna del maestro" (p. 34), yet insists that in Foscolo "sorge di contro alle società politiche . . . un nuovo consorzio più veramente umano: . . . La solitudine dell'eroe alfieriano è dissolta, ed egli si ritrova uomo fra gli uomini . . ." (p. 38).

17 All the works cited dealing with Foscolo's debt to Goethe and Rousseau treat this point. See particularly Fubini, *Lettura dell' "Ortis,"* p. 41; also pp. 17–18 of Luigi Russo's introduction to the second half of the novel, included in his *Ugo Foscolo: prose e poesie* (Florence, 1951), as well as the notes, pp. 45–50.

18 The nature of heroic, as opposed to sentimental, suicide is suggested by Jacopo's contrasting of himself with Odysseus. Alike in being exiles wandering through worlds of savage destruction, the two differ in that Jacopo is a creature of passion who cannot devote himself to his own preservation and who must feel the sufferings of others as agony in his own heart. Odysseus is a realist who accepts what he must; Jacopo is an idealist who protests. "God preserve you from my madness," says Jacopo of Odysseus, "and I pray with all the strength of my soul that I may be preserved from your *cleverness*" (p. 246). Jacopo's home is not Ithaca but death, for he inhabits a tragic world. Parini's last words are: "The only comfort I can give you is my compassion." Men like Parini and Jacopo can cling only to their shared feeling that there should be a life better than that provided by the senseless mechanism of nature to which "realistic" men submit.

19 Foscolo translated *The Sentimental Journey* into Italian and there can be no question that Sterne's influence on him is significant, though mostly exerted after the publication of the second edition of *Jacopo Ortis*. See

Giuseppe de Robertis' essay in his *Primi studi manzoniani*; Claudio Varese's *Linguaggio sterniano e linguaggio foscoliano* (Florence, 1947) (slightly disappointing); and the fine discussion of the problem by Mario Fubini (ed.), *Prose varie d'arte, Opere di Ugo Foscolo*, Vol. V, Edizione Nazionale (Florence, 1951), pp. xxxvi–lviii. The most perceptive suggestions as to the significance of Sterne for late eighteenth- and early nineteenth-century writers are those of Earl R. Wasserman in *The Subtler Language* (Baltimore, 1959), esp. pp. 170–71. The subject deserves further study.

20 Hence this kind of suicide stands as the necessary limit of certain actions. By recognizing this limit the rebel frees himself from the necessity of forcing the point. If circumstances demand it, he can, like Socrates, face his death with serenity, but until such time death is divested of its dark temptation. Foscolo, like many of his contemporaries, by working out the theme of suicide in his art, freed his life from its morbid influence. The point is of some significance, because two members of Foscolo's immediate family did commit suicide. On the relation of Romantic individualism to Romantic "social morality," see Morse Peckham, "Toward a Theory of Romanticism: II. Reconsiderations," *Studies in Romanticism,* I (1961), 6.

21 Russo, *Ugo Foscolo*, p. 64, note to l. 1347. The influence of Vico on Foscolo is enormous but most difficult to evaluate. One difficulty is that, as Mario Fubini says (*Romanticismo italiano* [Bari, 1953], p. 115), "L'Alfieri . . . preparó il Foscolo a intendre il Vico: . . ." I should risk the generalization that the distinctive character of late eighteenth-century and early nineteenth-century Italian poetry is due in large measure to Italian writers' knowledge of Vico. His influence on the rest of Europe was of course much less direct. See Erich Auerbach's essay in his *Scenes from the Drama of European Literature* (New York, 1959).

22 Although I try to keep to an obvious and generally accepted meaning of "natural law," I am aware that the term is ambiguous and has been the focus for bitter debates. These have not all been theological, and, in fact, I suspect that for the literary historian of the early nineteenth century it is the legal disputes which matter most. See F. L. Windolph, *Leviathan and Natural Law* (Princeton, 1951).

23 See Peckham, in *Studies in Romanticism*, I, 2–4.

24 See Gambarin, *Opere*, Vol. IV, Ed. Naz., p. 274, where the decrepit old woman reappears and Jacopo discusses nature and death.

CHAPTER II

1 See Geoffrey H. Hartman, *The Unmediated Vision* (New Haven, 1954), p. 6: "Wordsworth is the first English poet to consider and use personal experience as his 'sublime argument.' Before him, autobiography did not enter into serious poetry without being legitimized by a score of mythological references, or being set into the explicit frame of the Christian religion." As to the character of Wordsworth's "autobiography" in *The*

Prelude, see R. D. Havens' famous study, *The Mind of a Poet* (Baltimore, 1941), pp. 270–87.

2 Nevertheless, the change in Wordsworth's political attitudes is significant. One must not lose sight of the simple rightness of Zera S. Fink's remark that Wordsworth began his career as what most people would call a liberal and ended it as what most people would call a reactionary. See Zera S. Fink, "Wordsworth and the English Republican Tradition," *Journal of English and Germanic Philology*, XLVII (1948), 107–26, esp. 126. This fine article on the intellectual background of Wordsworth's politics, along with Fink's earlier *The Classical Republicans* (Evanston, 1945), esp. pp. 28–51, is essential for an understanding of Wordsworth's positions. It must be obvious, however, that I agree with Carlos Baker's remark that "no one can read Wordsworth for very long without the conviction that at the deeper levels his democracy never wavers."—"Sensation and Vision in Wordsworth," in *English Romantic Poets*, ed. Meyer H. Abrams (New York, 1960), p. 101. One should not forget, either, that *The Prelude* was begun in the 1790's, a decade which produced a large number of "apocalyptic epics": Blake's *The French Revolution* and *America*, Southey's *Joan of Arc* (to which Coleridge contributed), and Landor's *Gebir*, to mention but four. While *The Prelude* transcends this background, it can be fully appreciated only in relation to this efflorescence of anti-epical epics, which are not merely prophetic, utopian, and pacifistically anti-British but which are also notable for structural and metrical innovations and a tendency toward the celebration of personal fulfillment as opposed to social success. So far as I know there is no thorough study of this significant literary phenomenon.

3 Meyer H. Abrams, "The Correspondent Breeze: A Romantic Metaphor," pp. 37–54 in *English Romantic Poets*, has dealt most fully with the point. All quotations, except where specially noted, are from the 1805 version of *The Prelude*, ed. Ernest de Selincourt, 2d ed., revised by Helen Darbishire (Oxford, 1959). My references are to the 1805 text because I am juxtaposing *The Prelude* and *Jacopo Ortis* and I feel it is appropriate to use versions of the two works written contemporaneously.

4 John Jones, *The Egotistical Sublime* (London, 1954), p. 24: ". . . his understanding of the relationship of inner and outer is Wordsworth's principal claim to greatness."

5 Norman Lacey, *Wordsworth's View of Nature and Its Ethical Consequences* (Cambridge, 1948), p. 12: "*The Prelude* then is a study . . . of the interaction of Nature and mind." See Chapter VII of this book.

6 See for example, Leone Vivante, *English Poetry* (London, 1950), p. 102: "Wordsworth does not derive mind from sensation; rather, *he sees mind in sensation*." Vivante is a sometimes bizarre philosopher-critic, but he is often exciting. A sounder, solider treatment of the subject is to be found in Albert Gérard, *L'idée romantique de la poésie en Angleterre* (Paris, 1955); see for example p. 201. For the expression of this view in Wordsworth's

language and figures, see Carl Robinson Sonn, "An Approach to Wordsworth's Earlier Imagery," *ELH*, XXVII (1960), 208–22.

7   R. A. Foakes, *The Romantic Assertion* (New Haven, 1958), has much of importance to say on why poets like Wordsworth wrote long poems and how these poems tend to be built around a "structural image" (p. 49).

8   Vivante, *English Poetry,* p. 99: "The principle of synthesis is not abstractly inferred; . . . it is 'force.'"

9   Louis Bonnerot, "De quelques livres récents sur Wordsworth," *Études anglaises,* XI (1958), 310–22, p. 320.

10 An excellent discussion of *The Prelude* may be found in William Walsh, *The Use of the Imagination* (London, 1959). On the present point, see p. 34: "Wordsworth's witness to the originating energy which makes the mind a shaper and not just a receptacle of its experience is the more telling because he had in some respects a keener sense than Coleridge of the mind's dependence upon the world outside itself."

11 Although no scholar has commented on the relation between the form of that Romantic poetry in which spontaneity is stressed and the form of the eighteenth-century epistolary novel, the connection seems to me important. In the epistolary novel for perhaps the first time the illusion of spontaneity could be given an appropriate and effective structure.

12 Although it is important to notice Bennett Weaver's distinction: "He must treat the past after his true nature, letting his living mind proceed creatively into the past and not allowing the dead past to come into his mind." —"Wordsworth's *Prelude*: The Poetic Function of Memory," *Studies in Philology,* XXXIV (1937), 552–63. My debt to several of Weaver's articles on *The Prelude* will be apparent. On memory see Chapter V. My disagreements with David Ferry's lengthy analysis of *The Prelude* in *The Limits of Mortality* (Middletown, 1959), pp. 112–71, are obvious, but Ferry makes many good points, especially on "time"; see pp. 117, 123, 125, and *passim.*

13 See for example Gérard, *L'idée,* p. 320.

14 See Newton P. Stallknecht, *Strange Seas of Thought* (Bloomington, 1958), p. 14: "No object, no event, no living thing, not even the human soul exists or can exist by itself: each depends on all." But see also p. 68: "Neither Wordsworth nor Boehme and his followers dismiss discursive reason as wholly false." My understanding of Wordsworth has been much shaped by Stallknecht's work.

15 Hartman, *The Unmediated Vision,* p. 16.

16 Melvin M. Rader, *Presiding Ideas in Wordsworth's Poetry,* University of Washington Publications in Language and Literature, Vol. 8, No. 2 (Seattle, 1931), 121–216, esp. p. 125: "Especially significant . . . is Wordsworth's emphasis upon the unity of consciousness. Thought has no beginning, because it is rooted in the mind, an integer to itself, which is implicated in each mental process. To find the beginning, therefore, would be to find the origin of mind itself." Rader's work is of great significance for all thoughtful studies of Wordsworth's ideas.

17 The classic statement on this point is that of A. N. Whitehead, *Science and*

the Modern World (New York, 1925), p. 279. See also Stallknecht, *Strange Seas of Thought,* p. 9 and *passim.*

18   Edwin Morgan, "A Prelude to *The Prelude,*" *Essays in Criticism,* V (1955), 341–53, deals with this matter. See for example p. 346: ". . . emotion is unabstractable from circumstance." A reply to Morgan is Kenneth Muir's "An Epilogue to *The Prelude,*" *Essays in Criticism,* VI (1956), 243–45.

19   Youth primarily "receives," maturity primarily "gives," but only one capable of giving can receive and only one able to receive can give. This in barest outline is Wordsworth's "system" for the proper human development from childhood to maturity. It is worth noticing that at all stages there must be active reciprocity, hence Wordsworth stresses active powers by the use of verbs, for example, "to feel" and "to create." The very grammatical emphasis of some modern systems, such as Buber's "I" and "Thou," would be uncongenial to Wordsworth.

20   Although Wordsworth does not actually use the word "imagination" here. See also on page 30 the comment on the lines in Book VI commemorating the passage across the Alps.

21   See Walsh, *The Use of the Imagination,* p. 31; also p. 36, where he distinguishes between "the tenacity of the young mind" and "conscious memory."

22   Compare Leopardi's *Canto Notturno,* and see Chapter VII of this book.

23   Insufficient attention has been paid to Wordsworth's praise of fairy stories. Their inspirational value as he defines it may usefully be compared, for example, to Keats's and Foscolo's attitudes toward ancient literature and mythology. See Chapters VIII and IX of this book.

24   See Rader, *Presiding Ideas in Wordsworth's Poetry,* p. 157. Albert Gérard, "Coleridge, Keats and the Modern Mind," *Essays in Criticism,* I (1951), 249–61, asserts that "the Romantics . . . firmly believed that *within* 'mankind' there is room for a faculty that goes *beyond* reason. This is the basic assumption of Romanticism" (p. 253). As for geometry and poetry, compare Northrop Frye, *Anatomy of Criticism* (Princeton, 1957), pp. 350–52, for a lucid presentation of a "very speculative suggestion" that there is a significant analogy between literature and mathematics.

25   See De Selincourt, *Prelude,* 2d ed., pp. 198–200; the passage seems to have been written in 1806.

26   *Ibid.,* p. 200; lines 48–75 on MS. A.

27   As John E. Jordan, "Wordsworth's Minuteness and Fidelity," *PMLA,* LXXII (1957), 433–45, says in discussing changes in the different versions of *The Prelude*: "Wordsworth wanted the details . . . but he wanted also the unity of design."

28   A good discussion of Wordsworth's treatment of London will be found in F. H. Langman, "On the Scope of the Prelude," *English Studies in Africa,* I (1958), 195–204. "Wordsworth stands between Blake and Eliot, on the threshold of our world: more modern—more involved—than Blake, less modern than Eliot" (p. 198).

29 See Basil Willey, *The Seventeenth Century Background* (New York and London, 1950), pp. 296–309; and Chapter VI of this book.

30 The same remark could be applied to Foscolo, and, indeed, to most early nineteenth-century poets, who are exiles from Arcady, not—like Dr. Johnson—enemies of the pastoral world.

31 See Albert Gérard, *"Resolution and Independence:* Wordsworth's Coming of Age," *English Studies in Africa,* III (1960), 8–20, p. 9.

32 This is perhaps why "In trying to communicate the experience of true freedom through imagination, and in defending the national conditions of this freedom, Wordsworth wrote well."—Carl R. Woodring, "On Liberty in the Poetry of Wordsworth," *PMLA,* LXX (1955), 1033–48, p. 1039.

33 See F. M. Todd's remarks on Wordsworth's reactions to his 1820 visit to Switzerland, *Politics and the Poet* (London, 1957), p. 181.

34 Sir Henry Taylor, "Essay on the Poetical Works of Mr. Wordsworth," *Quarterly Review,* LIV (1834), 317–58, observed more than a century ago that Wordsworth did not invent any metaphysical system and that what is original and significant in Wordsworth is "not so much in reasoning as in judgment; not so much in the exposition of abstract truths as in his manner of regarding the particulars of life as they arise and of generalising them into one truth or another as the one or the other harmonises with his moral temperament and habitual and cherished states of feeling." I am indebted to Mr. Don Harper Hensley for calling my attention to this excellent, early study of Wordsworth.

35 "Although many romantic careers look like a working back to what had been originally rejected, it would be a mistake to suppose that the position returned to could ever again be the same as the original position. For the position returned to has been *chosen.*"—Robert Langbaum, *The Poetry of Experience* (London, 1957), p. 20.

36 Rader, *Presiding Ideas in Wordsworth's Poetry,* p. 169: "One of the supreme articles of his thought . . . is simply this idea: if imagination is once active, if the mind informs the senses, then a genuine and imperishable increment of power is added to existence." Rader is commenting specifically on the "spots of time" passage.

37 *Ibid.,* p. 165: "The significant fact is that synthesis is not effected by the mind *after* sensation, but the sensations appear to enter into consciousness already synthesized." See also Florence Marsh, *Wordsworth's Imagery: A Study in Poetic Vision* (New Haven, 1952), for example, p. 118: ". . . the mere fact must always be converted by the power of the imagination."

38 See the article by Jordan in *PMLA,* LXXII, 433–45.

39 One should not forget that Foscolo's country was defeated by physical force, that his cause failed under external pressure. This helped him to retain his overt "liberalism." Public oppression sometimes helps to preserve personal integrity. In the early 1790's Wordsworth hoped France would defeat England, because he believed France rather than England stood for true liberty. By 1805, Wordsworth had revised his ideas about

what constituted true liberty, but also by 1805 it seemed to many intelligent men that, as between England and France, true liberty now stood more with the former.

40 "Romantic poetry endeavors to lay bare the unusualness of the usual, and conversely the usual in the unusual."—R. H. Fogle, "A Note on Romantic Oppositions and Reconciliations," *The Major English Romantic Poets,* ed. Clarence D. Thorpe *et al.* (Carbondale, 1957), pp. 17–23, esp. pp. 19–20.

41 "Wordsworth's chief strength lies in that his greatest verse heightens our sense of communion with nature and humanity and thus offers a compelling motivation of democratic loyalties, making other ways of thought seem shabby, even inhuman, by contrast."—Newton P. Stallknecht, "Wordsworth and the Quality of Man," *Major English Romantic Poets,* pp. 52–73, p. 54. And see Whitehead, *Science and the Modern World,* p. 279: "Wordsworth presents a philosophy of individualism . . . but it is an individualism to be realized in community. . . . Everywhere individualism is tempered and enriched by an emphasis on the community of men and things."

42 See Walsh, *The Use of the Imagination,* p. 32; and Gérard, *L'idée,* p. 256. Walsh's sentence, "The poet is the standard of humanity, not the standard man," sums up Wordsworth's attitude splendidly. See also Peter Burra, *Wordsworth* (London, 1936), p. 70.

43 "Wordsworth believed that all inanimate nature shared, if to an infinitely less degree, the consciousness of life which man variously possesses. . . . Man to him was both a sensitive and a creative being. . . . It was this ideal reciprocity between all living things . . . which seemed to him the only quality necessary to happiness . . . in which man lived both in vital harmony with his neighbor and with the phenomenal universe."—Hugh I'Anson Fausset, *Studies in Idealism* (London, 1923), pp. 187–88.

44 Much of Stallknecht's work is relevant to this point.

45 See E. D. Hirsch, Jr., *Wordsworth and Schelling* (New Haven, 1960), p. 17.

46 The phrase is from the remarkable paragraph in Wordsworth's *Essay upon Epitaphs* (see the *Complete Poetical Works,* ed. Ernest de Selincourt and Helen Darbishire [Oxford, 1952], V, 444–56) in which he speaks of "feelings which, though they seem opposite to each other, have another and a finer connection than that of contrast.—It is a connection formed through the subtle progress by which, both in the natural and the moral world, qualities pass insensibly into their contraries, and things revolve upon each other. As, in sailing upon the orb of this planet, a voyage towards the regions where the sun sets, conducts gradually to the quarter where we have been accustomed to behold it come forth at its rising; and, in like manner, a voyage towards the east, the birthplace in our imagination of the morning, leads finally to the quarter where the sun is last seen when he departs from our eyes; so the contemplative Soul, travelling in the direction of mortality, advances to the country of everlasting life; and, in like manner, may she continue to explore those cheerful tracts, till she is brought back,

for her advantage and benefit, to the land of transitory things—of sorrow and of tears" (pp. 447–48).

What I have been saying of Wordsworth may suggest that I am disregarding Foscolo's emphasis upon "illusion." This is not my intention, which is, however, to stress the somewhat neglected positive implications of *Jacopo Ortis* (see note 49 below). In Chapter IX, I attempt to do more justice to the complexity of Foscolo's mature views.

47   The rhythm of *The Prelude* as a whole depends on a kind of ebb and flow between the unremarkable and the visionary, between "peace" and "excitation," which represents the pulsation of a vital cosmos at once *"stable et mouvant."* This rhythm is reflected in the counteractive forces of the poem's structure, the most obvious of which are the chronologically forward thrust of the autobiographical narrative and the chronologically backward thrust of the poet's creative memory (see Chapters V through VII).

48   The kind of beauty one finds in *The Tempest*. On the quality of Wordsworthian fear, see Walsh, *The Use of the Imagination*, p. 42.

49   Fausset, *Studies in Idealism*, p. 209: "Translated into human terms, she [Nature] was worthy of admiration and imitation; so far as man accepted her materially, . . . she was detestable." On this point Wordsworth's and Foscolo's views are surprisingly similar.

50   See Bennett Weaver, "Wordsworth's *Prelude*: The Shaping Spirit," *Studies in Philology*, XXXVII (1940), 75–87, esp. p. 78, "The fabric . . . is solidly enough set upon the substantial earth; yet the beauty expressed through that fabric is not of the earth but of that gracious reality which exists only in the creative intelligence." See also Francis Christensen, "Creative Sensibility in Wordsworth," *Journal of English and Germanic Philology*, XLV (1946), 361–68.

51   Abbie Findlay Potts, discussing the "plot" of *The Prelude*, says, ". . . the change in fortune is also accompanied by a discovery, the Poet's recognition that he himself and every other human being is by nature a poet, . . . This is the main discovery." *Wordsworth's* Prelude: *A Study of Its Literary Form* (Ithaca, 1953), p. 381. This is the best book on the literary background of *The Prelude*.

52   "The violent death of a king and of his executioner is at the center of Wordsworth's political preoccupations."—Jonathan Bishop, "Wordsworth and the 'Spots of Time,'" *ELH*, XXVI (1959), 45–65. Mr. Bishop is an unabashed follower of extreme modern psychological theory, but his judgments are often sensitive and original.

53   "If we can rid ourselves of the prejudices of Victorian progressives, Wordsworth's 'apostasy' appears in a new light. We, too, have our God that Failed. . . . He abandoned the Revolution only after the Revolution abandoned its ideals."—Langman, in *English Studies in Africa*, I, 200–201.

54   Fausset, *Studies in Idealism*, pp. 192–93: "Everything which prevented the expression of a man's whole self, or developed one of his faculties at the cost of another, was to him a cause of stumbling."

55 Gérard, *L'idée,* p. 241. And see his later important article, "Romance and
    Reality: Continuity and Growth in Keats's View of Art," *Keats-Shelley
    Journal,* XI (1962), 17–29, for example, in reference to the *Grecian Urn,*
    p. 26: "The note of mystery is indeed conspicuous: the meaning of life,
    suffering, and death is impenetrable; . . . [but there is] the indirect intima-
    tion that, although the ultimate truth about human destiny is unknowable,
    nevertheless life has a meaning, which is essentially spiritual and re-
    ligious. . . ." See Chapters IV and VI of this book.

56 The extensive treatment of this theme in *The Excursion* makes the poem
    a significant document of early nineteenth-century literature, and I should
    discuss it. But today few critics believe in the validity of any long poems.
    Most of our critical techniques serve to reduce length; we seem to prefer
    thin, clean skeletons (symbolic structures) to large living bodies complete
    with warts and moles. But Wordsworth regarded the cosmos as a vitally
    existential reality, and as such it cannot be summarily symbolized. He
    regarded the mind not as a *tabula rasa* but as a developing force, something
    that does not lend itself to succinct representation either. So when Words-
    worth undertook to define the place of the individual in the cosmos he
    embarked on a work of some length and one for whose form he saw no
    preëxistent model. In *The Excursion* he gave up the autobiographical form
    which he had used in the "preparatory" *Prelude* and attempted "some-
    thing of a dramatic form." By this he meant, I believe, something like a
    Platonic dialogue, which is not theatrical but which does dramatize move-
    ment of mind. This new form was necessarily accompanied by something
    of a new style, one that may be called intellectual—not in the sense of
    being metaphysical but in the sense that it is shaped to express principally
    consciousness and self-consciousness. I hope this much will make it clear
    to the reader why I could not fully discuss *The Excursion* in less than a
    chapter. Analogous reasons have restrained me from discussing important
    works by Foscolo, Leopardi, and Keats that are not incorporated in this
    study.

CHAPTER III

1   Comment upon and discussion of *Dei Sepolcri* is extensive, and I shall list
    here only those works to which I am most indebted for my reading of the
    poem. Most significant for me is the work of Mario Fubini, especially his
    Ugo Foscolo, 3d ed. (Florence, 1962), and his *Lettura della poesia fosco-
    liana* (Milan, 1949). The extensive commentary of Severino Ferrari in
    Ugo Foscolo: liriche scelte: i Sepolcri e le Grazie, 2d ed. revised by Oreste
    Antognoni and prepared for reprinting by Sergio Romagnoli (Florence,
    1957), is basic, even though the original date of publication was 1891.
    Walter Binni's review and anthology of Foscolo criticism, *Foscolo e la
    critica* (Florence, 1957) is indispensable. Also helpful are: Eugenio Dona-
    doni, *Ugo Foscolo, pensatore, critico, poeta,* 2d ed. (Palermo-Rome, 1927);
    the work of Franceso Flora, especially in *Storia della letteratura italiana*
    (with L. Nicastro) (3 vols.; Milan, 1940), III, 28–81; and Attilio Momi-

gliano, "La poesia dei Sepolcri di Ugo Foscolo," *Rivista d'Italia*, II (1928), 3–13. N. Sapegno in *Compendio di storia della letteratura italiana* (3 vols.; Florence, 1947), III, emphasizes Foscolo's attempt to overcome the "Alfierian gap" between the real and the ideal. On the relevance of Foscolo's *Commento alla chioma di Berenice*, see Aldo Vallone, *Genesi e formazione dei Sepolcri* (Asti, 1946). C. F. Goffis, *Studi foscoliani* (Florence, 1942), stresses the connection between *Dei Sepolcri* and *Le Grazie*. R. Ramat's two books, *Itinerario ritmico foscoliano* (Città di Castello, 1946) and *Discorso sulla poesia romantica italiana* (Lucca, 1950), discuss the "romantic religion of harmony" and, somewhat against the trend of modern criticism, rate *Dei Sepolcri* above *Le Grazie*. Two articles not specifically concerned with *Dei Sepolcri* which, nonetheless, have influenced my reading of the poem are Antonio Viscardi, "Note foscoliane," *La Cultura*, VII (1928), 349–52, and E. de Negri, "La logica della necessità e l'estetica della libertà del Foscolo," *Civiltà moderna*, XII (1940), 97–125, 269–87. Finally, mention may be made of Vittore Pisani, *Sulla poesia di Ugo Foscolo* (Milan, 1946), and Aldo Vallone, *Linea della poesia foscoliana* (Florence, 1957).

2 On Foscolo's politics and political activities see, for example, Giuseppe Chiarini's sound and readable biography, *La vita di Ugo Foscolo,* new ed. (Florence, 1927); Luigi Russo's two articles (containing excellent perceptions of Foscolo's character), "Foscolo politico," *Belfagor*, I (1946), 437–59 and II, 137–69; C. Morandi, "L'attività politica del Foscolo nel triennio repubblicano," and D. Spadoni, "Il Foscolo cospiratore nel 1813–14," both in *Studi su Ugo Foscolo editi a cura della Università di Pavia nel primo centenario della morte del poeta* (Turin, 1927), an indispensable collection of articles almost large enough to justify its title, which I shall shorten hereafter to *Studi di Pavia*; Paul Hazard's *La révolution française et les lettres italiennes* (Paris, 1910) has some value for the discussion of the political significance of *Jacopo Ortis*.

3 On Foscolo's exile in England, E. R. Vincent's *Ugo Foscolo: An Italian Exile in Regency England* (Cambridge, 1953) is outstanding, though Harry W. Rudman's brief treatment of Foscolo in England in *Italian Nationalism and English Letters* (New York and London, 1940), pp. 179–86, is sound. Foscolo's own writings, political and literary, during the period 1811–16 are being edited in Vol. VIII of the Edizione Nazionale and those of the English period in Vols. X–XII.

4 I make no claim to have mastered Foscolo's critical writings, which are extensive and nearly as contradictory as Coleridge's. My discussion of his critical position follows Fubini closely, his seventh chapter in *Ugo Foscolo*, his *Lettura della poesia*, and his chapter in *Romanticismo italiano* (Bari, 1953), "Introduzione alla critica foscoliana," pp. 106–60, serving as my chief guides. René Wellek's brief discussion of Foscolo as a critic in *A History of Modern Criticism: The Romantic Age* (New Haven, 1955), pp. 265–72, essentially agrees with Fubini; for example: "Foscolo is saved from the consequences of mere emotionalism or Platonic idealism by his

intense consciousness of the word, of the role of language and style in poetry. . . . Foscolo's chief importance, especially for Italy, lies in his attempt to see this conception of poetry as a part of history, of a philosophy of human development, and thus as the basis of a scheme for Italian literary history and a program for his own time" (p. 268). Foscolo's criticism is being collected in Vols. VIII, X, XI, and XII of the Edizione Nazionale, and lists of his articles in English are to be found in both Rudman and Vincent.

5   My translation of *The Sepulchres* and other of Foscolo's poems is based on the text in Luigi Russo's *Ugo Foscolo: prose e poesie* (Florence, 1951). This is an unpretentious edition, but it is inexpensive and obtainable in this country. Russo is a conscientious scholar, his notes are full, lucid, and helpful, and his presentation of *Le Grazie* provides more lines of the poem than any other available.

6   See G. Patroni, *La poesia e la figura d'Omero nei Sepolcri* in *Studi di Pavia*; G. Barbarisi, "Introduzione alle versioni omeriche del Foscolo," *Giornale Storico della letteratura italiana*, LXXXII (1955), 568–609.

7   This relating of "past" to "future" of course foreshadows the complexities of *The Graces*—see Chapter IX.

8   The standard work on this subject is O. Micale, *Thomas Gray e la sua influenza sulla letteratura italiana* (Catania, 1935). See also Donadoni, *Ugo Foscolo,* pp. 473–75.

9   Ernesto Grillo, *I Sepolcri* (London and Glasgow, 1928), p. 2, suggests more influence of Cesarotti than is warranted.

10   As is suggested by Carducci's judgment given at the beginning of this chapter. The sentence is quoted by Alberto Corbellini, "Il Foscolo e Pindaro" in *Studi di Pavia*, the fullest and most interesting treatment of the subject that I have read. Probably the centers of controversy for Foscolo's own comments, outside of his letters, are his original notes to the poem and his later *Lettera a Monsieur Guillon*, information on which is to be found in Ferrari's notes. Also relevant is Foscolo's *Osservazioni sul poema del Bardo del Monti.*

11   Here and throughout this discussion I am heavily indebted to Corbellini and to *Pindaro, le odi e frammenti*, trans. Ettore Romagnoli (2 vols.; Florence, 1921). See esp. I, xxiv and xix.

12   See R. G. Collingwood, *The Idea of History,* Galaxy ed. (New York, 1956), pp. 14–45, for a fascinating view of the historians of antiquity, all of whom, however, are post-Pindar.

13   Perhaps one should say a different phase of civilization. It is difficult for someone like myself, who finds Vico an exciting but baffling writer, to indicate briefly the nature of his influence on Foscolo. The interested reader would perhaps be best advised to look at the remarkable translation by T. G. Bergin and M. H. Fisch of *The New Science of Giambattista Vico* (Garden City, 1961), the Doubleday Anchor redaction of the same authors' complete translation, particularly Sections II and III of Book I, pp. 18–56, noting especially paragraph 337: ". . . what a great principle

of humanity burial is . . . with good reason burials were characterized by the sublime phrase 'compacts of the human race' . . . and . . . 'fellowships of humanity.' " See also Fubini, *Ugo Foscolo,* pp. 239–40.

14 See Robert Langbaum, *The Poetry of Experience* (London, 1957), esp. pp. 42, 47.

15 See the last part of Chapter VII for a further discussion of Romantic myth.

16 See for example Fubini, *Romanticismo italiano,* p. 126: "Lingua e stile perderanno nel Foscolo la loro astrattezza. . . . [Foscolo ha] una teoria della lingua italiana . . . la storia di una lingua non può tracciarsi se non nella storia letteraria della nazione." And p. 150: ". . . la sua personale esperienza di vita lo induce a negare con violenza la dottrina dell'arte come imitazione."

17 Foscolo's failure in critical consistency, a failure typical of many early nineteenth-century poets (Wordsworth being an obvious example), is frequently deplored by modern scholars. But the question of chief interest to anyone not concerned with ax-grinding is: why were the Romantics inconsistent in their criticism of their own poetry? The best answer, I believe, is suggested by Fubini's comment on Foscolo's remarks about *The Graces* (*Ugo Foscolo,* pp. 223–24): "Chi legge . . . senza preconcetti . . . le molte pagine abbozzate o stese con ordine dal Foscolo sul suo poema ha l'impressione di trovarsi di fronte ad un poeta possente, creatore di una nuova e originale forma d'arte e un critico esitante, che non riesce . . . a giustificarla criticamente. . . . L'incertezza sua . . . non sta a provare la originalità grande di quella poesia?" It is characteristic of early nineteenth-century poets that their poetry preceded their poetics, though their need to find a justifying critical theory ought not to be underestimated (see Chapter VII).

18 See Fubini's chapter in *Romanticismo italiano* and, for a discussion of Foscolo's use of literary references, his *Lettura della poesia,* pp. 112–23. Cf. also De Negri, in *Civiltà moderna,* XII: "[Foscolo] finisce per concepire la lingua comme un prodotto individuale" (p. 284). "L'estetica foscoliana mantiene sempre il carattere . . . di essere un' estetica della libertà" (p. 285).

19 Fubini sees Foscolo's conception of poetry's enormous "cultural" significance as deriving from Vico by way of Alfieri: see *Romanticismo italiano,* p. 115.

20 Fubini, *Romanticismo italiano,* pp. 117–18: "L'autonomia dell'arte e l' individualità inconfondibile di ogni opera poetica sono concetti sempre presenti alla mente del Foscolo. . . ." See also Foscolo's article on Dante, *Edinburgh Review,* XXIX (February, 1818), 453–74.

21 Corbellini, in *Studi di Pavia,* p. 67, suggests the term "assimilation" for this process.

22 See Fubini, *Romanticismo italiano,* pp. 118 ff.

23 Fubini makes this the root of Foscolo's insistence on the "chiaroscuro" of great art.

24 Fubini specifically identifies translation and the theory of translation as the factors which carried Foscolo beyond Locke. Fubini calls attention to the

importance of Foscolo's *L'esperimento di traduzione dell'Iliade di Omero* (Brescia, 1807), containing parallel translations by Foscolo, Monti, and Cesarotti. For Foscolo, as Fubini says, "translation is a recreation of a world, not a literary exercise," since words are the "creation of a particular poet at a particular historical moment."

25 For further illustration of this important point see the discussion of Foscolo's *ekphrasis* in Chapter IX.

26 Corbellini, in *Studi di Pavia*, p. 71, points out that Pindar celebrates sacrifice only once, while Foscolo is "il poeta umanissimo del valore sventurato."

27 In the Italian original the consoling trees of the poem are associated with women by use of feminine genders. I know of no way to reproduce this subtle effect in translation.

28 Langbaum's treatment of this kind of poetry, in *The Poetry of Experience*, is admirable.

CHAPTER IV

1 But it would be absurd to deny that Foscolo influenced Leopardi. See Walter Binni, *La nuova poetica leopardiana* (Florence, 1947), esp. p. 141, n.1. Also E. Guidi, *Leopardi e l' "Ortis"* (Genoa, 1947), and Giulio Natali, "Spiriti foscoliani nella poesia del Leopardi," *Rivista d'Italia*, III (1927), 41–57. Also relevant is Fernando Figurelli, "Le due canzoni patriottiche del Leopardi e il suo programma di letteratura nazionale e civile," *Belfagor*, VI (1951), 20–39, esp. p. 29.

2 My translations are from the edition of the *Canti* edited by Giuseppe de Robertis for Le Monnier (Florence, 1954, nuova ristampa). My chief reason for using this edition, besides its inexpensiveness and availability in this country, is that I have found De Robertis' notes most helpful. De Robertis does not lay much stress on sources; instead he concentrates on the elucidation of verbal connotations and musicality, and for the American reader unsure of his Italian nothing is more helpful. De Robertis is of course a fine scholar, see for example his *Saggio sul Leopardi* (Florence, 1960). Francesco Moroncini edited the two-volume *Canti di Giacomo Leopardi* (Bologna, 1927), which serves as a kind of variorum text. Mario Fubini's introduction to his edition of the *Canti* (Turin, 1945) is valuable, as is Benedetto Croce's article on Leopardi in *La critica*, XX (1922), 193–204, afterwards in *Poesia e non poesia*, 6th ed. (Bari, 1955), pp. 100–116. Of special relevance to *La ginestra* are Walter Binni, "La poesia eroica di Giacomo Leopardi," *Il Ponte*, XVI (1960), 1729–51, and, though quite old, Michele Losacco, "Per gli antecedenti della 'Ginestra,'" *Giornale Storico della letteratura italiana*, XLIII (1896), 289–340.

3 J. H. Whitfield, *Giacomo Leopardi* (Oxford, 1954), p. 251: "Leopardi's dismay is the gauge also of his affirmation. . . . No statement of Leopardi is greater than its opposite, and if the tragedy in which man is involved is immense for Leopardi, it is because the stature of man partakes of that immensity."

4 But see U. Bosco, *Titanismo e pietà nella poesia di Giacomo Leopardi* (Florence, 1960).

5 Binni, in *Il Ponte*, XVI, 1744. Binni's work during the past fifteen years has stressed the need to see Leopardi as something more than just the poet of the idylls and is, in my opinion, the most significant development in Leopardi criticism in this century.

6 Francesco Flora, "Natura e società in Giacomo Leopardi," *Quaderni ACI*, VI (1951), 49–74, p. 71: "L'uomo non deve ingannare se stesso: la natura lo ha creato alla morte e all'affanno; nè egli deve illudersi di aver miglior destino, dopo la morte . . . proprio qui . . . [Leopardi] inserisce l'idea della società umana, non più come quella di una corruzione della natura, ma di una difesa contro l'empietà della natura."

7 Binni, in *Il Ponte*, XVI, 1747: "Non più eroi della storia illustre classica: *Bruto minore* o *Saffo*, ma un'entità naturale delicata e modesta, risoluta e antiretorica, che oppone alla violenza della natura il suo esistere senza superbia e sensa servilismo . . . L'uomo cosciente della situazione umana. . . ." See also the very interesting article by Luigi Sturniolo, "Affinità e differenze nelle concezioni pessimistiche di Pindaro, Lucrezio e Leopardi," *Il mondo classico*, XIV (1947), 159–66, arguing that "Leopardi e Lucrezio sono assai vicini come poeti e non come pensatori" (p. 163).

8 See Bruno Biral, "Il significato di 'Natura' nel pensiero di Leopardi," *Il Ponte*, XV (1959), 1264–80.

9 See Emilio Bigi, "Lingua e stile dei 'Grandi Idilli,' " *Belfagor* VI (1951), 489–508, esp. pp. 500–505, with references to earlier studies by Fubini, Levi, and Colagrosso.

10 Robert Langbaum, *The Poetry of Experience* (London, 1957), p. 54. Langbaum, p. 39, quotes Dr. Johnson's observations (from the "Life of Denham") and comments on them. My indebtedness to Professor Langbaum should be plain.

11 For example, Douglas Bush, *John Keats, Selected Poems and Letters* (Boston, 1959), p. 346; Leonidas M. Jones, "The *Ode to Psyche*: An Allegorical Introduction To Keats's 'Great Odes,' " *The Keats-Shelley Memorial Bulletin*, IX (1958), 22–26. Jones, however, following James R. Caldwell in *John Keats' Fancy* (Ithaca, 1945), and John Holloway in "The Odes of Keats," *Cambridge Journal*, V (1952), 416–26, links *Psyche* to the other odes, whereas E. C. Pettet, *On the Poetry of Keats* (Cambridge, 1957), p. 317, puts *Psyche* into a special category. In recent years *Psyche* has been well and often defended, perhaps most effectively by Kenneth Allott, "The *Ode to Psyche*," *John Keats: A Reassessment*, ed. Kenneth Muir (Liverpool, 1958), pp. 74–94. Mr. Allott disposes of the difficulties raised by H. W. Garrod's celebrated reading of the last lines (pp. 77–79) and calls attention to some overlooked praise of the poem, notably that of Bridges and of Eliot (p. 74). See also Max Schulz, "Keats's Timeless Order of Things," *Criticism*, II (1960), 55–65; and Charles W. Hagelman, Jr., "Keats's Medical Training and the Last Stanza of the 'Ode to Psyche,' " *Keats-Shelley Journal*, XI (1962), 73–82.

12 See C. L. Finney, *The Evolution of Keats's Poetry* (Cambridge, Mass., 1936), II, 614–15; and Allott in *John Keats: A Reassessment,* pp. 83–85. Adolf Hoffman, *Das Psyche-Märchen des Apuleius in der englischen Literatur* (Strasbourg, 1908), analyzes various renderings of the Cupid and Psyche story in English. Hoffman treats both Mrs. Tighe's *Psyche* (Earle V. Weller, "Keats and Mary Tighe," *PMLA,* XLII [1927], 963–85, provides parallel passages) and Hudson Gurney's less noticed *Cupid and Psyche* (1799) which may have influenced Keats, e.g., Cupid as "Eternal beauty veil'd in man," and the reference to "Hesperian gardens" (Hoffman, p. 61). See also B. Ifor Evans, "Keats and *The Golden Ass," Nineteenth Century,* C (1926), 263–71.

13 "Since this book of Lucius is a figure of a man's life and toucheth the nature and manners of mortal man, egging them forward from their asinal form to their human and perfect shape (besides the pleasant and delectable jests therein contained) . . . I trust that the matter shall be esteemed by such as not only delight to please their fancies in recording the same, but also take a pattern thereby to regenerate their minds from brutal and beastly custom." This passage from Adlington's preface is quoted by Robert Graves in the introduction to his lively translation of *The Golden Ass,* Cardinal ed. (New York, 1952), p. ix.

14 ". . . a neat philosophical allegory of the progress of the rational soul towards intellectual love"—*ibid.,* p. xvi. For a discussion of the relation of this kind of allegory to folk-narrative and legend see Andrew Lang's introduction to *The Most Pleasant and Delectable Tale of the Marriage of Cupid and Psyche* (this is Adlington's version), London, 1887. Elizabeth H. Haight, *Apuleius and His Influence* (New York, 1927), traces the influence of *The Golden Ass* upon philosophy and the fine arts, though her sixth chapter deals with various renderings of Cupid and Psyche in English literature. For a scientific study of the folklore involved see Dudley David Griffith, *The Origin of the Griselda Story,* University of Washington Publications in Language and Literature, Vol. 8, No. 1 (Seattle, 1931), 1–120.

15 All quotations are from H. W. Garrod, *The Poetical Works of John Keats,* 2d ed. (Oxford, 1958).

16 It appears to me that Psyche is for Keats more closely associated with beauty than with the soul, although I do not wish entirely to exclude the latter nor to separate the poem from the famous "soul-making" passage in the long journal letter of February 14–May 3, 1819. See H. B. Forman (ed.), *The Letters of John Keats,* 2d ed. (Oxford, 1935), pp. 335–36. G. Wilson Knight in his critique of *Psyche* in *The Starlit Dome* (London, 1959), pp. 301–4, stresses the mingling of beauty with love to produce the religious effect of the poem's conclusion: "Keats's poetry is priest-like, with the selfless pomp and unperturbed assurance of a celebrant at a Christian Mass. His whole work moves to this point, challenging our limited sense not of the beautiful but of the sacred" (p. 304).

17 An interesting reading of *Psyche* with special emphasis upon "the gar-

dener Fancy" is to be found in Harold Bloom's *The Visionary Company* (Garden City, 1961), pp. 389–97. Mr. Bloom rightly insists on the importance of "feign" in the line "With all the gardener Fancy e'er could feign," comparing it to Yeats's "artifice," and pointing out that "the natural gardener breeds only in finite variety, but the abundance of the imagination is endless, and each imaginative breeding is unique" (pp. 395–96).

18 See Bloom, *The Visionary Company,* pp. 390–93, for an excellent detailed analysis of the passage in contrast to the nearly identical lines in the preceding stanza. Mr. Bloom may go too far in defining the first passage as "deliberately . . . ludicrous" and "faintly ridiculous," but the movement of "internalization" he traces seems indisputable. Perhaps his definition of Keats's "communion" as "natural supernaturalism" slightly blurs the distinction Keats draws between himself and the ancient rhapsodists. On this point see the commentaries of Knight and of Graham Hough, *The Romantic Poets* (London, 1953), pp. 172–73.

19 In the traditional story Cupid and Psyche met in the dark, but Keats's Psyche will be given "a bright torch"—perhaps to distinguish the "new" divinity from the old. This explanation of a puzzling point fits my reading of the poem so neatly that I am almost suspicious of it.

20 My reading of the odes has been most influenced by the studies of Mario Fubini, *Lettura della poesia foscoliana* (Milan, 1949), and the earlier study "Il 'dolce stil nuovo' di Ugo Foscolo," *La Cultura,* VII (1927), 52–62, later in *Ugo Foscolo,* 3d ed. (Florence, 1962). See also G. Citanna, *La poesia di Ugo Foscolo* (Bari, 1920), pp. 15–23; and Benedetto Croce, *Poesia e non poesia,* pp. 72–86.

21 Fubini, "Il 'dolce stil nuovo,' " p. 54.

22 *Ibid.,* p. 59.

23 But see, for example, R. D. Havens, "Of Beauty and Reality in Keats," *ELH,* XVII (1950), 206–13, for suggestions as to changes in the word's connotations in Keats's later work; and Archibald Lampman, "The Character and Poetry of Keats," *University of Toronto Quarterly,* XV (1946), 356–72, esp. pp. 357–59.

24 Notice the relationship of this "localizing" to the "translating" discussed in the preceding chapter. See also Chapter X.

25 On the first stanza see David Perkins, *The Quest for Permanence* (Cambridge, Mass., 1959), pp. 285–86. A good discussion of the ode's musicality is to be found in M. R. Ridley's fine study *Keats's Craftsmanship* (Oxford, 1933), pp. 232–40.

26 This circumstance provides one argument for associating the composition of *Melancholy* with *To Autumn* and not with the other odes of the Spring of 1819.

27 Bernard Blackstone, *The Consecrated Urn* (London, 1959), p. 352, treats the final stanza somewhat differently.

28 F. R. Leavis, *Revaluations* (London, 1936), p. 246: "Actually, when we re-read it we find that it moves outward and upward toward life as strongly as it moves downward to extinction."

29 Two good general discussions of the odes as a group may be found in John Holloway, *Cambridge Journal*, V, 416–26; and in Kenneth Muir, "The Meaning of the Odes," *John Keats: A Reassessment,* ed. Kenneth Muir (Liverpool, 1958), pp. 63–73.

30 I find it almost impossible to determine what my reading of this ode and of the *Ode on a Grecian Urn* owes to other critics. I shall briefly list those I am sure have influenced me and trust to the generosity of critics and scholars whose work I have inadvertently used without giving credit. Perkins, *The Quest for Permanence,* pp. 244–57; R. H. Fogle, "Keats's *Ode to a Nightingale,*" *PMLA,* LXVIII (1953), 211–22; H. M. McLuhan, "Aesthetic Patterns in Keats's Odes," *University of Toronto Quarterly,* XII (1942–43), 167–79; Thomas P. Harrison, "Keats and a Nightingale," *English Studies,* XLI (1960), 353–59. Most of my discussions of Keats's poetry owe something to Earl R. Wasserman's *The Finer Tone* (Baltimore, 1953) and to Douglas Bush's *Mythology and the Romantic Tradition* (Cambridge, Mass., 1937; reprinted by Pageant Books, New York, 1957) and his splendid little paperback edition of Keats cited in note 11, above. More specialized articles are those of Janet Spens, "A Study of Keats's 'Ode to a Nightingale,' " *Review of English Studies,* III, New Series (1952), 234–43, on the influence of Hazlitt and Wordsworth, and James D. Boulanger, "Keats's Symbolism," *ELH,* XXVIII (1961), 244–59, esp. 245–48, which discusses the ode in relation to W. K. Wimsatt's "Concrete Universal"—see *The Verbal Icon* (Lexington, 1954).

31 For an interesting discussion of these "perilous seas" see Newell F. Ford, "Keats's Romantic Seas: 'Ruthless' or 'Keelless'?" *Keats-Shelley Journal,* I (1952), 11–22.

32 McLuhan, in *University of Toronto Quarterly*, XII, 179: "[Keats was unable to] finally reject anything less than a total view of his experience. It is just such a totality . . . which is the concern of these odes. The odes have no message. They are actions."

33 Fogle, in *PMLA,* LXVIII, 218, points out the significance of the early version of the last line, "Was it a vision *real* or waking dream." Fogle's analysis succeeds in never destroying the balance of forces which creates the action of the ode: "The principal stress of the poem is a struggle between ideal and actual: . . . both pleasure and pain are deliberately heightened and meet in a common intensity."

34 R. H. Fogle, in his important book, *The Imagery of Keats and Shelley* (Chapel Hill, 1949), considers carefully (with full references to earlier studies) the problem of empathy, which is related to the point I am making, see esp. p. 139. Fogle distinguishes between the *Nightingale* as "sympathetic" and the *Urn* as "empathetic" (pp. 170 ff.).

35 Langbaum, *The Poetry of Experience,* p. 51.

36 I follow Garrod's ordering of the stanzas. See his discussion of the manuscript problem, p. 447.

37 Unless Knight, *The Starlit Dome,* p. 296, implies it.

38 D. G. James, *Scepticism and Poetry* (London, 1937), pp. 192–95; Robert

Berkelman, "Keats and the Urn," *South Atlantic Quarterly,* LVII (1958), 354–58; Martha Hale Shackford, "The *Ode on a Grecian Urn,*" *Keats-Shelley Journal,* IV (1955), 7–14 (the stress here on the ode as a celebration of form seems to me appropriate); J. M. Murry's latest development of his long work on Keats, *Keats* (London, 1955); Kenneth Burke, *A Grammar of Motives* (New York, 1935); Cleanth Brooks, *The Well Wrought Urn* (New York, 1947), and C. M. Bowra, *The Romantic Imagination* (Cambridge, Mass., 1949), provide some of the more celebrated interpretations of the ode. I believe more influential on my reading of the poem are the articles of Charles I. Patterson, "Passion and Permanence in Keats's 'Ode on a Grecian Urn,'" *ELH,* XXI (1954), 208–20, and Leo Spitzer, "The 'Ode on a Grecian Urn,' or Content vs. Metagrammar," *Comparative Literature,* VII (1955), 203–25. Spitzer, disagreeing with Wasserman's interpretation in *The Finer Tone,* argues rightly, I think, for this distinction: "The *archaeological* message of the urn is dead, its *aesthetic* message is alive 'for ever' . . . ." (p. 214). ". . . all readers of Keats's ode ought to become passers-by, pausing before the immortal urn and listening to its consoling message" (p. 221). "I believe that the unity of the poem remains intact and that the final lines are indeed the quite naturally developed abstract formulation of the actual experience of the work of art by the poet dramatically portrayed in this ode of *ekphrasis*" (p. 223). I think Spitzer's point is strengthened if one recognizes that there is a "Romantic ekphrasis"—as distinct from the classical prototype (see my discussion of Foscolo's *The Graces* below). Much of what Patterson says (Spitzer apparently was unaware of the article) substantiates Spitzer's point. "What the urn says it says *to men*; without them it could never be nor *be heard,* for men made it in the first place, and more men must be born if it is to have an audience in the future. . . . Keats proclaimed several times that the poet speaks to men, not to himself or other artists" (pp. 216–17). "But the art experience of the urn, understood for just what it is worth and no more, has helped his cognitive imagination to realize this truth. The urn has been to his mind what light is to the eyes, has made insight possible" (p. 219). I did not see Albert Gérard's important essay "Romance and Reality: Continuity and Growth in Keats's View of Art," *Keats-Shelley Journal,* XI (1962), 17–29, until after I had written my paragraphs on the *Grecian Urn.* Gérard's essay in some ways anticipates my view, but since our angles of attack are parallel rather than identical, I have decided to let my remarks stand.

39 Gérard's discussion of this point in the essay cited in the note above is most valuable.

40 What I try to define here and elsewhere is similar to Albert Gérard's *tertium quid;* see *L'idée romantique de la poésie en Angleterre* (Paris, 1955), pp. 140, 161, and *passim.*

41 On the textual problem underlying the interpretations see the articles by Alvin Whitley, in the *Keats-Shelley Memorial Bulletin,* V (1953), 1–2, and Jack Stillinger, in *PMLA,* LXXIII (1958), 447–48. I do not find convincing

the interpretation of the last lines proposed by Robert M. Adams in *Strains of Discord* (Ithaca, 1958): ". . . the last words of the poem are spoken not *by* but *to* the urn . . ." (p. 70). But I believe Mr. Adams' effort to evaluate what he calls "open-formed literary works" makes a contribution to our understanding of much early nineteenth-century literature. Gérard's (*Keats-Shelley Journal*, XI, 28–29) stress on the final words, especially "on earth" seems to me thoroughly justified.

42 See Roberta D. Cornelius, "Keats as a Humanist," *Keats-Shelley Journal*, V (1956), 87–96, especially her definition: "A humanist is one who is concerned with the nature and life of man, who believes in man's dignity and worth, and who attaches supreme importance to such expression of man's capabilities as will contribute to the lasting enrichment of human life. . . . In this large view and also in the narrower interpretation of the word, Keats was a true humanist." In a somewhat similar fashion Whitfield stresses the humanism of Leopardi: "Life is made for life, and not for death; and man's prime interest is in man. The kernel of Leopardi's thought is an exclusive humanism" (p. 196). See also p. 263.

CHAPTER V

1 There are many studies of "topographical" poetry; those I have found most useful, aside from studies mentioned in later notes, are: Robert Arnold Aubin, *Topographical Poetry in Eighteenth Century England* (New York, 1936); John Arthos, *The Language of Natural Description in Eighteenth Century Poetry* (Ann Arbor, 1949); Walter John Hipple, Jr., *The Beautiful, the Sublime, and the Picturesque* (Carbondale, 1957); Wylie Sypher, *From Rococo to Cubism* (New York, 1960), esp. pp. 48–59 and for later developments pp. 82–109; H. M. McLuhan, "Tennyson and Picturesque Poetry," *Essays in Criticism,* I (1951), 261–82, and "The Aesthetic Moment in Landscape Poetry," *English Institute Essays* (New York, 1951), pp. 168–81. Not so specifically concerned with my subject but providing much relevant information are Marjorie Hope Nicolson, *Mountain Gloom and Mountain Glory* (Ithaca, 1959), and Jean Hagstrum, *The Sister Arts* (Chicago, 1958). Earl R. Wasserman's chapters on *Cooper's Hill* (pp. 45–100) and *Windsor Forest* (pp. 101–68) in *The Subtler Language* (Baltimore, 1959) are thought-provoking and original.

2 Probably the best study of the concept of landscape is Sir Kenneth Clark's *Landscape into Art* (Pelican Book, Harmondsworth, 1956), but E. H. Gombrich's *Art and Illusion* (New York, 1960) treats with wit and lucidity many of the fundamental aesthetic problems involved in any consideration of the development of landscape art.

3 I believe that one can trace a development from pastoral poetry through "garden" poetry to a poetry concerned with progressively "wilder" nature— but that must be the subject of another study.

4 C. P. Ramaswami Aiyar, *Treatment of Landscape in Eastern and Western Poetry* (Baroda, 1956), observes that "In the Chinese language, the word for landscape is composed of two ideographic symbols, one for mountain

and the other for water" (p. 10), and he compares Wordsworth's comments on the landscape of Switzerland.

5 Clark, *Landscape into Art*, p. 35. Also p. 46: "[Ruysdael] felt the grandeur and pathos of simple nature. . . . This feeling he expressed, as all great landscape painters have done, through the large dispositions of light and dark."

6 An essential element in Wordsworth's originality is suggested by Jacques Maritain, *Creative Intuition in Art and Poetry*, "Bollingen Series," XXXV, 1 (New York, 1953), 144–45: "They [earlier poets] were not interested in reflexive self-awareness. The *reflex age*, the age of *prise de conscience*, which roughly speaking began for mysticism at the time of St. Teresa of Avila and St. John of the Cross, came later for poetry. When it began, at the time of Romanticism, it brought to completion the slow process of 'revelation of the Self' which had developed in the course of modern centuries."

7 See Fredrick A. Pottle's important article, "The Eye and the Object in the Poetry of Wordsworth," *Wordsworth, Centenary Studies*, ed. Gilbert T. Dunklin (Princeton, 1951), pp. 23–44, esp. pp. 32–33: "It is a great mistake to consider Wordsworth a descriptive poet." See also Robert Langbaum's specific comments on the opening lines of *Tintern Abbey* in *The Poetry of Experience* (London, 1957), p. 48.

8 This of course is one of the principal subjects of Meyer H. Abrams' monumental study *The Mirror and the Lamp* (New York, 1953); see esp. pp. 103–13.

9 See John F. Danby, *The Simple Wordsworth* (London, 1960), p. 97. His discussion of *Tintern Abbey* will be found on pp. 93–96 of this excellent little book. Other studies that may possibly have influenced my reading are John B. McNulty, "Autobiographical Vagaries in *Tintern Abbey*," *Studies in Philology*, XLII (1945), 81–86; James Benziger, "Tintern Abbey Revisited," *PMLA*, LXV (1950), 154–62; Harold Bloom, *The Visionary Company* (Garden City, 1961), pp. 127–36.

10 The phrase "not . . . As is a landscape to a blind man's eye" may present problems of interpretation because it summarizes a basic figurative pattern in the poem upon which depend differences and likenesses between "sight" and "vision."

11 See Charles Harold Gray, "Wordsworth's First Visit to Tintern Abbey," *PMLA*, XLIX (1934), 123–34, for a study of the dates in the poem, particularly with reference to evidence of *The Prelude*.

12 See Albert Gérard, "*Resolution and Independence*: Wordsworth's Coming of Age," *English Studies in Africa*, III (1960), 8–20, p. 9. Also E. D. Hirsch, Jr., *Wordsworth and Schelling* (New Haven, 1960), pp. 71–73. The poem "spirals," or "expands and contracts," or moves "cyclically" because it follows the action of the mind.

13 Wordsworth always employs the subjunctive with care and precision, and it seems to me that an understanding of the uses to which he puts the subjunctive carries one to the heart of his poetic method. Two important

studies bearing on the matter are: Carl Robinson Sonn, "An Approach to Wordsworth's Earlier Imagery," *ELH*, XXVII (1960), 208–22, esp. p. 217; H. W. Piper, *The Active Universe* (London, 1962), esp. pp. 115, 122, and 210 ff.

14 Nothing said in this discussion is intended to derogate the achievement of Neoclassical descriptive poetry. On the contrary, I want to suggest that we are likely to undervalue this poetry because we read it in the light of Wordsworth's art, from which most "nature" poetry of the last century and a half derives.

15 Again, my intention is to describe, not to criticize. But a description of the change I am concerned with can be easily distorted, and I think some critics have failed to do justice to the realism of Neoclassic poetic language. See Bonamy Dobree, *English Literature in the Early Eighteenth Century, 1700–1740,* (Oxford, 1959), esp. p. 161: ". . . the inclusive phrase, the epithet-noun combination: 'feathered tribe,' 'fleecy care,' 'finny breed' and so on, [are] used not, it must be insisted, in the interests of generalization and a soothing vagueness, but on the contrary, of precision, or of more attentive observation."

16 Langbaum, *The Poetry of Experience,* pp. 48–49.

17 Compare the discussion of Foscolo's language in Chapter III.

18 Geoffrey H. Hartman, *The Unmediated Vision* (New Haven, 1954), pp. 24–25, analyzes not only verbal redundancies but also sound repetitions in the poem. See also Charles J. Smith, "The Contrarieties: Wordsworth's Dualistic Imagery," *PMLA,* LXIX (1954), 1181–99.

19 John Jones, *The Egotistical Sublime* (London, 1954), p. 35, calls attention to Wordsworth's use of the word "things." On the potency of Wordsworthian passivity, see Morse Peckham, *Beyond the Tragic Vision* (New York, 1962), pp. 116–17, and compare the discussion of Keats's *Indolence* ode in the preceding chapter.

20 I believe this point could be sustained by a contrast between eighteenth- and nineteenth-century painting.

21 It is plain that I differ from Josephine Miles on this high point, but my thinking on this subject has been much influenced by her work. Of special relevance here are *The Vocabulary of Poetry, Three Studies,* University of California Publications in English, Vol. XII (Berkeley, 1946), and "Wordsworth: The Mind's Excursive Power," in *The Major English Romantic Poets,* ed. Clarence D. Thorpe *et al.* (Carbondale, 1957), pp. 35–51. Also important here is the study of R. A. Foakes, *The Romantic Assertion* (New Haven, 1958); note esp. in this context p. 35. See also Chapter III of this book.

22 See R. H. Fogle in *The Major English Romantic Poets,* pp. 19–20. Note also Walter Raleigh's observation, in *Wordsworth,* 8th ed. (London, 1921), p. 126: "The experiences that Wordsworth takes for his poetic material are those which adapt themselves least readily to verbal expression."

23 I admit that the preceding paragraph does not paraphrase any critical statement of Wordsworth's and that he wrote rather contradictorily of

these matters. But my "defense" is not manufactured out of whole cloth;
see Jones, *The Egotistical Sublime,* p. 67, and Newton P. Stallknecht,
Strange Seas of Thought (Bloomington, 1958), p. 39. One must remember
of Wordsworth that, "after all, he had never wanted to be a critic."—
George Watson, *The Literary Critics* (Pelican Book, Harmondsworth,
1962), p. 117.

24 Basil Willey, *The Seventeenth Century Background* (New York and
London, 1950), pp. 296–309.

25 Albert Gérard, *L'idée romantique de la poésie en Angleterre* (Paris, 1955),
p. 66, stresses that joy is essential to the English Romantics while Welt-
schmerz is essential to the German Romantics. One of the best things in
this fine book is the skill and accuracy with which Gérard distinguishes
between British and German Romanticism; see, for example, p. 274 on the
place of the "fragment" in Germany and Britain.

26 Melvin M. Rader, *Presiding Ideas in Wordsworth's Poetry,* University of
Washington Publications in Language and Literature, Vol. 8, No. 2
(Seattle, 1931), 121–216, esp. p. 125; Gérard, *L'idée,* p. 373.

27 Stallknecht, *Strange Seas of Thought,* p. 83.

28 "Infinity" was enormously important to Wordsworth. See for example
his famous letter to Landor, *The Letters of William and Dorothy
Wordsworth: The Later Years,* ed. Ernest de Selincourt (3 vols.; Oxford,
1939), I, 134–35.

29 Langbaum, *The Poetry of Experience,* pp. 31–32: "They [the Romantics]
were out to transform reality, to show that it had no existence apart from
the emotional apprehension of it." See also p. 28. See also D. G. James,
"Wordsworth and Tennyson," *Proceedings of the British Academy,*
1950, pp. 113–30, esp. p. 126: "[we see] landscape raised by Wordsworth's
imagination into an impassioned revelation."

30 Georges Poulet, "Timelessness and Romanticism," *Journal of the History
of Ideas,* XV (1954), 3–22, speaks directly to this point: "The Romantics
did not want to describe in their poems an ideal world. . . . They wanted
to express their own concrete experiences, their own immediate realities,
and to reflect in their poetry not the fixed splendor of God's eternity but
their own personal confused apprehension, in the here and now, of a
human timelessness. They took hold of the idea of eternity; but they
removed it from its empyrean world into their own" (p. 7). This article
and Poulet's earlier *Studies in Human Time* (Baltimore, 1956) are major
contributions which have considerably influenced my thinking. But I must
confess that I find myself in disagreement not alone with some of Poulet's
conclusions but also with parts of his assertions. For example, I do not
believe that *Tintern Abbey* expresses Wordsworth's "own personal
confused apprehension," even though I heartily agree with the principle
point of the passage above. Romantic apprehension at its best is logically
surprising, paradoxical, but not confused.

31 Norman Lacey, *Wordsworth's View of Nature and Its Ethical Consequences* (Cambridge, 1948), p. 5.

32 I have attempted to translate the Italian demonstratives literally. I should like to remind the reader that John Heath-Stubbs's translations are excellent poetic renderings.

33 My interpretation is heavily indebted to Adriano Tilgher, *La Filosofia di Leopardi* (Rome, 1940).

34 *Ibid.*, p. 149. Relevant here is the article by E. Raimondi, "Modi leopardiani," *Convivium*, XVI (1948), 524–35.

35 Francesco de Sanctis, *La letteratura italiana nel secolo XIX*, Vol. III, *Giacomo Leopardi*, ed. Walter Binni (Bari, 1953), p. 115.

36 *Ibid.*, p. 116.

37 *Ibid.*, p. 117. Interesting here, though not, I confess, entirely convincing to me, is Alessandro Parronchi, "Il muro di Berkeley e la siepe di Leopardi e la nascita della 'veduta indiretta.' "—*Paragone*, IX (1959), 3–29. A critique of the poem in English is to be found in Domenico Vittorini, *High Points in the History of Italian Literature* (New York, 1958).

38 Compare Wordsworth's *Two April Mornings*.

39 This attitude is expressed again in other poems, e.g., *Il passero solitario*, where the memories of old age are called painful.

40 See the reference to Bennett Weaver, note 12, Chapter II. Fernando Figurelli in an important book, *Giacomo Leopardi, poeta dell'idillio* (Bari, 1941), stresses the importance of creative memory, and points out (p. 77): "Il Leopardi non è mai poeta dell' esperienza immediato e quando l'ha tentato è restato inferiore a se stesso. Egli non canta la sua vita ma il ricordo di essa, . . ." See also pp. 35 ff. Two studies by Piero Bigongiari should be noted here also: *L'elaborazione della lirica leopardiana* (Florence, 1937) and "La costituzione dell' 'ottica' idillica," *Paragone*, VIII (1958), 19–76. Few modern psychologists seem to have devoted attention to the concept of creative memory. Herbert Marcuse is an exception. In his difficult but intriguing book *Eros and Civilization* (Boston, 1955) he observes: "The psychoanalytic liberation of memory explodes the rationality of the repressed individual. As cognition gives way to re-cognition, the forbidden images and impulses of childhood begin to tell the truth that reason denies. Regression assumes a progressive function. . . . The *recherche du temps perdu* becomes the vehicle of future liberation" (p. 19). His remark (p. 232) that "the ability to remember is a product of civilization—perhaps its oldest and most fundamental achievement" is directly in line with Wordsworth's and Leopardi's understanding of the nature of memory.

41 Professor Morse Peckham goes a little farther than I do in his extremely valuable article, "Toward a Theory of Romanticism: II. Reconsiderations," *Studies in Romanticism*, I (1961), 1–8: "Imagination is a means of grace, to be sure, but Nature does not redeem man. Rather, man, through the exercise of the imagination redeems Nature. Value enters the world through the self, which is not supported by any perceptible social or cosmic order, and the self projects upon the world an order which serves to symbolize that self-generated value" (p. 5). Peckham's verb, "projects,"

is misinterpreted if it is read as implying a total separation between "man" and "nature." The poets see man as *both* a natural creature *and* as a being of more than natural capacities. Man could not "redeem" nature were he not in part a natural creature—hence Peckham's assertion that the Romantic poet takes on "the role of Christ" (p. 6).

42 This point has been thoroughly established in recent years. See for example Abrams, *The Mirror and the Lamp,* pp. 291–92.

43 See Bruno Biral, "Il significato di 'Natura' nel pensiero di Leopardi," *Il Ponte,* XV (1959), 1264–80, esp. p. 1277.

44 See, for example, "The World Is Too Much With Us."

45 A good discussion of *La sera del dì di festa* will be found in Figurelli, *Giacomo Leopardi,* pp. 108–9.

46 The same process, although operating "culturally" rather than "personally," is at work in the conclusion of *The Sepulchres.* See Chapters VIII and IX for a discussion of our poets' treatment of the cultural past.

47 Langbaum's remarks (in *The Poetry of Experience*) on *Frost at Midnight* and *Tintern Abbey* are appropriate here: "The meaning of the poem is in all that has accrued since the original vision, in the gain in perception. But the gain is rather in the intensity of understanding than in what is understood" (p. 46). ". . . the revelation is not a formulated idea that dispels mystery, but a perception that advances in intensity to a deeper and wider, a more inclusive, mystery. . . . It is the whole purpose of the poem . . . to transform knowledge into experience" (p. 48).

48 Leopardi's pessimism has been much studied. An interesting and thoughtful article is that of Luigi Sturniolo, "Affinità e differenze nelle concezioni pessimistiche di Pindaro, Lucrezio e Leopardi," *Il mondo classico,* XIV (1947), 159–66.

CHAPTER VI

1 A valuable article of relevance here is that of Emilio Bigi, "Lingua e stile dei 'Grandi Idilli,' " *Belfagor,* VI (1951), 489–508. See esp. p. 492, n. 5, with its references to earlier studies of Leopardi's language by De Robertis and Contini. See also Fernando Figurelli, *Giacomo Leopardi, poeta dell'idillio* (Bari, 1941), pp. 81–84.

2 Francesco de Sanctis, *La letteratura italiana nel secolo XIX,* Vol. III, *Giacomo Leopardi,* ed. Walter Binni (Bari, 1953), p. 345.

3 Besides Bigi, in *Belfagor,* VI, pp. 496–99, see the important study by Cesare Galimberti, *Linguaggio del vero in Leopardi* (Florence, 1959), esp. p. 155.

4 One of the most useful studies of the "Lucy" poems is Herbert Hartman's "Wordsworth's 'Lucy' Poems: Notes and Marginalia," *PMLA,* XLIX (1934), 134–42. F. W. Bateson's rather strained and sensational interpretation is to be found in his *Wordsworth: A Re-Interpretation,* 2d ed. (London and New York, 1956). An excellent comparison between the "Lucy" poems and the "Matthew" poems is to be found in John F. Danby, *The Simple Wordsworth* (London, 1960), pp. 83–88.

5 C. M. Bowra, *The Romantic Imagination* (Cambridge, Mass., 1949), p. 11: "Their [the Romantics'] art aimed at presenting as forcibly as possible the moments of vision which give to even the vastest issues the coherence and simplicity of single events."

6 See Helen Darbishire, "Wordsworth's Significance for Us," *The Major English Romantic Poets*, Clarence D. Thorpe *et al.* (Carbondale, 1957), pp. 74, 75.

7 Some important studies of the poem: Albert Gérard, *"Resolution and Independence:* Wordsworth's Coming of Age," *English Studies in Africa,* III (1960), 8–20; W. W. Robson, "Wordsworth: *Resolution and Independence"* in *Interpretations,* ed. John Wain (London, 1955); Richard Chase, *Quest for Myth* (Baton Rouge, 1949). I am most indebted, however, to the articles by Conran and Grob cited below, especially the latter.

8 Anthony E. M. Conran, "The Dialectic of Experience: A Study of Wordsworth's *Resolution and Independence,"* *PMLA,* LXXV (1960), 66–74, p. 72.

9 Compare the discussion of *Jacopo Ortis* as a philosophical novel in Chapter I.

10 Alan Grob, "Process and Permanence in *Resolution and Independence,"* *ELH,* XXVIII (1961), 89–100: "Both poems [*Elegiac Stanzas* and *Resolution and Independence*] are, in fact, poems of renunciation, statements of the unsuitability of nature's holy plan as a model of human conduct" (p. 90). Also: ". . . the Leech-gatherer has also found a spiritual existence alien to and transcending the very processes of nature . . ." (p. 97).

11 As A. C. Bradley remarked of a passage in *The Prelude,* "Everything here is natural, but everything is apocalyptic." *Oxford Lectures on Poetry* (London, 1909), p. 134.

12 See Robert Langbaum, *The Poetry of Experience* (London, 1957), p. 54; and Grob, in *ELH,* XXVIII, 97.

13 "It is the Romantic paradox, the main problem of Keats in his maturity: how to reconcile the world of the imagination with the dangerously humdrum world of everyday."—Conran, in *PMLA,* LXXV, 71.

14 Obviously I am in agreement with Grob's interpretation of the poem (though I am concerned here with illustrating a technique rather than with providing an interpretation): "Although the Leech-gatherer is just such a victim of natural decay as Wordsworth had foreseen as his own future, it becomes clear during the poet's questioning that the old man is not, after all, a kind of Doppelgänger figure giving substance to and confirming Wordsworth's earlier premonitions. . . . There has been no decay of inner life to correspond to that of the outer life . . ." (p. 99). I should add that the "dramatic" quality of the poem arises exactly from the anticlimactic nature of the Leech-gatherer: he is *not* a Doppelgänger— but he is significant. This pattern—build-up, anticlimax, and finally the discovery of unexpected significance in the trivial—is common in Wordsworth's poetry and is quite deliberate. It explains why a poem such as *Resolution and Independence* may be identified by Conran as "comic"

in the profoundest sense. It is a poem of recovery, of escape from an apparently tragic dilemma: "Wordsworth's admonishment comes about because he has unnecessarily limited the possible guides available to man, assuming that man must either follow self-interest or follow nature. What the Leech-gatherer represents is a third way . . ." Grob, *ELH,* XXVIII, 100.

15 Recent studies of this much-discussed poem are: Bernard Blackstone, *The Consecrated Urn* (London, 1959), pp. 275–88, which stresses the element of the initiation ritual in the poem; Jack Stillinger, "The Hood-winking of Madeline: Scepticism in 'The Eve of St. Agnes,'" *Studies in Philology,* LVIII (1961), 533–55; Norman Nathan, "Flesh Made Soul," *The Personalist,* XLII (1961), 198–202, which, without pretense at scholar-ship, defines with clarity and force the problem which Stillinger wrestles with at far greater length: "[The poem has all the] earmarks of a scandal story [in] today's tabloid. . . . The strange side of it all is that, despite the ruthlessness on the part of Porphyro and the lack of delicacy on the part of Madeline, the reader may feel that he has read a tale of the purest and most holy young love imaginable" (p. 198). I believe Stillinger is thoroughly justified in arguing for Keats's "scepticism" and against the excesses of the "metaphysical" critics, though he finally oversimplifies; see esp. p. 553 on the Nightingale and Grecian Urn odes.

16 On this point see G. Wilson Knight, *The Starlit Dome* (London, 1959), pp. 279–80.

17 See R. A. Foakes (one of Stillinger's "metaphysical" critics), *The Roman-tic Assertion* (New Haven, 1958), pp. 93–94.

18 Insofar as Bernice Slote, *Keats and the Dramatic Principle* (Lincoln, 1958), is willing to modify the traditional conception of "drama" in the direction I am suggesting, her argument for Keats as a "dramatic" poet is illuminating. Her long discussion of *Lamia,* pp. 138–92, implies this more sophisticated conception of "drama" to a greater extent than do the earlier portions of her book.

19 The conclusion of the poem has been intensively studied. See Earl R. Wasserman, *The Finer Tone* (Baltimore, 1953), pp. 122–30; and Cecil C. Seronsy, "The Concluding Stanzas of 'The Eve of St. Agnes,'" *Keats-Shelley Journal,* VI (1957), 12–13. Herbert Heinen, "Interwoven Time in Keats's Poetry," *Texas Studies in Literature and Language,* III (1961), 382–88, discusses Keats's shifting of tenses, particularly in Stanza XLI (pp. 383–84). Initiating the modern debate on the poem's ending are two articles in *Modern Language Review*: Herbert G. Wright, "Has Keats's 'Eve of St. Agnes' a Tragic Ending?" (XL, 1945, 90–94), and M. Whitely's answer, "The 'Tragic Ending' of Keats's 'Eve of St. Agnes'" (XLII, 1947, 123–25).

20 Hence I disagree with Stillinger when he says, "The realistic notes all seem to occur in the framework, and the main action is all romance. There is no interaction . . ." (p. 534). I do not believe "framework" and "main action" are so separable.

21 Stillinger's argument (*Studies in Philology*, LVIII, 538–46) that Porphyro uses a "stratagem" and is not undertaking a "pilgrimage," seems to me valid and important. But the point of the poem as I read it is that what *begins* as a "stratagem" ends in a kind of holiness, which is not Christian holiness and which does not "escape" from the realities of this world. Albert Gérard (in "Romance and Reality: Continuity and Growth in Keats's View of Art," *Keats-Shelley Journal,* XI, 1962, 17–29), building on William Empson's remark in *The Structure of Complex Words* (London, 1951), pp. 370–71, argues for this balance as the essence of Keats's mature art, in which we see "a revelation of the beautiful in the actual" (p. 28) and which "actualizes the ideal and . . . makes perceptible . . . the ideal in the actual" (p. 29).

22 R. H. Fogle, "A Reading of Keats's 'Eve of St. Agnes,'" *College English,* VI (1944–45), 325–28: "The story belongs to the remote past, the lovers are long dead; but this imaginative projection of the essential values of young love is immortal. And these values are arrived at not by forgetting what everyday existence is like, but by using the mean, sordid, and commonplace as a foundation upon which to build a high romance" (p. 328). I should add to this, again differing from Stillinger, who says ". . . the dreamer in the poems of 1819 is always one who would escape pain. [This is true.] . . . Either he comes to grief through his delusion, or he learns his lesson and wakes up" (p. 551), that Keats increasingly saw "vision" (something different, to be sure, from "delusive dreams") as the means of uniting "high romance" and "mean, sordid, and commonplace" reality. Madeline finally awakes from a most delightful trance to discover she has acquired a brave and honorable (though not perfect) husband. The interest and complexity of Keats's later work is that he simultaneously saw the danger of delusive dreaming *and* the danger of mere scepticism; neither "romance" alone nor "realism" alone was sufficient for his vision. See my discussion of *Hyperion* in Chapter VIII.

23 See Mario Fubini, *Lettura della poesia foscoliana* (Milan, 1949), p. 61.

24 I have read with interest the recent interpretations of Harold Bloom (*The Visionary Company* [Garden City, 1961], pp. 179–82) and David Perkins (*The Quest for Permanence* [Cambridge, Mass., 1959], pp. 82–84), but I have found more valuable E. D. Hirsch, Jr., *Wordsworth and Schelling* (New Haven, 1960), pp. 88–97. Hirsch relates "Peele Castle" to other of Wordsworth's poems and draws attention to some recurrent Wordsworthian techniques clearly illustrated by the elegy.

25 Here I differ from Hirsch, who asserts that the poet looks "toward the eternal city of God."

26 Darbishire, in *Major English Romantic Poets*, p. 99.

27 Martha Hale Shackford's *Wordsworth's Interest in Painters and Pictures* (Wellesley, 1945) is the fullest study of this subject.

28 *Ibid.,* p. 8. One of Meyer H. Abrams' most useful contributions in *The Mirror and the Lamp* (New York, 1953) is the careful definition of what different poets and critics mean by "creativity." For Wordsworth, as

opposed to Coleridge, see pp. 57–67 and 180–82. See also the discussions of "imagination" in *The Prelude* in Chapter II and of our poets' attitudes toward the art of earlier epochs in Chapter IX.

29 Here again Abrams' careful distinctions are helpful; see *The Mirror and the Lamp*, p. 65.

30 Sensitive readings of the poem are Perkins, *The Quest for Permanence*, pp. 290–94, and R. A. Brower, *The Fields of Light*, Galaxy ed. (New York, 1962), pp. 38–41. A thorough and compelling study of the poem as more than a descriptive piece, with much interesting material on the sources of its imagery, is Arnold Davenport's "A Note on 'To Autumn,'" in *John Keats: A Reassessment*, ed. Kenneth Muir (Liverpool, 1958), pp. 95–101. Douglas Bush, in "Keats and His Ideas," *English Romantic Poets*, ed. Meyer H. Abrams, Galaxy ed. (New York, 1960), sticks to the old idea of the poem as pure description (see pp. 336–37). Bush, I believe, is wrong in this instance, but he is surely right to warn against the confusion of poetry and biography illustrated, for example, by Robert Gittings, *The Living Year* (Cambridge, Mass., 1954), pp. 186–88.

31 Margaret Sherwood, *Undercurrents of Influence in English Romantic Poetry* (Cambridge, Mass., 1934), p. 263: ". . . a perfect expression of the phase of primitive feeling and dim thought in regard to earth processes when these are passing into a thought of personality."

32 Edith Hamilton, *The Greek Way to Western Civilization* (New York, 1942), p. 51, remarks on the third stanza of the poem: "The things men live with, noted as men of reason note them, not slurred over or evaded, not idealized away from actuality, and then perceived as beautiful—that is the way Greek poets saw the world."

33 As Keats in *The Eve of St. Agnes* transforms romance into a myth of romance, so in *Autumn* he transforms a mood into a myth of a mood.

34 Of special value in regard to this poem is Piero Bigongiari, *L'elaborazione della lirica leopardiana* (Florence, 1937).

35 See Francesco Flora, "Natura e società in Giacomo Leopardi," *Quaderni ACI*, VI (1951), 49–74.

36 See Figurelli, *Giacomo Leopardi*, p. 114, and Francesco Flora, *Orfismo della parola* (Rocca San Casciano, 1953), pp. 305–9.

37 Luigi Malagoli, *Leopardi* (Florence, 1960), pp. 47 ff.

38 See Nesca Robb, *Four in Exile* (London, n.d.), p. 68.

39 Compare Adriano Tilgher, *La Filosofia di Leopardi* (Rome, 1940), p. 114: "Per l'idealismo storicistico vichiano e hegeliano la civiltà si riduce in fondo all 'esplicazione di tendenze già posto nell 'uomo dalla natura, ma per Leopardi l'uomo facendo la civiltà *non* si limita a *svolgere* la sua natura, ma ne . . . crea un mondo interamente di sua fattura." On the intellectual background of Romantic myth-making see Albert J. Kuhn's valuable "English Deism and the Development of Romantic Mythological Syncretism," *PMLA*, LXXI (1956), 1094–1116.

40 See René Wellek, *A History of Modern Criticism: The Romantic Age* (New Haven, 1955), pp. 274 and 275.

CHAPTER VII

1   Iris Origo, *Leopardi* (London, 1953), quotes from Francesco Flora's introduction to *Leopardi: Poesie e Prose*: "The whole of Arcadia is freed; what was merely literature, becomes poetry" (p. 90). On Wordsworth's sympathy for Arcadianism see Chapter II.

2   I translate *fanciullo mio* here as "little brother" on the strength of De Robertis' comment "Come dicesse: figlio mio, fratello mio" (p. 249 of the text cited in note 12 below). I believe my translation properly expresses the development of thought and feeling in the conclusion of the poem— a development which depends in part on the distinction-in-similitude between "Garzoncello" in line 43 and "fanciullo" in line 48—but I have had to depart from the literal meaning of a significant word. I have taken a few similar liberties in other translations, but it would have been wearisome to justify each, and I trust that readers of Italian will accept the explanation above as sufficient evidence that I may have been misguided in my translating but at least not willful or thoughtless.

3   I know of no modern critic who disagrees with this point. For Leopardi's reminiscences of earlier works, see A. Zottoli, "Risonanze arcadiche e melodrammatiche nei versi di Giacomo Leopardi," *La Cultura*, II (1923), 49–57.

4   Nesca Robb, *Four in Exile* (London, n.d.): "In poem after poem Recanati becomes for its child a type of all human life" (p. 68). "And since he sees in it an image of humanity, the love, compassion and pain he feels in contemplating it are an image of the response he would make to all his kind" (p. 69).

5   "As between all levels, it is the lower ones that set the frame in which phenomena of superior level operate. The 'laws' or forces of the lower level do not per se 'produce' the upper-level phenomena; at any rate, these cannot be wholly derived from below; there is always a specific residuum, a sum of the parts, a combination or organization, that is of and in the level being considered. Thus organic processes of events conform wholly to physico-chemical process, but cannot be non-residually resolved in to them."—A. L. Kroeber and Clyde Kluckhohn, *Culture* (Cambridge, Mass., 1952), p. 148.

6   See the end of Chapter X for a discussion of one implication of this view.

7   J. H. Whitfield, *Giacomo Leopardi* (Oxford, 1954), p. 196: "Life is made for life and not for death; and man's prime interest is in man. The kernel of Leopardi's thought is an exclusive humanism."

8   Not only is it the last of the idylls but it is also the one to which Leopardi devoted the greatest care. It took him six months to compose it. He wrote *To Silvia* in two days and *Remembrances*, which is longer than the *Night Song*, in eighteen. See Angelo Monteverdi, "La composizione del 'Canto notturno,'" *La rassegna della letteratura italiana*, LXIV (1960), 207–17. On the figure of the "pellegrino" in Leopardi, see Cesare Galimberti, *Linguaggio del vero in Leopardi* (Florence, 1959), esp. pp. 20–21 with references to the earlier studies by Colagrosso and Ferrero.

Studies of general problems raised clearly in the *Night Song* are Ugo Dotti, "Valore esistenziale del paesaggio leopardiano," *Lettere italiane,* XII (1960), 459–66; and F. Grassi *Il sentimento della notte nella poesia del Leopardi* (Florence, 1960).

9 See Galimberti, *Linguaggio del vero,* pp. 85–91, esp. p. 87, n. 105, and pp. 88–89, n. 106.

10 See Origo, *Leopardi,* p. 24, for a discussion of Leopardi's fear of masks. It has long been a commonplace that the relatively juvenile poetry of the Romantics is often marred by clumsily transparent disguises, e.g., *Endymion.*

11 The chief exceptions for Leopardi are *Spavento Notturno* and the *Coro dei Morti* (both of these fascinating poems are well translated by Heath-Stubbs). For a discussion of "il colloquio" in Leopardi, see Fernando Figurelli, *Giacomo Leopardi, poeta dell'idillio* (Bari, 1941), esp. pp. 74–75.

12 Good discussions of Leopardi's language will be found in Francesco Flora's introduction to *Canti e prose scelte* (Milan, 1938); Mario Fubini's introduction to *Canti di Giacomo Leopardi* (Turin, 1945); and Giuseppe de Robertis' notes in his edition of the *Canti* (Florence, 1954), on which my translations are based. See also of course Emilio Bigi, "Lingua e stile dei 'Grandi Idilli,'" *Belfagor,* VI (1951), 489–508.

13 See Monteverdi, in *La rassegna della letteratura italiana,* LXIV, p. 215.

14 Whitfield, *Giacomo Leopardi,* p. 233: "It is not *noia* and *nulla* . . . that dominate the *Canti.*"

15 See Figurelli, *Giacomo Leopardi,* pp. 115–16.

16 See Whitfield's translations and discussion, *Giacomo Leopardi,* p. 192: "Life is made naturally for life and not for death. That is to say, it is made for activity and for all that there is most vital in the functions of the living creature."

17 Compare Albert Gérard's comments on the "questions" of the *Grecian Urn,* "Romance and Reality: Continuity and Growth in Keats's View of Art," *Keats-Shelley Journal,* XI (1962), 26.

18 See for example Giuseppe de Lorenzo, "Time and Space as Conceived by Leopardi," *East and West,* VI (1955), 249–53, and "The Cosmic Conceptions of Leopardi" in the same publication, V (1954), 198–204.

19 Walter Pater's remarks on Wordsworth are relevant here. "He has a power likewise of realizing and conveying to the consciousness of his reader abstract and elementary impressions, silence, darkness, absolute motionlessness, or, again, the whole complex sentiment of a particular place, the abstract expression of desolation in the long white road, of peacefulness in a particular folding of the hills. That sense of a life in natural objects, which in most poetry is but a rhetorical artifice, was, then, in Wordsworth the assertion of what was for him almost literal fact.

   .   .   .   .

He raises physical nature to the level of human thought, giving it thereby a mystic power and expression; he subdues man to the level of nature, but gives him therewith a certain breadth and vastness and solemnity."—

From a review of Morley's *Complete Works of Wordsworth,* in *The Guardian,* February 27, 1889. I have quoted from the Macmillan edition of Pater's works (London, 1914), *Essays from "The Guardian,"* pp. 98–100.

20   Compare Alan Grob, "Process and Permanence in *Resolution and Independence,*" *ELH,* XXVIII (1961), 89–100, esp. p. 100. His observations seem relevant here as well.

21   See C. M. Bowra's remark in *The Romantic Imagination* (Cambridge, Mass., 1949), p. 11, cited in note 5 to Chapter VI.

22   It appears to me that most inadequate modern judgments of the purposes and attainments of early nineteenth-century poetry are founded on a failure to perceive that to Romantic poets a man attains his identity by fully developing *all* his capacities and potentialities.

23   Here attention may be called to Wordsworth's somewhat neglected distinction between imagination and fancy in his note to *The Thorn* (see the *Complete Poetical Works,* ed. Ernest de Selincourt and Helen Darbishire [Oxford, 1952], II, 512): "Superstitious men are almost always men of slow faculties and deep feelings; their minds are not loose, but adhesive; they have a reasonable share of imagination, by which word I mean the faculty which produces impressive effects out of simple elements; but they are utterly destitute of fancy, the power by which pleasure and surprise are excited by sudden varieties of situation and an accumulated imagery." All of Wordsworth's best poetry "produces impressive effects out of simple elements."

24   I realize that this statement puts me in flat opposition to a traditional definition of the Romantic poet. See, for example, R. H. Fogle, "Keats's *Ode to a Nightingale,*" *PMLA,* LXVIII (1953), 211: "The *Nightingale* is a Romantic poem . . . in that it describes a choice and rare experience, intentionally remote from the commonplace." There is a difference between Romantic poets; a student once remarked to me that Wordsworth is always losing something and Keats is always finding something. But I should argue that much Romantic poetry, including Keats's odes, endeavors to make commonplace experience choice and rare.

25   Originally published in New York and London, 1950. My quotations are from the Doubleday Anchor edition (Garden City, 1953); see pp. 293–94 for this excerpt.

26   *Ibid.,* pp. 295, 300–301.

27   *Ibid.,* p. 294. "Mythology" for Willey means primarily Greco-Roman mythology. It was Douglas Bush (in *Mythology and the Romantic Tradition* [Cambridge, Mass., 1937; reprinted by Pageant Books, New York, 1957]), I believe, who first pointed out that Romantic poets were "deprived" not alone of the subject matter of classical mythology but also of its form, "forthright storytelling."

28   As is testified by the histories of criticism of Abrams, Wellek, and Watson.

29   See note 17, Chapter III, for Fubini's comment on this point.

CHAPTER VIII

1 Hence the variety of interpretations of the poem, to many of which my study is indebted. I should perhaps single out the following as most influential: Douglas Bush, *Mythology and the Romantic Tradition* (Pageant Books reprint, New York, 1957, of the original edition, Cambridge, Mass., 1937), pp. 115–28; Kenneth Muir, "The Meaning of Hyperion" in *John Keats: A Reassessment,* ed. Muir (Liverpool, 1958), pp. 102–22; Martha Hale Shackford, *"Hyperion," Sewanee Review,* XXII (1925), 48–60; D. G. James, *Scepticism and Poetry* (London, 1937), pp. 198–202; James R. Caldwell, "The Meaning of *Hyperion," PMLA,* LI (1936), 1080–97; Stuart Sperry, "Keats, Milton, and *The Fall of Hyperion," PMLA,* LXXVII (1962), 77–84. Bernard Blackstone's latest study, in *The Lost Travellers* (London, 1962), pp. 276–84, is disappointing after his discussion in *The Consecrated Urn,* cited below. All quotations are from H. W. Garrod, *The Poetical Works of John Keats,* 2d ed. (Oxford, 1958).

2 See for example G. R. Levy, *The Sword from the Rock* (London, 1953).

3 Bernard Blackstone, *The Consecrated Urn* (London and New York, 1959), p. 237: *"Hyperion* is to be a cosmogonic epic. It will 'unfold through images the theory of the world.'" Blackstone's emphasis is upon the relevance of Plato's *Timaeus.*

4 Two unpublished doctoral dissertations which deal with the influence of William Godwin's *Pantheon* on Keats's system of progressive evolution deserve mention: Sister Mary Carlin, "John Keats' Knowledge of Greek Art: a Study of Some Early Sources" (Catholic University of America, 1951) and Norman Anderson, "Bard in Fealty: Keats' Use of Classical Mythology" (University of Wisconsin, 1962).

5 See, of course, Bush, *Mythology and the Romantic Tradition,* pp. 115–28; also Ernest de Selincourt's edition of *The Poems of John Keats,* 4th ed. (New York, 1921), p. xlv: ". . . a story of the ancient world had to assume Elizabethan dress before it could kindle his imagination." Also, pp. xlvii–xlviii: ". . . The poems of Greek inspiration exhibit no trace of influence of classical literature, but are determined in each case by the influence of different models of English poetry." This last probably overstates an excellent point.

6 I use the word "synaesthesia" in its more general sense. R. H. Fogle, *The Imagery of Keats and Shelley* (Chapel Hill, 1949), drawing on Clarence D. Thorpe's work, analyzes with more intensity the significance of synaesthesia in Keats's art; see esp. p. 137.

7 See Caldwell, in *PMLA,* LI, 1093.

8 A good discussion of the Titans' "earthliness" is to be found in Lucien Wolff, *John Keats, sa vie et son œuvre* (Paris, 1910), p. 628. Though old, Wolff's book is still valuable.

9 Leone Vivante, *English Poetry* (London, 1950), provides a valuable definition of Keats's love for the new and unknown: "Keats describes . . . the moment of *novelty* as outstandingly representative of life and life's

value . . ." (p. 182). " 'Novelty' must be understood as laying stress on an intimate value of non-predeterminedness and potency, rather than on change" (p. 183).

10   "The assembled Titans themselves approximate to the chaos surrounding them: . . . Plainly *Hyperion* . . . is a macrocosmic model of the psyche in ignorance and enlightenment."—Blackstone, *The Consecrated Urn*, p. 238.

11   "What Oceanus proclaims is the imaginative center of the fragment."— Harold Bloom, *The Visionary Company* (Garden City, 1961), p. 385.

12   A. E. Powell (Mrs. E. R. Dodds), *The Romantic Theory of Poetry* (London, 1926), p. 229: "In their [the Titans'] very passion there is no conflict, no struggle to recreate their being out of tragedy. The 'vale of Soul-making' is not for these. They are like great natural forces, which governed by an overmastering law fulfil easily and unconsciously that for which they are formed. It is not theirs to win knowledge and by art to make, with all the agony and effort of creation. The new gods seem smaller, but more vivid . . . they are convulsed in making. . . . Art and knowledge have entered into their singing, so that it is able to express their complex life, with its active, conscious effort to shape things to its intent."

13   Bush, *Mythology and the Romantic Tradition*, p. 124: "The Titans, however benign and beneficent, had in a crisis behaved not like deities but like frail mortals; they had lost, and deserved to lose, the sovereignty of the world because they had lost the sovereignty over themselves." Note that Keats stresses Saturn's loss of "identity"; see I, 112–16.

14   "All is negative here. The divisions of the day are, as it were, obliterated: the four elements are presented in terms of silence and inaction. There is no air. The rhythms of the verse gyrate sluggishly."—Blackstone, *The Consecrated Urn*, p. 234.

15   On this point see D. G. James, *The Romantic Comedy* (London, 1948), p. 136.

16   *Ibid.*, p. 128: "The beauty of the new Gods is a more difficult and terrible beauty than that of the old; yet it is none the less greater. The Godhead of *Hyperion* is that which acknowledges for its own the world in which Lear suffered and Cordelia was hanged, and is yet no less a principle of Beauty and Order." I think this is the point toward which Dorothy Van Ghent moves in "Keats's Myth of the Hero," *Keats-Shelley Journal*, III (1954), 7–25 (pp. 10–16 on *Hyperion*), but I confess I do not fully follow her argument. See also R. D. Havens, "Of Beauty and Reality in Keats," *ELH*, XVII (1950), 206–13, for a discussion of how the connotations of "beauty" change in Keats's later poetry.

17   Caldwell, *PMLA*, LI, 1096.

18   Sperry, *PMLA*, LXXVII, 80: "The life-and-death struggle with which the first *Hyperion* ends is carried over and expanded in the second. But its context is changed in such a way as to lead one more and more to consider Keats's allegory within the framework of sin and redemption." My only disagreement with Mr. Sperry's excellent point is that he seems to make it exclusive; without denying the relevance of "sin and redemption" to

The Fall of Hyperion, I should say that some less orthodoxly religious conceptions are as important.

19 *Ibid.*, p. 77.

20 John D. Rosenberg, "Keats and Milton: The Paradox of Rejection," *Keats-Shelley Journal*, VI (1957), 87–95. Rosenberg argues that the principal change between the two *Hyperions* is to be traced to Keats's effort "to humanize the poem" (p. 91).

21 Bloom, *The Visionary Company*, p. 412: "Keats implies that the fanatic and the savage are imperfect poets, with a further suggestion that religious speculation and mythology are poetry not fully written." Page 413: "Moneta . . . is a priestess of intense consciousness doing homage to the dead faiths which have become merely materials for poetry."

22 Sperry, *PMLA*, LXXVII, 78: ". . . the *true* poet, as the closing lines of the paragraph make clear, is the very opposite of the fanatic who speaks merely to a 'sect.' True poetry implies not only imaginative activity but the perception of value and meaning relevant to all mankind. 'In dreams,' Keats seems to say with Yeats, 'begins responsibility,' and the special obligation of the poet to society is destined to become, particularly through Moneta's urging, the major concern of Keats's dreamer."

23 For a recent example, David Perkins, *The Quest for Permanence* (Cambridge, Mass., 1959), pp. 276–82.

24 A most important and helpful article on this matter is that of Brian Wicker, "The Disputed Lines in *The Fall of Hyperion*," *Essays in Criticism*, VII (1957), 28–41. A famous discussion of the lines is that of J. M. Murry, "The Poet and the Dreamer," now in *Keats* (London, 1955), pp. 238–49.

25 This imagery fits in with the pattern of sickness-medicine imagery, so far as I know unnoticed by the critics, which runs throughout the second version of *Hyperion*. For example, by Moneta's "propitious parley" the poet is "medicin'd/In sickness not ignoble," and later the face of the goddess is described as "bright blanch'd/By an immortal sickness which kills not; . . . deathward progressing/To no death . . ."

26 Note G. K. Chesterton's discussion of the "new" poetry (*Robert Browning* [London, 1926], p. 185), the "practical" value of which, he says, is that it "can realise motives" and express "beyond the power of rational statement a condition of mind" from which actions may arise.

27 Rosenberg, in *Keats-Shelley Journal*, VI, 93: "He [Keats] reveals an instinctive historical sense and faith in the collective development of mind."

28 Albert Gérard, "Coleridge, Keats and the Modern Mind," *Essays in Criticism*, I (1951), 249–61, emphasizes the general significance of this point. For example: "The Romantics . . . firmly believed that *within* 'mankind' there is room for a faculty that goes beyond reason. This is the basic assumption of romanticism" (p. 253).

29 "*The Fall of Hyperion* must be regarded as one of the major attempts within European romanticism to reconcile the imagination with a realistic and humane awareness of the suffering of mankind."—Sperry, *PMLA*, LXXVII, 83. Mr. Sperry's insistence on the poem's adherence to the

orthodox pattern of sin and redemption leads him to stress the dark side of *The Fall*—he speaks of Keats's final attitude as "closer to resignation than to hope—perhaps even despair." I wish to emphasize the element of reaffirmation within Keats's admittedly ever more tragic view of life.

30 For example, Mario Fubini remarks, in *Lettura della poesia foscoliana* (Milan, 1949), p. 77: ". . . Foscolo considera . . . la poesia come espressione della più profonda umanità del poeta e come tale per sua natura rara . . ."

31 Compare Earl R. Wasserman's comments on the "creative" poet, in *The Subtler Language* (Baltimore, 1959), esp. pp. 11, 173, 175.

CHAPTER IX

1 Luigi Russo's general introduction to *Ugo Foscolo: prose e poesie* (Florence, 1951) and his specific introduction to *Le Grazie* tell something of the history of the poem, as does the section on *Le Grazie* in Mario Fubini's *Lettura della poesia foscoliana* (Milan, 1949). Michele Barbi in *La nuova filologia e l'edizione dei nostri scrittori da Dante al Manzoni* (Florence, 1938) describes some of the problems involved in establishing an edition of the poem, problems which are dramatized in the monograph of Francesco Pagliai cited in note 15, below.

2 Foscolo's essay *Di un antico Inno alle Grazie* of 1822 probably represents the poet's most detached intellectual consideration of the poem. See Russo, *Ugo Foscolo*, pp. 161–62.

3 Michele Barbi, "L'edizione nazionale del Foscolo e le Grazie," *Pan*, XIII (1934), 481–503, esp. pp. 484–85. See also M. Sterpa, *Le Grazie di Ugo Foscolo* (Catania, 1930); Giulio Natali, *Dal Guinizelli al d'Annunzio* (Rome, 1942), pp. 256–77; and Fubini, *Lettura della poesia*, p. 135, as well as the chapter on *Le Grazie* in *Ugo Foscolo*, 3d ed. (Florence, 1962), pp. 203–48.

4 I may have given the impression that De Sanctis' criticism of nineteenth-century literature is valueless except for his work on Leopardi. This is not true, as the reader can prove by turning to his volume *La letteratura italiana nel secolo XIX* in the edition annotated by Benedetto Croce (Naples, 1922). Croce's most interesting commentary on *The Graces* may be found in *Poesia antica e moderna*, 3d ed. (Bari, 1930), pp. 366–72. An earlier study by Croce is "Foscolo," *La Critica*, XX (1922), 129–39, later in *Poesia e non poesia*, 6th ed. (Bari, 1955).

5 Line references are to Russo's edition.

6 The poem is dedicated to Canova; see Giulio Natali, "Canova e Foscolo," *Orpheus*, V (1958), 31–34, and the earlier study of E. Montanari discussed by Fubini, *Ugo Foscolo*, p. 318, n. 15.

7 E. de Negri, "La logica della necessità e l'estetica della libertà del Foscolo," *Civiltà Moderna*, XVIII (1940), 285; also Francesco Flora, "La rivolta romantica e la poesia come verità," *Letterature moderne*, VII (1957), 5–34.

8 Russo, *Ugo Foscolo*, p. 164, note to l. 8. At stake is not solely a change in

political attitude but also a stylistic maturation; Foscolo has outgrown his earlier Alfierianism.

9   At the risk of causing unnecessary confusion, I sometimes use "civility" (an archaic meaning of which is "civilization") rather than "civilization" in connection with *The Graces* because *civility*—"behaviour proper to the intercourse of civilized people, politeness" (*Oxford English Dictionary*)— is the key to *civilization* as Foscolo understands it. I hope some connotations of the "modesty" and "discretion" he praises are conveyed by "civility," which by its very ambiguity may suggest something of the balance maintained throughout *The Graces* between the personal and the universal.

10 Russo describes this third realm as "metahistorical." The movement distinguishes *The Graces* from *The Sepulchres*; see Mario Martelli, *Linee generali per uno studio su "Le Grazie,"* (Siena, 1947), pp. 28 ff.

11 Fubini, *Lettura della poesia*, p. 142.

12 Fubini, *Ugo Foscolo*, pp. 217 and 229.

13 "La poesia non è lo specchio della vita, bensì il suo superamento. . . ." Fubini, *Lettura della poesia*, p. 131. Many of Fubini's best critical observations concern this point, though he never underestimates the influence of classical writers on Foscolo; see pp. 143–48 for the relation of Propertius and Catullus, for example. Giuseppe de Robertis, "Per un frammento delle 'Grazie,' " *Studi* (Florence, 1944), pp. 126–35, points out (p. 126) that although Foscolo's statements about poetry often have a Neoclassical ring, in *The Graces* his poetry transcends his poetics. De Robertis also observes that Foscolo is to be distinguished from the more conservative Monti by his creative use of words (p. 128). In his *Cinque Saggi* (Florence, 1945), Attilio Momigliano provides an interesting contrast between Foscolo's poem and the *Amori* of Savioli; see also Fubini, *Lettura della poesia*, pp. 164–68.

14 Martelli, *Linee generali per uno studio su "Le Grazie,"* p. 8. Hence the mixture of sorrow and joy in the poem's final prayer, epitomized in the concluding ". . . i grandi/ Occhi fatali al lor natio sorriso." See Fubini, *Lettura della poesia*, pp. 130, 137–38; and Russo, *Ugo Foscolo*, p. 262, notes to III, 272 and 274–75.

15 E. Chiorboli, "Il Foscolo nel velo delle Grazie e nel sogno del guerriero," *Giornale Storico della letteratura italiana*, CIX (1937), 253–62, esp. pp. 257–58. Fubini, *Lettura della poesia*, p. 157: ". . . esso è un' altra raffigurazione di quella virtù della compassione."

16 The most complete discussion, with full references, is to be found in Francesco Pagliai, "I versi dei Silvani," *Studi di filologia italiana, Bollettino dell'Accademia della Crusca*, X (1952), 145–412. Two hundred and seventy pages of discussion for nine lines of poetry may seem excessive, but Pagliai is in the process of editing the volume of Foscolo's poetry for the Edizione Nazionale, and his monograph (which includes all possible variants) illustrates the problems of trying to edit conscientiously *Le Grazie.*

17 This version is to be found in Pagliai, in *Studi di filologia italiana*, X, 267. On the significance of the first person see pp. 333–34. Just to prove that no literary analysis is ever complete I worked out a lengthy vowel-pattern and sentence-structure analysis of Foscolo's progress to the final version— in which it becomes obvious that the stops occur with progressive frequency and that with increasing clarity "i" and "o" sounds, dominant in the first five lines, are replaced by "a" and "e" sounds in the last lines. I am sure the reader will be grateful for my decision to keep my analysis to myself.

18 Douglas Bush's comments on "The World Is Too Much With Us," in *Mythology and the Romantic Tradition* (Cambridge, Mass., 1937; reprinted by Pageant Books, New York, 1957), pp. 58–59, are relevant here.

19 By now, I trust, the reader will have understood my reason for using words such as "suprarational," "suprapersonal," and "supranatural." I do not like these terms, but the poets I study strive to go beyond the rational, the personal, and the natural—without merely falling back on older systems of transcendence. To say, for example, that Leopardi is attracted to the "supernatural" is misleading because of the connotations which surround the word. He is, however, attracted to that which goes beyond nature in a fashion not clearly imagined before the beginning of the nineteenth century, to the "supranatural."

20 Russo, *Ugo Foscolo,* note to l. 127, p. 203.

21 Antonio Viscardi, "Note foscoliane," *La cultura,* VII (1928), 349–52, p. 349: ". . . Foscolo esprime di un paesaggio non già gli aspetti immutabili, bensì gli aspetti momentanei, fugacissimi." Page 350: ". . . la rappresentazione foscoliana nasce sempre da impressioni immediate e vivacissime." Page 351: "L'immagine espressiva è, in fondo, quasi un rivelare a sè stessi, un concretare plasticamente il processo sentimentale e fantastico avviato dalla sensazione: . . ." Viscardi thus tries to distinguish Foscolo from Poliziano on one side and d'Annunzio on the other, that is, to place Foscolo between "formalists" and "spiritualists," and to explain his union of the sensory and the literary. It is in this union that the similarity between Foscolo and Shelley is perhaps most apparent. Compare also Albert Gérard's comment on Keats's success at making "immortal an intensity of passion which is essentially transient," in "Romance and Reality: Continuity and Growth in Keats's View of Art," *Keats-Shelley Journal,* XI (1962), 17–29, esp. p. 24.

22 Fubini, *Ugo Foscolo,* p. 229.

23 But see Fubini's discussion, *Lettura della poesia,* pp. 154 ff., based on Foscolo's own comments in *Di un antico Inno alle Grazie,* where he differentiates his method from that of Homer and Hesiod by emphasizing that he does not describe, but that Flora herself designs the scenes. As Fubini justly remarks, Foscolo distinguishes between "description" and "evocation." "Non è però un puro artificio tecnico quello del Foscolo, bensì una forma poetica che ben risponde al dinamismo della sua poesia . . ." (p. 154).

CHAPTER X

1   Lionel Trilling, *The Liberal Imagination* (New York, 1950), pp. 129–59.

2   Gilbert Highet, *The Powers of Poetry* (New York, 1960), pp. 228–35.

3   This of course is involved with a special way of seeing, as H. W. Piper has observed in his recent study, *The Active Universe* (London, 1962); notice especially pp. 210–22 of this valuable book. Piper's philosophic explanations are complemented (in the case of Wordsworth) by Carl Robinson Sonn's "An Approach to Wordsworth's Earlier Imagery," *ELH*, XXVII (1960), 208–22, which discusses the metaphoric structure of Wordsworth's language.

4   *Complete Poetical Works,* ed. Ernest de Selincourt and Helen Darbishire (Oxford, 1952), IV, 464. Surely one reason early nineteenth-century poets admired Plato was that he was a myth-*maker*. But on the non-Platonic quality of Wordsworth's vision see Morse Peckham, *Beyond the Tragic Vision* (New York, 1962), p. 118.

5   Of course I have loaded the dice; one would expect Italian poets to be more "Mediterranean" than "Germanic." I believe, nonetheless, that what I call the Mediterranean impulse can be found in German poets of the early nineteenth century. I hope that I shall be able later to test (and undoubtedly to modify) my conclusions in this work through a study of French and German Romanticism.

Boldface page numbers indicate the principal discussion of a subject.

Style: poetic, **i–xx, 174–76**, and *passim*;
in *Jacopo Ortis*, 5–6; dreams and, 149
Suicide: and Foscolo, 15; heroic, 15, 17,
67, 192*n18*, 193*n20*
Sunday Evening, **101–103**; translation
of, 100–101; and *Tintern Abbey*, 102–3

Tempest, The, 81–82, 199*n48*
Time, **87–101**; and space-time in *Tintern
Abbey*, 91; in *The Infinite*, 97–98; in
Immortality ode, 172
Tintern Abbey, **87–96**; time in, 89–91;
space-time in, 91; joy in, 93–94; mysti-
cism in, 95–96; and *To the Moon*, 98–
99; and *Sunday Evening*, 102–3
Titanism, 65
To a Friend Restored to Health, **74**
To Autumn, **114–16**; and *The Graces*,
164
To Luigia Pallavicini, **73–74**; and *To
Silvia*, 106
To Silvia, **105–6**; translation of, 104–5;
and *To Luigia Pallavicini*, 106; and
"Lucy" poems, 107
To the Moon, **98–100**; translation of, 98
To Zante, **111–12**; translation of, 111;
Odysseus in, 111; *Divine Comedy* and,
112
Translation: and early nineteenth-cen-
tury poetry, xviii, **47–61**, 170; and
Sepulchres, 47–61 *passim*; and civiliza-
tion, 50–51; and creativity, 56–58; and
Immortality ode, 170; and Foscolo,
203–4*n24*
Trilling, Lionel, 168

Vico, Giambattista: and *Jacopo Ortis*,
17; and *The Graces*, 156; and Foscolo,
193*n21*, 203*n19*. SEE ALSO Civilization
Village Saturday, The, **120–22**; translation of, 120
Vision: and visionary poetry, xvii; and
myth, xix; in *Prelude*, 23, 40–41; in
Ode to Psyche, 72–73; and dream in
Elegiac Stanzas, 114; and secular
myth, 118–19; and early nineteenth-
century poetry, 130–31; in *Fall of Hyperion*, 147–49; and dream and civilization, 152–53; imaginative, in Keats
and Foscolo, 158; in *The Graces*, 164;
in *Immortality* ode, 171; and dream in
Ode on a Grecian Urn, 208*n33*; in *Eve
of St. Agnes*, 218*n22*

Wasserman, Earl R., xv
Wellek, René, 190*n12*
Werther: popularity of, xiv; and *Jacopo
Ortis*, 3–4
Whitehead, Alfred North, 147
Willey, Basil, 94, 131–32
Wordsworth, William. SEE *Elegiac Stan-
zas*; "Lucy" poems; *Ode: Intimations
of Immortality; Old Cumberland Beg-
gar, The; Prelude, The; Resolution
and Independence; Tintern Abbey*

Yeats, William Butler, 206–7*n17*, 225*n22*

Zante: in *To a Friend Restored to
Health*, 74

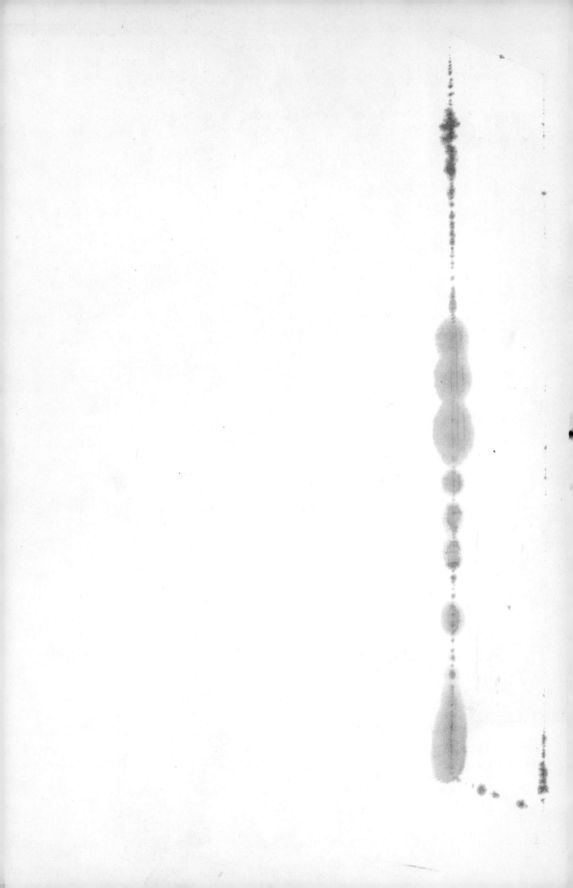